Second Language Learning and Teaching

Series editor

Mirosław Pawlak, Kalisz, Poland

Aims and Scope

The series brings together volumes dealing with different aspects of learning and teaching second and foreign languages. The titles included are both monographs and edited collections focusing on a variety of topics ranging from the processes underlying second language acquisition, through various aspects of language learning in instructed and non-instructed settings, to different facets of the teaching process, including syllabus choice, materials design, classroom practices and evaluation. The publications reflect state-of-the-art developments in those areas, they adopt a wide range of theoretical perspectives and follow diverse research paradigms. The intended audience are all those who are interested in naturalistic and classroom second language acquisition, including researchers, methodologists, curriculum and materials designers, teachers and undergraduate and graduate students undertaking empirical investigations of how second languages are learnt and taught.

More information about this series at
http://www.springer.com/series/10129

Liliana Piasecka • Małgorzata Adams-Tukiendorf • Przemysław Wilk
Editors

New Media and Perennial Problems in Foreign Language Learning and Teaching

Springer

Editors
Liliana Piasecka
Małgorzata Adams-Tukiendorf
Przemysław Wilk
Instytut Filologii Angielskiej
Uniwersytet Opolski
Opole
Poland

ISSN 2193-7648   ISSN 2193-7656 (electronic)
ISBN 978-3-319-07685-0   ISBN 978-3-319-07686-7 (eBook)
DOI 10.1007/978-3-319-07686-7
Springer Cham Heidelberg New York Dordrecht London

Library of Congress Control Number: 2014957157

© Springer International Publishing Switzerland 2015
This work is subject to copyright. All rights are reserved by the Publisher, whether the whole or part of the material is concerned, specifically the rights of translation, reprinting, reuse of illustrations, recitation, broadcasting, reproduction on microfilms or in any other physical way, and transmission or information storage and retrieval, electronic adaptation, computer software, or by similar or dissimilar methodology now known or hereafter developed. Exempted from this legal reservation are brief excerpts in connection with reviews or scholarly analysis or material supplied specifically for the purpose of being entered and executed on a computer system, for exclusive use by the purchaser of the work. Duplication of this publication or parts thereof is permitted only under the provisions of the Copyright Law of the Publisher's location, in its current version, and permission for use must always be obtained from Springer. Permissions for use may be obtained through RightsLink at the Copyright Clearance Center. Violations are liable to prosecution under the respective Copyright Law.
The use of general descriptive names, registered names, trademarks, service marks, etc. in this publication does not imply, even in the absence of a specific statement, that such names are exempt from the relevant protective laws and regulations and therefore free for general use.
While the advice and information in this book are believed to be true and accurate at the date of publication, neither the authors nor the editors nor the publisher can accept any legal responsibility for any errors or omissions that may be made. The publisher makes no warranty, express or implied, with respect to the material contained herein.

Printed on acid-free paper

Springer is part of Springer Science+Business Media (www.springer.com)

Preface

The aim of the volume is to discuss the ways in which New Media, accessible through communication and information technologies, shape practices and expectations in foreign language classrooms along with problems that have always accompanied foreign language learning and teaching. Digital natives or the new-millennium learners—frequently foreign language learners—have been growing with computers, mobile phones and the Internet that are essential components of their reality, educational reality included. According to the 2009 PISA results, the percentage of students who have at least one computer at home has grown considerably, which means that learners have easy access to New Media. Most importantly, New Media allow a fast and cheap access to information and to multiple multimodal sources of foreign language input that can enhance foreign language comprehension and production, thus contributing to more effective communication. Learners have an unprecedented opportunity to choose the sources of information and the ways of communication they prefer. Moreover, New Media have altered the ways in which people communicate, blending orality with literacy, which means that language and social skills necessary for effective communication are of particular concern for language learners and teachers. New Media also concern the learners' development of lifelong learning skills which affect their minds and skills concerning intercultural communication outside the formal educational system although the intercultural contact does not have to result in intercultural understanding. This needs time, effort and motivation to develop.

However, learning and communicating by means of New Media has not eliminated the challenges that foreign language learners have always faced such as the need to learn vocabulary, think while learning, pay attention to the form of the language or critically approach information available in textbooks whose style and design have been shaped by popular culture forms, to mention just a few.

The focus of the book, then, is two-tailed: on the one hand, the authors discuss the impact of the New Media on foreign language learning practices and comprehension of abstract concepts; on the other hand, they are concerned with perennial issues pertaining to the role of vocabulary, corrective feedback, textbooks and inner speech in the process of language learning and use.

The uniqueness of the book stems from the fact that every chapter reports original empirical research on issues related to aspects of foreign language learning and teaching in various countries (in Europe and outside) and by various age groups. The studies are based on qualitative and quantitative research designs, e.g. survey analyses, quasi-experimental treatments, case studies, an empirical corpus-driven analysis of frequency distributions and recurrent patterns of language use, multimodal discourse analysis, or think-aloud protocols. The authors, both novice and experienced researchers and academic teachers, demonstrate how using social networks (e.g. *Facebook*), videoconferencing, mobile phones, wikis, and computer-mediated interaction contribute to the development of language skills, negotiated interaction, autonomy, and intercultural competence.

The book is divided into two parts. Part One, entitled "New Media and foreign language development", focuses on the use of the new media in foreign language learning, teaching and communication. It consists of six sections and opens with a chapter on teenage foreign language learners' use of *Skype*, *Facebook*, *YouTube*, emails, and TV programmes in learning English. Polish, German, and Spanish adolescents most frequently listen to music, watch films, and use YouTube and Internet sites. As shown by the results of Magdalena Szyszka's study, these media contribute to the development of L2 skills and enhance learner autonomy and motivation for learning.

Cross-cultural and intercultural issues emerge in the chapter "Advanced Learners' Intercultural Experience Through Computer-Enhanced Technology: A Study of Polish and Romanian Students" which focuses on computer-mediated communication (CMC) as an effective way of developing intercultural competence through an L2. According to Aleksandra Wach, the development of intercultural awareness is particularly significant in today's increasingly multilingual and multicultural world, with English as a lingua franca of intercultural communication among native and non-native users. The participants of the study, Polish and Romanian students of English, frequently engaged in CMC in English by emails, instant messaging, and social networking sites, were provided with an intensive and meaning-oriented contact with the target language. Engaging in CMC, the participants comprehended and produced language in meaningful contexts of seeking cultural information, but also reflecting on cultural norms, values, and beliefs.

The chapter "Wikis and New Perspectives for Collaborative Writing" is devoted to the development of academic writing skills in a foreign language through a wiki, based on the idea of collaborative writing in which a text is created and edited asynchronously by many authors. Basing on the concepts of scaffolding and languaging, Małgorzata Marzec-Stawiarska argues that they can be effectively incorporated into collaborative writing of a wiki and contribute to language growth. L2 learners engaged in the activity enjoyed the opportunities for error correction and for discussing the process of writing. They also realised the importance of audience in writing and reflected on the nature of collaboration.

Videoconferencing as a new dimension of learning and as a means of providing L2 learners with modified input and feedback (repair of communication breakdown, repair of learner error, and discourse management) that are conducive to language production and negotiation of meaning is introduced in the chapter "The Foreign Language Classroom in the New Media Age: Videoconferencing and Negotiated Interaction Among L2 Learners". Videoconferencing is similar to face-to-face communication because of the audiovisual channel that allows the users to rely not only on verbal but also on non-verbal clues in immediate communication. Moreover, the learners have an opportunity to use English in genuine communicative contexts with other learners of English. The participants of the study used the foreign language—English—as a lingua franca because they had different L1s and English was the language they shared and could use for successful communication. The reported study is international as the participants were Polish and Spanish learners of English. Thus it also allowed Barbara Loranc-Paszylk to draw cross-cultural conclusions.

Emails, *Facebook*, and mobile phones play an important role in classroom communication between learners, as well as learners and their teachers. Following the assumption that successful communication supports success in language learning, Anna Kozioł analyses satisfaction with teacher–student communication at schools and preferences in the choice of means of communication. The participants of her study prefer face-to-face communication albeit they successfully communicate by means of computer technologies. This has important implications for foreign language learning practices which might incorporate new technologies to vary language input and opportunities for language use.

Facebook, online communication, and the use of English are central in the final paper of Part One. Johnny George observes that the worldwide expansion of *Facebook* has greatly influenced the dominance of English as a lingua franca for online communication. The results of the study of Japanese university English majors show that they use English to communicate with other Japanese students by means of *Facebook* although their confidence in the use of the L2 is absent in face-to-face communication.

Part Two, entitled "Perennial issues in foreign language development", consists of six sections that refer to thought processes in foreign language learning, effective ways of teaching collocations, development of lexical competence, as well as the description of vocabulary characteristic of pharmaceutical English. Since learning a new language entails making mistakes and using textbooks, these issues are also addressed.

The part opens with a text by Danuta Gabryś-Barker who recognises the impact of New Media on foreign language learning which, regardless of technological support, requires thinking. Therefore, she makes inner speech—a verbalised form of thinking—the focus of her inquiry. Inner speech is particularly intriguing in the case of foreign language learners as the choice of language for thinking shows how a bi/multilingual mind works, and how it processes language for comprehension and production. It also sheds light on the language progress of learners and reveals their emotions. The data obtained from multilinguals through think-aloud protocols show how L1 and L2 input tasks shape inner speech, how the language of input affects the language of processing, what languages are activated during different processing sequences, and what language choices are made in the different types of comment.

Errors are one of the perennial issues addressed in this part. Lech Zabor and Agnieszka Rychlewska show how the ways of communicating errors impact foreign language learners' use of a specific language form, i.e. articles, in writing. According to the principles of *Counterbalance Hypothesis*, which they follow, the learners' ability to notice the gap between the ill-formed utterance produced in their interlanguage and the target linguistic form is enhanced by the shift in their attentional focus from meaning to form in a meaning-focused context and from form to meaning in a form-oriented setting. The study the authors carried out, focusing on the effects of varied corrective feedback, revealed that all the participants benefitted from the treatment. Moreover, written meta-linguistic corrective feedback provided in the inductive way and targeting a single linguistic feature improved the learners' accuracy in the use of notoriously misused articles.

Polish EFL learners' problems with both noticing and using English collocations—an important aspect of communicative competence—are discussed by Paweł Szudarski. Form-focused instruction on collocations is suggested to make learners more sensitive to them. The author reports results of a mixed-method pedagogic intervention which aimed at teaching learners selected English collocations. The results of the qualitative part of the study show that reading while listening and input enhancement are more effective in teaching collocations than reading only. These findings are corroborated by the interviews with the learners whose awareness of collocations has grown. Their teacher was satisfied with the effects of the experimental treatment.

Communicating via images, or via the picture modality, has become an integral part of communication in the New Media age. Illustrating how three cognitive mechanisms, i.e. conceptual metaphor, metonymy, and blending, facilitate conceptualizations of a highly abstract phenomenon of the EU crisis, Przemysław Wilk argues for the development of learners' figurative language competence across modalities. He also believes that since primacy is given to the human sense of vision in conceptualising the reality, the picture modality is a reasonable starting point for the development of learners' figurative language competence.

The following contribution refers to the design and analysis of Cultural and Media Studies textbooks for college students. Katarzyna Molek-Kozakowska notes that these textbooks, more and more multimodal, universalised, informalised, and entertaining, show how this domain of academic discourse is being colonised by pop-cultural forms. This crossover between popular media culture and academia may negatively affect students' critical literacy that enables the student to deconstruct meanings and demystify hegemonic ideologies inscribed in texts via various semiotic resources. The analysis of selected university textbooks (four case studies) within the framework of multimodal discourse analysis indicates a move from literacy towards visuality and orality in textbook design and style. This aims at developing functional rather than critical literacy and the changes in textbook formats that imitate popular media culture may hinder students' critical skills.

Part Two closes with a paper that reports a preliminary study aiming at a description of key vocabulary and phraseology in English for Specific Purposes, focusing on pharmaceutical texts. Łukasz Grabowski presents a corpus-driven

Preface ix

description of vocabulary and phraseology (key words, lexical bundles, and phrase frames) in clinical trial protocols and European public assessment reports, written originally in English. Identifying register features and their functions in these two text types provides new data for a description of English used for pharmaceutical purposes, which matters in teaching English for Specific Purposes, translators' training or lexicography, for example.

We hope that this volume will stir interest in how new technologies can be used to promote understanding of the complex, multimodal realities in which we exist. As we have been living with the New Media for a relatively short time (in comparison with print resources), there are also ample research opportunities and perspectives that can trigger further research. Last but not least, some authors have provided descriptions of new-media-based activities that can be implemented in foreign language classrooms to support linguistic, personal, and social development of learners.

The Editors

Contents

Part I New Media and Foreign Language Development

Multimedia in Learning English as a Foreign Language as Preferred by German, Spanish, and Polish Teenagers   3
Magdalena Szyszka

Advanced Learners' Intercultural Experience Through Computer-Enhanced Technology: A Study of Polish and Romanian Students 21
Aleksandra Wach

Wikis and New Perspectives for Collaborative Writing 39
Małgorzata Marzec-Stawiarska

The Foreign Language Classroom in the New Media Age: Videoconferencing and Negotiated Interaction Among L2 Learners 57
Barbara Loranc-Paszylk

E-mail, Facebook, and Mobile Phones as Essential Tools for Lower Secondary School Students' Communication 73
Anna Kozioł

***Facebook* to *Facebook* Encounters in Japan: How an Online Social Network Promotes Autonomous L2 Production** 91
Johnny George

Part II Perennial Issues in Foreign Language Development

Communicating with Oneself: On the Phenomenon of Private/Inner Speech in Language Acquisition 115
Danuta Gabryś-Barker

The Effectiveness of Written Corrective Feedback in the Acquisition of the English Article System by Polish Learners in View of the Counterbalance Hypothesis 131
Lech Zabor and Agnieszka Rychlewska

Formal Instruction in Collocations in English: Mixed Methods Approach 151
Paweł Szudarski

Some Implications for Developing Learners' Figurative Language Competence Across Modalities: Metaphor, Metonymy and Blending in the Picture Modality 169
Przemysław Wilk

Design and Style of Cultural and Media Studies Textbooks for College Students 189
Katarzyna Molek-Kozakowska

Towards Teaching English for Pharmaceutical Purposes: An Attempt at a Description of Key Vocabulary and Phraseology in Clinical Trial Protocols and European Public Assessment Reports 209
Łukasz Grabowski

Contributors

Małgorzata Adams-Tukiendor, Ph.D. is an Assistant Professor at Department of Applied Linguistics, English Philology, University of Opole, Opole, Poland. She holds a Ph.D. in linguistics. She specialises in foreign language acquisition. Her main research interests are cognitive and affective factors influencing writing in a foreign language and the role of intelligence and creativity in learning a foreign language and specifically in learning to write. Her current interests focus also on the role of reflection in the teaching profession. She runs teacher training courses for ELT students and practitioners and teaches academic writing at the university. She is a co-author of a writing manual for EFL students (*Developing writing skills*) and an author of numerous articles on selected issues which reflect her research interests. Apart from her academic work she also practises coaching in education for students, teachers, and school headmasters at all educational levels.

Danuta Gabryś-Barker is Professor of English at the University of Silesia, Katowice, Poland, where she lectures and supervises M.A. and Ph.D. theses in applied linguistics, psycholinguistics, and especially in second language acquisition. Her main areas of interest are multilingualism and applied psycholinguistics. As a teacher trainer she lectures on research methods in second language acquisition and TEFL projects. Prof. Gabryś-Barker has published over 100 articles nationally as well as internationally and the books *Aspects of multilingual storage, processing and retrieval* (2005) and *Reflectivity in pre-service teacher education* (2012). She has edited nine volumes, among others for Multilingual Matters, Springer, and the University of Silesia Press. Prof. Gabryś-Barker is the editor-in-chief (together with Eva Vetter) of the *International Journal of Multilingualism* (Taylor & Francis/Routledge).

Johnny George is an Associate Professor in the Humanities division of the University of Tokyo. As a linguist, his research areas include anthropological linguistics and sociolinguistics, particularly in the area of linguistic Politeness. During his term as an Assistant Professor in the language department of Nagoya University of Business and

Commerce (NUCB), he served for 2 years as the editor of the *NUCB Journal of Language, Culture, and Communication* and developed an increased interest in TESOL research. His current interest in the area of TESOL involves the examination of the communicative practices of L2 learners in natural language contexts.

Łukasz Grabowski, Ph.D. is an Assistant Professor at the Institute of English at Opole University, Poland, where he teaches undergraduate and postgraduate courses in sociolinguistics, corpus linguistics, and English-to-Polish translation. His research interests include corpus linguistics, translation studies (theoretical and applied), and phraseology.

Anna Kozioł, M.A. graduated from Opole University in 2011. Currently, she is a Ph.D. student in the Department of Philology at Opole University. She is doing research on the topic of group dynamics and language success in junior high schools, taking into consideration the aspect of gender. She also works as an English teacher at a primary and a junior high school. Incorporating innovative methods of teaching into the foreign language classroom along with stimulating and motivating teaching techniques are her field of research interest.

Barbara Loranc-Paszylk, Ph.D. works as an Assistant Professor at University of Bielsko-Biala, Poland. She accomplished her Ph.D. in Applied Linguistics in 2008. Her research interests include investigation on effectiveness of Content and Language Integrated Learning, as well as innovative uses of new technologies and e-learning resources in teaching foreign languages.

Małgorzata Marzec-Stawiarska, Ph.D. works as an Assistant Professor at the English Department at the Pedagogical University in Cracow. Her Ph.D. thesis analysed the role of summarising in developing reading and writing skills in a foreign language. Lately her research interest has been connected with developing language skills in a foreign language classroom context, primarily speaking and writing, by engaging students into collaborative work. She is also interested in the role of affective domain in learning foreign languages. Her recent studies have investigated language-skill-specific anxiety experienced by teacher trainees and also by teachers of EFL.

Katarzyna Molek-Kozakowska, Ph.D. is an Assistant Professor at the Institute of English, Opole University, Poland. Trained as a linguist, she now specialises in discourse analysis and media studies. She has published on various aspects of mass-mediated political discourse, rhetorical and stylistic properties of contemporary journalism, and critical literacy.

Liliana Piasecka is Professor of English at the Institute of English, Opole University (Poland), where she works as an applied linguist, researcher, and teacher trainer. She teaches SLA and ELT courses and supervises M.A. and Ph.D. theses. Her research interests include second/foreign language acquisition issues, especially L2 lexical development, relations between L1 and L2 reading, gender, and identity. She has published two books, numerous articles, and co-edited two collections of essays.

Agnieszka Rychlewska, M.A. is currently a Ph.D. student in the Faculty of Philology at Wroclaw University, Poland. She holds an MA degree in applied linguistics from the same faculty. She is also a graduate of the Postgraduate Studies in the EU Educational Programmes from the Faculty of Social Sciences and she also completed the Postgraduate Studies in Translation at Wroclaw University. Ms. Rychlewska has been professionally involved in teaching English for 10 years, currently at the secondary school and Wroclaw Academy for the Dramatic Arts. Her research interests pertain to ELT methodology, specifically oral and written corrective feedback.

Paweł Szudarski, Ph.D. is currently based at Teacher Training College of Foreign Languages in Września, Poland. Recently he has completed his Ph.D. studies at the University of Nottingham, UK. He has also worked for the Center for Applied Linguistics in Washington, DC. His research interests include second language acquisition, lexis, instruction of English Language Learners and corpus linguistics.

Magdalena Szyszka, M.A. is currently working on her Ph.D. at Opole University where she also teaches. Being involved in EFL teaching and teacher training for several years, she is interested in second/foreign language acquisition and, in particular, language learning strategies, language anxiety, and English pronunciation. Her recent publications on the self-perceived pronunciation competence and language anxiety as well as on variability in pronunciation learning strategies' use reflect her interests mentioned above.

Aleksandra Wach, Ph.D. works as an Assistant Professor at the Faculty of English, Adam Mickiewicz University, Poznań, Poland. Apart from teaching English as a foreign language at University level, she conducts EFL didactics courses and is involved in training pre-service and in-service English teachers. Her current professional interests include second language acquisition processes, the development of intercultural competence in the process of learning and teaching a foreign language, the application of new technology in foreign language learning and teaching, learning and teaching grammar, and the role of L1 in learning a foreign language.

Przemysław Wilk, Ph.D. is an Assistant Professor at the Institute of English, Opole University. His research interests range from discourse studies to cognitive linguistics. Specifically, his research concentrates on the application of cognitive linguistics in Critical Discourse Analysis as well as on cognitive lexical semantics. Recently, he has gained interest in figurative language competence in the context of foreign language instruction.

Lech Zabor, Ph.D. teaches applied linguistics at Wroclaw University, Poland. His principal interests are in second language learning, specifically the acquisition of English articles. His recent research focuses on the role of semantic and discourse universals in the perception of definiteness by speakers of Slavic and Romance languages. He has published articles on these topics in journals such as *Belgrade English Language and Literature Studies,* and *Copenhagen Studies in Language.* As a visiting academic he taught courses and lectured on language acquisition at the universities in Poland, Denmark, Ireland, Italy, France, Lithuania, Russia, Spain, the Czech Republic, and the UK.

Part I
New Media and Foreign Language Development

Multimedia in Learning English as a Foreign Language as Preferred by German, Spanish, and Polish Teenagers

Magdalena Szyszka

Abstract This paper presents the findings of a small-scale study investigating the preferences of German, Polish, and Spanish teenage English as a foreign language (EFL) learners concerning their use of multimedia, such as *Skype*, *Facebook*, *YouTube*, e-mails, and TV-programmes in learning English. A group of 88 respondents was requested to complete an on-line questionnaire in order to specify how often some selected types of multimedia are used by adolescents in their autonomous EFL learning, and to determine their views on the extent to which some selected multimedia affect the development of their language skills (reading, writing, listening, and speaking) and their English pronunciation. The outcomes confirm culture-specific preferences and provide some interesting insights into adolescents' favourable tools for autonomous EFL learning which are invaluable for language teachers, researchers, and course designers. The results also show that the respondents view watching films and listening to music as very influential in improving their listening skills.

Keywords Multimedia • Computer assisted language learning (CALL) • Language skills • Learner preferences

1 Introduction

A learner in the twenty-first century may have an extraordinary selection of stimuli for learning a foreign language compared to the learner of the previous pre-Internet époque. These tools, limited earlier (that is even 20 years before) to paper (books, copybooks, letters, diaries), video or audio recordings, have been flourishing and multiplying since 1990s. The burst of technological development, especially the advent of the Internet, has largely affected the area of foreign language education, where the application of multimedia might be viewed within the realm of computer assisted language learning (CALL), understood originally as "the search for and study of applications of the computer in language teaching and learning" (Levy

---

M. Szyszka (✉)
University of Opole, Opole, Poland
e-mail: mszyszka@uni.opole.pl

© Springer International Publishing Switzerland 2015
L. Piasecka et al. (eds.), *New Media and Perennial Problems in Foreign Language Learning and Teaching*, Second Language Learning and Teaching,
DOI 10.1007/978-3-319-07686-7_1

1997: 1). A more recent approach, adopted in this study, equates CALL with "any process in which a learner uses a computer and, as a result, improves his or her language" (Beatty 2003: 7). Although this process may be performed with or without an overt user's intention to learn a foreign language, EFL learners are aware that a range of multimedia may be used as a medium in social communication or as a tool to get information in a target language.

The new multimedia attracts particularly younger groups of learners, frequently called digital natives (Prensky 2001) or the new-millennium learners (Howe and Strauss 2000). The data of the 2003 PISA report (Wastlau-Schlüter 2005), investigating the access to information technologies among adolescent groups of learners, confirm that 99.31 % of 15-year old Europeans have already used a computer, either at school or at home. The countries which took part in the 2009 PISA research, Germany, Spain and Poland among others, note a considerable increase (from 72 % in 2000 to 94 % in 2009) in the percentage of students who have at least one computer at home (OECD 2011). The 2009 PISA research also shows that on average less than 1 % of students taking part in the study have never used a computer. Therefore, it may be assumed that virtually all teenage European L2 learners have already been in contact with a computer. What is more, Otta and Tavella (2010) indicate that new-millennium learners are able to clearly specify their preferred ways of applying the software tools. They use information and communications technology (ICT) not only to learn and work but also to socialise, to get information and to entertain (Stevens 2010). In other words, adolescent EFL learners constitute the age group particularly prone to purposefully exploiting the multimedia and technological applications for international communication, leisure, and learning, which may directly or indirectly lead to the development of their foreign language skills. Hence, the approach of non-structured (without setting clear objectives, timing or teacher's support), informal learning, which may be either intentional or random, is followed in this study.

This study's objective is to examine the adolescents' beliefs on how multimedia augment their development of English language skills, such as reading, writing, speaking, and listening, as well as their English pronunciation. The purpose of the investigation is also to identify the multimedia that is most frequently applied by them for learning EFL and to explore the use of thereof in three different nationality groups: German, Polish, and Spanish.

2 The Application of Multimedia in Foreign Language Learning

The three sample nationality groups differ with respect to several educational aspects stemming from their cultures. Stevens' (2010) report on the impact of ICT and new media on language learning places Germany among the countries that exemplify a high level of multilingualism, educational attainment, perceived effectiveness of language learning at school and ICT penetration, although the data in the report indicate that German students' exposure to languages through foreign media is low. Spain scores low or very low in most of the areas mentioned above with the exception of a medium level of ICT penetration. The levels of these educational aspects in Poland might be closer to the Spanish context (cf. Krajka et al. 2010). Therefore, it is interesting to investigate how the adolescent EFL learners from these countries perceive the impact of ICT on their EFL learning processes.

A number of CALL technologies might be applied in order to develop four language skills: speaking, listening, reading, and writing. A plethora of applications, such as *Skype* or Voice Over Internet Protocol (VOIP), serves "to mediate communication via voice, to transmit audio or video through audio and video conferencing, or to facilitate user participation and interaction via text chat, voice chat, audio blogs, or voiced bulletin boards" (Levy 2009: 771). E-mails, which may be used as authentic tools in transferring information in the target language, are reported to enhance communicative skills (Liu et al. 2002). Digitised video (e.g. *YouTube*) and audio files (e.g. audiobooks), TV and radio programmes available on-line provide an infinite source of authentic materials for L2 listening. Apart from word processors, L2 writing in CALL might be enhanced via email, student-designed websites, PowerPoint presentations, weblogs, and wikis (Levy 2009). What is interesting, applications designed for the use of one skill may aid in the development of another. For example, a mild positive influence of real-time conversational text exchange (e.g. a chat), which entails the direct use of writing ability, on L2 speaking has been reported (Payne and Ross 2005; Payne and Whitney 2002). Finally, computer-based L2 reading may benefit enormously from a range of authentic materials and tools. Several technologies may be useful for developing this skill:

> electronic dictionaries, software that provides textual, contextual and/or multimedia annotations, computer-based training programs that aim to accelerate and automatize word recognition, Web-based activities that seek to teach a variety of components (from text structures and discourse organization to reading strategies) and the Internet as a source of materials for extensive reading (Chun 2006: 69)

In pronunciation CALL, frequently referred to as computer-aided pronunciation training (CAPT), Hubbard (2009) enumerates three types of applications. The first one, a digital voice recorder, allows learners to listen to a native speaker's pronunciation and record the imitated version of a learner's voice in order to compare it with the native one and practice pronunciation further. Speech visualisation is the second application useful for pronunciation practice and awareness raising. Here a native speaker's voice spectrogram indicates various parameters for the analysis thereof. The third one is automatic speech recognition (ASR), where the learner is given feedback on "how close a learner's speech is to a norm for native speakers" (Hubbard 2009: 7). CAPT applications implemented in direct pronunciation training have been reported to trigger higher awareness and motivation in L2 learners (Lai et al. 2009; Fang and Lin 2012). However, other computer applications, such as digitised video (films, *YouTube*) or audio (radio programmes, audiobooks) recordings may also have the potential for developing motivation for learning L2 pronunciation, as they not only serve as the source of native pronunciation models but are also embedded in context.

Although the bulk of research into CALL investigates its correlation with L2 learning outcomes (e.g. Beatty 2003; Garrett 2009; Hubbard 2009; Jafarian et al. 2012; Pearson et al. 2011), and students' attitudes to CALL applications in the process of language learning (Cunningham 2000; Mahmoudi et al. 2012), there is a need for more studies directed at learners' opinions and insights into CALL (Lasagabaster and Sierra 2003). Bulut and AbuSeileek (2007) claim that researching learners' opinions is one of the best ways to evaluate CALL. Hubbard (2009: 14) is of the opinion that "more attention should be given to how students use computers on their own and what training content and processes can help them be more successful." That knowledge may lead to effective steps taken by L2 teachers and educators in developing autonomous L2 learning paths through CALL. Therefore, a great deal of further empirical research is needed. This study attempts to investigate which of the computer applications EFL learners use most frequently in their independent, autonomous L2 language learning. It also addresses the issue of how EFL learners perceive CALL's influence on their L2 skills and learning of pronunciation.

3 Method

The empirical part delineates the participants, the design of the instrument, the procedure, and the results of the research. To attain the objective, the following three research questions are proposed. (1) Which of the selected multimedia are most/least frequently used among teenage EFL learners? (2) What are the cross-cultural (Spanish, German, Polish) similarities and differences in the frequency of use of the selected multimedia? (3) Which multimedia, in the respondents' views, affects their speaking, listening, reading, writing, and pronunciation most? The above research questions constituted the basis for posing the following hypotheses: H1—there are significant differences in the frequency of use of the selected multimedia among teenage EFL learners, H2—there are culture-based differences in the frequency of use of the selected multimedia.

3.1 Participants

The participants in this study were 88 EFL students (48 female, 36 male, and 4 indicated neither) from three different countries: Germany, Poland and Spain. The same number of 34 students responded to the survey in Spain and Poland. There were 20 respondents from Germany. The age of the participants ranged from

14 to 18 with an average of 16. The mean age of the Spanish participants was 14.6, German teenagers were 16.4 and Polish 17.4 years old on average. Proficiency levels of the respondents were established on the basis of a self-report scale, from excellent through very good, good, satisfactory to unsatisfactory. Most Polish, German and Spanish teenagers evaluated their English level as very good (14, 6 and 6 subjects, respectively) and good (14, 13 and 16, respectively). However, in the Spanish group 6 students declared unsatisfactory and 4 satisfactory levels of English; whereas none of German and Polish subjects ticked off unsatisfactory level of English, and only 1 German and 3 Polish subjects viewed their L2 level as satisfactory.

3.2 Instruments

An on-line questionnaire (see Appendix A) was designed in English so that the same form of it should reach the respondents from the three different nationalities. However, care was taken to formulate the items suitable for the intermediate level, B1/B2, EFL learner. It was constructed to compile three types of information: the basic bio data of the respondents, their frequency of use of the selected multimedia, and their opinions on how far computer applications affect their L2 learning skills and pronunciation. Ten questions and sub-questions were organised into three sections: demographic questions (gender, age, nationality, starting age of learning English, L2 proficiency self-evaluation), a question on frequency of use of the selected multimedia (How often do you use the following multimedia when you learn English out of school?), and questions on the impact of multimedia on particular language skills and pronunciation (e.g. Which multimedia make you better at pronunciation?).

In the first set of questions the adolescents were requested to either fill in the information or tick off the answers listed. The second one, designating the frequency of use of multimedia, operated on a 5-point Likert scale, where 1 indicated 'never' and 5—'very frequently'. In the last set of questions the respondents were to choose one out of four options, 'not at all,' 'a little,' 'somewhat' or 'a lot,' referring to the degree the selected multimedia modify their L2 speaking, listening, reading, writing, and pronunciation. The responses pertained to the following types of multimedia: TV programmes, electronic dictionaries, *Skype*, *Facebook*, e-mail, *YouTube*, the Internet sites, computer software, music, films, audiobooks and computer games. The number of potential computer applications has been restrained in the questionnaire due to the limitations caused by the design of a manageable instrument.

3.3 Procedure

The questionnaire was published in May 2012 and the responses were collected until the end of September 2012. The link to the on-line address of the questionnaire was attached to the personal correspondence sent to English teachers from Germany, Poland, and Spain. The author distributed the link among her adolescent EFL students in Poland, as well. The teachers were informed that the approximate time of filling in the anonymous questionnaire might be 8 min, and they were requested to encourage their students to respond to it. The online design of the survey assured anonymity.

3.4 Data Analysis

The data collected from the online questionnaire on multimedia used by adolescent EFL learners were computed by means of percentages, mean frequencies and standard deviations. Moreover, one-way ANOVA was calculated to test the first null hypothesis stemming from the first research question: (H10) there are no significant differences in the frequency of use of the selected multimedia among teenage EFL learners. Additionally, a *t*-test for independent samples was applied in order to establish whether the EFL learners from three different countries used the selected multimedia significantly differently. If this is the case, the second null hypothesis stating that (H20) there are no culture differences in the frequency of use of the selected multimedia will be rejected. Finally, to address the third more descriptive research question, mean values were calculated to investigate the views of the respondents on the influence of multimedia on L2 reading, writing, speaking, listening and pronunciation.

4 Results

The research findings are provided in this section in order to address the research questions and hypotheses. Firstly, the frequency of the use of selected multimedia is considered and analysed. Secondly, the results of a *t*-test for independent samples are discussed. Thirdly, an analysis of the multimedia that, in the opinion of the respondents, affects most their development of L2 speaking, listening, reading, writing, and pronunciation is provided.

The outcomes of the questionnaire items focusing on how often the selected multimedia is used by teenagers taking part in the research are shown in Table 1. Here the variance (F) values of one-way ANOVA, testing whether the 12 selected multimedia are used statistically differently at $\alpha = 0.05$, are provided. Additionally, mean frequency (M) of the respondents' use of particular multimedia and standard

Multimedia in Learning English as a Foreign Language as Preferred by German... 9

Table 1 Results of one-way ANOVA of EFL learners' declared use of the 12 multimedia

Multimedia		N	Σ	M	SD	F
TV programmes		88	235	2.7	1.2	1.5
Electronic dictionaries		88	274	3.1	1.2	1.5
Skype		88	174	2	1.3	1.7
Facebook		87	258	3	1.5	2.2
E-mail		88	221	2.5	1.3	1.6
YouTube		87	312	3.6	1.3	1.8
Internet sites		88	320	3.6	1.2	1.4
Computer software		88	254	2.9	1.4	1.9
Music		88	337	3.8	1.4	2
Films		87	308	3.5	1.3	1.7
Audiobooks		88	174	2	1.2	1.4
Computer games		88	227	2.6	1.5	2.2
Source of variation	SS	df	MS	F	P-value	F crit.
Between groups	380	11	34.5	19.8	1.47 E-36	1.8
Within groups	1,817	1,041	1.7			
Total	2,197	1,052				

deviations (SD), showing how far the individuals' responses vary from the mean, are included.

The most frequently used multimedia by adolescent respondents is music, with a mean of 3.8 and SD = 1.4. *YouTube* (M = 3.6 and SD = 1.3) and the Internet sites (M = 3.6 and SD = 1.2), with the declared use of just above the middle value between sometimes and frequently take the second place. The least frequently applied items are *Skype* (M = 2 and SD = 1.3) and audiobooks (M = 2 and SD = 1.2).

Further analysis discloses that almost half of the respondents (48.9 %) use music applications very frequently and 18.2 % implement them frequently. Only 10 out of 88 EFL learners (11.4 %) never exploit this type of multimedia. Similarly, 48 respondents (54.6 %) acknowledge frequent or very frequent use of *YouTube* and 59.1 % of Internet sites. A considerable number of adolescents also declare frequent or very frequent application of the following multimedia: films (58 %), electronic dictionaries (39.7 %), and *Facebook* (38.6 %).

The least popular computer application, *Skype*, is never used by 53.4 % of German, Polish, and Spanish teenagers taking part in the research. Most of them are never or rarely concerned with audiobooks (75 %), e-mails (55.6 %) and, interestingly, computer games (55.7 %).

The above discrepancies in the use of the 12 multimedia are confirmed by the results of one-way ANOVA. The variance calculated between groups of multimedia reaches the value (F = 19.8) greater than the critical variance (F crit. = 1.8), which means that the first null hypothesis (H10) is rejected. Teenage L2 learners use the above multimedia significantly differently.

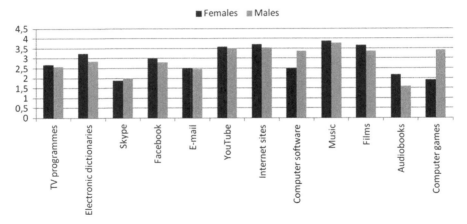

Fig. 1 Gender differences and frequency of the selected multimedia use (5 = very frequently, 4 = frequently, 3 = sometimes, 2 = rarely, 1 = never)

The frequency of the declared use of the selected multimedia has been analysed with reference to gender (see Fig. 1). The differences between the declared use of CALL applications of females and males are insignificant. However, the boys exceed the girls in their use of computer software and games; whereas the girls declare a slightly more frequent use of electronic dictionaries and audiobooks.

In order to address the second null hypothesis concerning cultural differences in the declared use of multimedia, the responses of adolescent EFL learners from Germany (DE), Poland (PL), and Spain (ES) were calculated separately. Subsequently, they were paired up to apply a t-test for independent or unmatched samples, which indicates mean differences between two groups. This statistical test was applied for each pair of the nationality groups: Polish and German (PL vs. DE), German and Spanish (DE vs. ES), as well as Polish and Spanish (PL vs. ES). The results shown in Table 2 provide only statistically significant results at $p < 0.05$.

Statistically significant differences in the frequency of use of TV programmes, *Facebook*, *YouTube*, Internet sites, music, and films are observed among Polish and German respondents. Polish adolescents declare significantly more frequent application of the above multimedia. German learners differ statistically significantly from Spanish learners in the use of electronic dictionaries, *YouTube*, and films. The former indicate that they relate to electronic dictionaries and watch films more often than the latter. Spanish teenagers, however, exploit *YouTube* significantly more frequently than their peers from Germany. Finally, Polish respondents differ from the Spanish in their greater use of electronic dictionaries, *Facebook*, Internet sites, music, and films. Since not all t-test results were statistically significant, the second null hypothesis (H20) is only partially rejected.

The numerical data related to the views on how far the 12 selected multimedia affect adolescents' English pronunciation are presented in Fig. 2. A considerably

Multimedia in Learning English as a Foreign Language as Preferred by German... 11

Table 2 Statistically significant differences in the use of multimedia among German (DE), Polish (PL) and Spanish (ES) EFL teenage learners ($p < 0.05$)

	M1	M2	SD1	SD2			
Group 1 vs. Group 2	Group 1	Group 2	Group 1	Group 2	t	df	p
TV programmes							
PL vs. DE	2.9	2.2	0.97	0.96	2.3	52	0.02
Electronic dictionaries							
DE vs. ES	3.5	2.3	0.94	1.21	3.7	52	0.00
PL vs. ES	3.7	2.3	0.93	1.21	5.3	66	0.00
Facebook							
PL vs. DE	3.7	2.7	1.34	1.34	2.5	52	0.01
PL vs. ES	3.7	2.4	1.34	1.43	3.7	65	0.00
YouTube							
PL vs. DE	4.0	2.8	1.11	1.15	3.8	52	0.00
ES vs. DE	3.6	2.8	1.47	1.15	2.0	51	0.04
Internet sites							
PL vs. DE	4.2	3.2	0.81	1.15	3.8	52	0.00
PL vs. ES	4.2	3.3	0.81	1.29	3.5	66	0.00
Music							
PL vs. DE	4.3	3.4	1.06	1.42	2.8	52	0.00
PL vs. ES	4.3	3.5	1.06	1.59	2.4	66	0.01
Film							
DE vs. ES	3.65	2.69	1.04	1.35	2.7	51	0.00
PL vs. DE	4.29	3.65	0.79	1.04	2.6	52	0.01
PL vs. ES	4.29	2.69	0.79	1.35	5.9	65	0.00

high value on a 4-point scale is ascribed to films ($M = 3.22$) and music ($M = 3.12$) by the three nationality groups, as well as TV programmes ($M = 2.8$), which to Polish and German learners are more than somewhat influential as far as English pronunciation is concerned. *Skype* ($M = 1.65$) and electronic dictionaries ($M = 2.08$), however, are undervalued here by most adolescents.

In order to identify which of the 12 types of multimedia improve, according to EFL learners, their English reading, writing, speaking, and listening abilities, a 4-point Likert scale ($1 =$ not at all, $2 =$ a little, $3 =$ somewhat, $4 =$ a lot) was used in the questionnaire. Table 3 presents means calculated for the three nationality groups (Polish $=$ PL, German $=$ DE and Spanish $=$ ES) and the means of all the responses (Total) referring to a particular medium and skill.

Most responses connected with the extent to which the selected types of multimedia affect the development of reading abilities are placed around the value 'a little,' with the exception of Internet sites, which are more than somewhat important for Polish ($M = 3.3$), though less than for the German ($M = 2.7$) and the Spanish ($M = 2.4$) EFL learners. E-mail ($M = 2.3$), *Facebook* ($M = 2.4$), and electronic dictionaries ($M = 2.4$) are not considered very valuable in improving reading in English by all three groups of respondents. Generally, adolescent EFL learners do

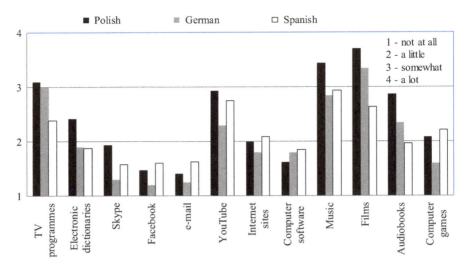

Fig. 2 Mean values assigned to multimedia affecting English pronunciation in the view of EFL learners

not perceive the multimedia enumerated in the questionnaire as strongly affecting their reading abilities.

In developing writing the respondents find electronic dictionaries (M = 2.6), Internet sites (M = 2.5), *Facebook* (M = 2.5), and e-mail (M = 2.5) more than a little helpful, although the average values do not exemplify very high figures. Of all the groups only German learners note that electronic dictionaries somewhat exert an influence over their writing (M = 3). Polish teenagers find electronic dictionaries (M = 2.8), e-mails (M = 2.9), and Internet sites (M = 2.8) quite useful in developing their English writing.

Speaking is believed to be developed through films (M = 3) and TV programmes (M = 2.9). However, Polish and German EFL learners appreciate these two types of multimedia more than their Spanish peers, who assign lower values to them (M = 2.5 and M = 2.5 respectively). *YouTube* (M = 2.7) and music (M = 2.6) are also considered somewhat important in the development of speaking skills by all EFL learners taking part in the research.

Finally, the adolescents participating in the study declare that several multimedia highly affect their EFL listening skills. The highest total value is assigned by all three EFL groups to films (M = 3.4), which, as learners acknowledge, promote their listening most. Interestingly, the other highly appreciated media believed to improve listening skill are music (M = 3.3) and *YouTube* (M = 3.3).

Table 3 The mean values assigned to multimedia affecting reading, writing, speaking and listening in the view of Polish (PL), German (DE) and Spanish (ES) EFL learners

Multimedia	Reading				Writing				Speaking				Listening			
	PL	DE	ES	Total	PL	DE	ES	Total	PL	DE	ES	Total	PL	DE	ES	Total
TV programmes	1.5	1.8	1.9	**1.7**	1.5	1.6	1.6	**1.6**	3	3.1	2.5	**2.9**	3.5	3.5	2.9	**3.3**
Electronic dictionaries	2.5	2.6	2.2	**2.4**	2.8	3	2.1	**2.6**	1.9	2.4	1.8	**2**	1.8	1.7	1.7	**1.7**
Skype	1.7	1.4	1.8	**1.7**	1.9	1.6	1.8	**1.8**	2.5	1.8	1.9	**2.1**	2.5	1.8	1.9	**2.1**
Facebook	2.6	2.4	2.3	**2.4**	3	2.2	2.2	**2.5**	1.9	1.7	1.8	**1.8**	1.5	1.4	1.7	**1.5**
E-mail	2.3	2.4	2.2	**2.3**	2.9	2.5	2.1	**2.5**	1.6	1.8	1.7	**1.7**	1.2	1.4	1.5	**1.4**
YouTube	2.2	1.9	2.6	**2.2**	2	1.6	2.1	**1.9**	2.6	2.8	2.7	**2.7**	3.5	3.2	3.2	**3.3**
Internet sites	3.3	2.7	2.4	**2.8**	2.8	2.4	2.4	**2.5**	1.9	1.9	2.1	**2**	1.9	1.9	2.2	**2**
Computer software	2.3	2.2	2	**2.2**	2	1.8	2	**1.9**	1.7	1.6	1.9	**1.7**	1.5	1.6	1.8	**1.6**
Music	1.8	1.7	2.2	**1.9**	1.6	1.6	1.8	**1.6**	2.7	2.5	2.5	**2.6**	3.7	3.3	3	**3.3**
Films	2.3	2.4	2.3	**2.3**	1.8	2	1.9	**1.9**	3.1	3.3	2.5	**3**	3.8	3.6	2.9	**3.4**
Audiobooks	1.8	1.8	1.8	**1.8**	1.5	1.8	1.8	**1.7**	2.4	2.3	1.8	**2.2**	3.1	3	2	**2.7**
Computer games	2.1	1.6	2.3	**2**	1.8	1.5	2.1	**1.8**	1.9	1.6	1.9	**1.8**	2.1	1.5	2.2	**1.9**

5 Discussion

The first null hypothesis has been rejected; therefore the results of this study confirm that various types of multimedia are used significantly differently by teenagers from Germany, Poland and Spain. Further analysis of the data leads to the response to the first research question concerning the frequency of use of multimedia by adolescent EFL learners, which may provide food for thought in selecting motivational teaching aids from among a range of multimedia. The unquestionable winner in this category is music, which, of all the multimedia listed in the survey, is most frequently used by teenagers from Germany, Poland, and Spain. The respondents also state that music improves their English pronunciation, speaking, and listening skills. The second most frequently used computer applications are *YouTube* and Internet sites, which provide an infinite written and oral target language data for language learning. However, to apply them successfully in the EFL classroom, there is a need to investigate them further in order to narrow down the scope, for example, by considering the type, length, and motivational factor of the contents.

The findings of this study generally confirm culture differences in the choice of multimedia addressed in the second research question and formulated in the second null hypothesis, partially rejected. Not all but several types of multimedia, e.g. films and electronic dictionaries, are used significantly differently by the EFL learners of the three nationalities. Polish and German adolescents use multimedia significantly differently in six categories, Polish and Spanish in five, whereas German and Spanish groups differ statistically significantly in the use of three types of multimedia—electronic dictionaries, *YouTube*, and films. The outcomes indicate that Spanish EFL learners declare the least frequent use of multimedia of all three groups, which only partially mirrors Stevens' (2010) report on the impact of ICT and new media on language learning, where Spain is placed at the medium level of ICT penetration. Another explanation of this outcome may be rooted in the declared level of L2 proficiency. Spanish participants viewed their level of English as lower than German and Polish teenagers. Therefore, they might not perceive the potential of multimedia in L2 learning and simply be less motivated to learn English through multimedia in general. However, contrary to expectations, Polish respondents declared a comparatively higher frequency of multimedia use. This fact may stem from the profile of the Polish group of respondents, who were high school students with general positive attitude to self-development and L2 learning. Nevertheless, there are CALL applications, such as *Skype*, e-mail, computer software, audiobooks, and computer games, which are used similarly by German, Polish, and Spanish adolescents. Therefore, considering the choice of multimedia in EFL learning and teaching process, it is essential to take cultural background into account.

The third research question investigates the adolescents' beliefs concerning the influence of multimedia on their English pronunciation and speaking, listening, reading, and writing skills. In the view of the respondents, films, music, and TV programmes most affect the development of English pronunciation. These types of media provide authentic and meaningful contexts for pronunciation practice, as the EFL learner's attention is directed "to the overall utterance, not to how the word or segment in isolation is uttered" (AbuSeileek 2007: 18). Although none of the above types of multimedia specifically aims at overt pronunciation practice, EFL learners view them as useful. Moreover, the focus on pronunciation fluency at the discourse level reflects a more recent approach to pronunciation teaching which encourages the use of fluency-building and multisensory techniques supplemented by technology (cf. Celce-Murcia et al. 2010). Therefore, EFL teachers should feel encouraged to adapt excerpts from films, music, and TV programmes to promote pronunciation learning imbedded in authentic contexts.

Of all the language skills, listening is the one that EFL learners in this study find comparatively strongly affected by a number of multimedia. Music, TV programmes, *YouTube*, and films are believed to exert the greatest influence on listening. Interestingly, EFL adolescent learners choose the same types of multimedia when addressing the issue of speaking, though the medium values calculated in the study for speaking are slightly lower than for listening, which means that the respondents recognise the same media as augmenting their listening skills more than speaking. The study outcomes confirm that the most influential types of multimedia referring to writing turn out to be electronic dictionaries, e-mail, *Facebook*, and Internet sites, whereas EFL reading development is mostly affected by Internet sites, electronic dictionaries, and *Facebook*. In other words, these are the same types of media with a diverse degree of influence. Briefly, in this study oral communication (i.e. listening and speaking) is viewed to be stimulated by music, TV programmes, *YouTube*, and films; whereas written communication (i.e. reading and writing) is enhanced by electronic dictionaries, *Facebook*, and the Internet sites.

Conclusion

The results of the study provide information that might be directly implemented by EFL teachers. Learners' preferences and choices of CALL instruments are important for creating resources for language learning and designing curricula optimal for effective EFL learning in adolescent groups. Classroom applications of the preferred multimedia may raise learners' motivation towards learning language skills (Smith 2000) and pronunciation (Pennington 1999). Also, the data collected in this study may affect the choice of language teaching tools for developing learning autonomy, since learning with the help of CALL may stimulate students' autonomous, self-paced language learning (Schwienhorst 2002). One more advantage of CALL is that it creates a non-threatening environment for studying because the learners choose where and when they prefer to develop their target language skills (Lasagabaster and Sierra 2003).

(continued)

Although the findings of the study may trigger an array of practical ideas on how to implement CALL applications in the process of English language learning, they should be interpreted with caution for the following reasons. First of all, the sample was limited to 88 respondents, so it should be extended to provide more reliable data for statistical analysis. Moreover, the instrument might be improved by broadening the list of multimedia because newer and newer applications are used every year, especially with the emergence of iPhones and smartphones, which learners use as substitutes for computers. Finally, the survey might additionally include open response options to collect qualitative data helpful to building a multifaceted picture of how teenage groups of learners respond to CALL.

The present study focuses on EFL learners' declared use of CALL applications. This approach follows Blake's (2009: 822) suggested direction of investigation within the realm of technology, which in "itself does not constitute a methodology, researchers cannot directly test the question 'Does it work?' without first addressing the question of how technology is used." Therefore, the outcomes indicating the choices that adolescent EFL learners make with reference to CALL may serve as a springboard for further, more detailed investigations. Firstly, more attention might be devoted to age and gender differences in the choice and extent of CALL applications. Secondly, it might be interesting to investigate not only national but also regional and social differences in the use of multimedia to provide a more comprehensible picture. Finally, the study might further investigate the extent of adolescents' autonomous application of CALL with reference to their linguistic performance.

Appendix 1: Multimedia in EFL learning

The aim of this research is to help us better understand what kind of multimedia young people use to learn English. There is no right or wrong answer to any of these questions. Please, read each item of the questionnaire carefully and respond.

Tick the box

☐ I agree to take part in this survey

Gender:

☐ Female
☐ Male
☐ I do not want to answer

Age: ....
Nationality: ....
At what age did you start learning English? ......

How do you evaluate your level of English?

☐ excellent
☐ very good
☐ good
☐ satisfactory
☐ unsatisfactory

How often do you use the following multimedia when you learn English out of school?

	Never	Rarely	Sometimes	Frequently	Very frequently
TV programmes	☐	☐	☐	☐	☐
Electronic dictionaries	☐	☐	☐	☐	☐
Skype	☐	☐	☐	☐	☐
Facebook	☐	☐	☐	☐	☐
E-mail	☐	☐	☐	☐	☐
YouTube	☐	☐	☐	☐	☐
Internet sites	☐	☐	☐	☐	☐
Computer software	☐	☐	☐	☐	☐
Music	☐	☐	☐	☐	☐
Films	☐	☐	☐	☐	☐
Audiobooks	☐	☐	☐	☐	☐
Computer games	☐	☐	☐	☐	☐

Which multimedia make you better at English pronunciation/reading/writing/speaking/listening?[a]

	Not at all	A little	Somewhat	A lot
TV programmes	☐	☐	☐	☐
Electronic dictionaries	☐	☐	☐	☐
Skype	☐	☐	☐	☐
Facebook	☐	☐	☐	☐
E-mail	☐	☐	☐	☐
YouTube	☐	☐	☐	☐
Internet sites	☐	☐	☐	☐
Computer software	☐	☐	☐	☐
Music	☐	☐	☐	☐
Films	☐	☐	☐	☐
Audiobooks	☐	☐	☐	☐
Computer games	☐	☐	☐	☐

[a]These items are originally published as separate subparts of the on-line questionnaire

References

AbuSeileek, A.F. 2007. Computer-assisted pronunciation instruction as an effective means for teaching stress. *The JALT CALL Journal* 3: 3–24.

Beatty, K. 2003. *Teaching and researching computer-assisted language learning*. New York: Longman.

Blake, R.J. 2009. The use of technology for second language distance learning. *The Modern Language Journal* 93: 822–835.

Bulut, D., and A.F. AbuSeileek. 2007. Learner attitude toward call and level of achievement in basic language skills. *Journal of Institute of Social Sciences of Erciyes University* 23: 103–126.

Celce-Murcia, M., D.M. Brinton, J.M. Goodwin, and B. Griner. 2010. *Teaching pronunciation: A course book and reference guide*. New York: Cambridge University Press.

Chun, D.M. 2006. CALL technologies for L2 reading. In *Calling on CALL: From theory and research to new directions in foreign language teaching*, CALICO monograph series, vol. 5, ed. L. Ducate and N. Arnold, 69–98. San Marcos, TX: CALICO.

Cunningham, K. 2000. Integrating CALL into the writing curriculum. *The Internet TESL Journal* 6. http://iteslj.org/Articles/Cunningham-CALLWriting. Accessed 28 Jan 2013.

Fang, T., and C. Lin. 2012. Taiwan EFL learners' pronunciation strategies in two learning contexts. *Journal of Language Teaching and Research* 3: 888–897.

Garrett, N. 2009. Computer-assisted language learning trends and issues revisited: Integrating innovation. *The Modern Language Journal* 93: 719–740.

Howe, N., and W. Strauss. 2000. *Millennials rising: The next great generation*. New York: Vintage Original.

Hubbard, P. 2009. A general introduction to computer assisted language learning (1–20). In *Computer assisted language learning: Critical concepts in linguistics, volumes I-IV*, ed. P. Hubbard. London: Routledge. http://www.stanford.edu/~efs/callc/callcc-intro.pdf. Accessed 30 Dec 2012.

Jafarian, K., A. Soori, and R. Kafipour. 2012. The effect of computer assisted language learning (CALL) on EFL high school students' writing achievement. *European Journal of Social Sciences* 27: 138–148.

Krajka, J., M. Kurek, and S. Maciaszczyk. 2010. *Media społecznościowe a nauka języków obcych: przekonania i wykorzystania na Łotwie, w Polsce i w Rumunii [Social media and foreign language learning: Beliefs and use in Latvia, Poland and Romania]*. Warszawa: Szkoła Wyższa Psychologii Społecznej.

Lai, Y.S., H.H. Tsai, and P.T. Yu. 2009. A multimedia English learning system using HMMs to improve phonemic awareness for English learning. *Educational Technology and Society* 12: 266–281.

Lasagabaster, D., and J. Sierra. 2003. Students evaluation of CALL software programs. *Educational Media International* 40: 293–304.

Levy, M. 1997. *Computer-assisted language learning: Context and conceptualization*. Oxford: Oxford University Press.

Levy, M. 2009. Technologies in use for second language learning. *The Modern Language Journal* 93: 769–782.

Liu, M., Z. Moore, L. Graham, and S. Lee. 2002. A look at the research on computer-based technology use in second language learning: A review of the literature from 1990–2000. *Journal of Research on Technology in Education* 34: 250–273.

Mahmoudi, E., A.A. Samad, and N.Z. Razak. 2012. Attitude and students' performance in computer assisted English language learning (CAELL) for learning vocabulary. *Procedia: Social and Behavioral Sciences* 66: 489–498. doi:10.1016/j.sbspro.2012.11.293.

Organisation for Economic Co-operation and Development (OECD). 2011. PISA 2009 results: Students on line: Digital technologies and performance (Volume VI). doi:10.1787/9789264112995-en. Accessed 30 Apr 2013.

Otta, M., and M. Tavella. 2010. Motivation and engagement in computer-based learning tasks: Investigating key contributing factors. *World Journal on Educational Technology* 2: 1–15.

Payne, J.S., and B.M. Ross. 2005. Synchronous CMC, working memory, and L2 oral proficiency development. *Language Learning and Technology* 9: 35–54.

Payne, J.S., and P.J. Whitney. 2002. Developing L2 oral proficiency through synchronous CMC: Output, working memory, and interlanguage development. *CALICO Journal* 20: 7–32.

Pearson, P., L. Pickering, and R. Da Silva. 2011. The impact of computer assisted pronunciation training on the improvement of Vietnamese learner production of English syllable margins. In *Proceedings of the 2nd pronunciation in second language learning and teaching conference*, ed. J. Levis and K. LeVelle, 169–180. Ames, IA: Iowa State University.

Pennington, M. 1999. Computer-aided pronunciation pedagogy: Promise, limitations, directions. *Computer Assisted Language Learning* 12: 427–440.

Prensky, M. 2001. Digital natives, digital immigrants. *On the Horizon* 9: 1–9.

Schwienhorst, K. 2002. Why virtual, why environments? Implementing virtual reality concepts in computer-assisted language learning. *Simulation and Gaming* 33: 196–209.

Smith, M. 2000. Factors influencing successful student uptake of sociocollaborative CALL. *Computer Assisted Language Learning* 13: 397–415.

Stevens, A. 2010. Study on the impact of ICT and new media on language learning. European Commission, UK. http://eacea.ec.europa.eu/llp/studies/documents/study_impact_ict_new_media_language_learning/final_report_en.pdf. Accessed 28 Jan 2013.

Wastlau-Schlüter, P. 2005. *How boys and girls in Europe are finding their way with information and communication technology? (No.3)*. Brussels: Eurydice.

Advanced Learners' Intercultural Experience Through Computer-Enhanced Technology: A Study of Polish and Romanian Students

Aleksandra Wach

Abstract In today's globalized world, the development of intercultural competence, which includes concepts such as cultural knowledge, curiosity about "otherness", intercultural sensitivity and openness to other cultures, is considered one of the basic objectives of education, including foreign language (L2) education. Computer-based technologies, embracing various forms of computer-mediated communication (CMC), appear to be particularly useful in promoting an intercultural approach, as they provide L2 users with opportunities to access cultural information and engage in authentic intercultural exchanges with other L2 users. The article reports the findings of a study that investigated whether and to what extent advanced EFL learners, English majors from Poland and Romania, made use of information and communication technology (ICT) to enhance their intercultural experience. The results indicate declared high levels of ICT use to get information about the culture of English-speaking countries, but also enhanced interest in other cultures, openness to cultural differences and willingness to communicate with foreigners through CMC. On the basis of the findings, conclusions are drawn about the potential benefits of online experience for the development of L2 learners' intercultural awareness, although intercultural training within formal instruction is needed to better prepare learners for pursuing intercultural competence development through online resources.

Keywords Intercultural competence • Intercultural experience • Information and communication technology • Culture teaching • English as a foreign language

---

A. Wach (✉)
Adam Mickiewicz University, Poznań, Poland
e-mail: waleks@wa.amu.edu.pl

© Springer International Publishing Switzerland 2015
L. Piasecka et al. (eds.), *New Media and Perennial Problems in Foreign Language Learning and Teaching*, Second Language Learning and Teaching,
DOI 10.1007/978-3-319-07686-7_2

1 Introduction

Becoming interculturally competent is a vital requirement for modern citizens and qualified professionals in the contemporary multicultural world. Due to the rapid pace of advancements in digital technology, the emergence of international media, and international academic and business cooperation, individuals nowadays need to be able to communicate effectively with people from other cultures. Only in this way will they be able to accommodate to the demands of an increasingly interconnected world and to participate in the global marketplace (Espinar et al. 2012; Perry and Southwell 2011; Sercu 2005). In order to succeed in this, they need to develop intercultural competence, defined as "the ability to interact effectively and appropriately with people from other cultures" (Perry and Southwell 2011: 455). In addition, in order to effectively communicate in intercultural situations, one needs to be a competent user of foreign languages; therefore, incorporating an intercultural approach into L2 education (and, particularly, into the teaching of English, which is the primary means of international communication today), seems especially adequate (Young and Sachdev 2011). Therefore, English as a Foreign Language (EFL) learners need to receive intercultural training in classroom-based activities as well as take advantage of opportunities for intercultural experiences outside the classroom, through visits abroad or through technology, as since the 1990s, the development of computer-based technology has made communication and mediation among individuals from different cultures considerably easier (Blake 2008; Kramsch 2011; O'Dowd 2007; van Compernolle and Williams 2009; Youngs et al. 2011).

Computer-enhanced technology is a valuable source of cultural information for L2 learners, as through various applications they gain access to literature, video, and online media which provide information about customs, lifestyles, or cultural representations; moreover, the Internet creates opportunities for L2 learners to engage in intercultural online interactions with native and other non-native users of the target language. The beneficial effects of engaging in online intercultural projects are largely confirmed by research (Elola and Oskoz 2008; Schuetze 2008; Zeiss and Isabelli-García 2005). It also needs to be noted that the out-of-class intercultural experience that L2 learners engage in may also contribute to an increased willingness to communicate with foreigners, openness to other cultures and deepened intercultural understanding.

In the article, the findings of a study which focused on the usefulness of computer-enhanced technology in the process of developing intercultural competence in Polish and Romanian advanced learners of English as a foreign language will be presented and analyzed. First, however, a brief discussion of the role of technology in fostering intercultural L2 education will be provided.

2 The Role of Technology in Fostering an Intercultural Approach in L2 Education

Although the development of intercultural competence has always been considered a vital aim of L2 teaching, the understanding of the term 'intercultural competence', and, consequently, of the aims of intercultural education, have changed over the decades (Castro and Sercu 2005; Byrnes 2010; Scarino 2010; Sercu 2010). As Sercu (2010) further explains, while in the past intercultural education denoted primarily the acquisition of knowledge about the target language culture, nowadays, in addition to this, it encompasses a much wider scope of abilities which lead the learner toward participation in intercultural and multilingual communities. Scarino (2010) summarizes this change as a move from a cultural to an intercultural orientation in L2 teaching.

Scarino (2010: 324) goes on to explain that in the process of becoming interculturally competent, L2 learners "come to understand culture not only as information about diverse people and their practices but also, and most importantly, as the contextual framework that people use to exchange meaning in communication with others and through which they understand their social world". Sercu (2005: 2) lists the following abilities as characterizing an interculturally competent person: "the willingness to engage with the foreign culture, self-awareness and the ability to look upon oneself from the outside, the ability to see the world through the others' eyes, the ability to cope with uncertainty". In another article, Sercu (2010) defines an interculturally competent person as interested in other cultures, open-minded, non-judgmental about cultural differences, respectful for "otherness", empathetic and flexible. In defining the concept of intercultural competence, Byram et al. (2002) list three crucial components: knowledge (culture-general and culture-specific), skill (which involves interpretation and interaction abilities, metacognitive strategies used in discovering cross-cultural differences and adjusting to them), and attitudes (motivation, openness and willingness to learn about other cultures). According to Perry and Southwell (2011), the concept of intercultural understanding encompasses knowledge about one's own and other cultures, positive attitudes (respect, empathy and curiosity) toward other cultures, and an appreciation of differences among cultures. In their definitions, the conception of intercultural competence involves behavior and communication skills, and largely denotes "the ability to interact effectively and appropriately with people from other cultures" (Perry and Southwell 2011: 455). Hence, as highlighted by many researchers (Byram et al. 2002; Sercu 2010), intercultural communicative competence also involves the ability to use a foreign language appropriately in various intercultural situations.

Therefore, within the intercultural approach in L2 education, opportunities need to be created for all of these components to be fostered in learners, as the development of intercultural communicative competence is considered to be a vital aim of L2 teaching nowadays. Baker (2012: 66) highlights that in today's increasingly multilingual and multicultural world, where English has become the lingua franca of intercultural communication among native as well as non-native users, the development of intercultural awareness is particularly significant "in expanding circle and global lingua franca contexts, in which cultural influences are likely to be varied, dynamic, and emergent". According to the Council of Europe (2001), an L2 learner is expected to develop "interculturality" by combining their own language and cultural competence with knowledge about the "ways of acting and communicating" in other languages they learn. This, in turn, leads to the emergence of intercultural awareness, which denotes "greater openness to new cultural experiences". Corbett (2003: 2) makes the point that within an intercultural approach to foreign language education, learners develop an ability "to view different cultures from a perspective of informed understanding".

Acknowledging the need to incorporate intercultural education into L2 instruction, Belz (2007: 157), notices that "the classroom is an insufficiently rich learning environment with regard to opportunities for apprenticeship into the diverse and complex forms of linguistic behaviour that both index and constitute intercultural competence". Similarly, Korhonen (2010) makes the point that very often in L2 classrooms the teaching of culture may be trivialized, neglected, or conducted in an artificial, teacher-centered way, providing learners with no real experience with other cultures. There are, of course, ways of applying appropriate teaching techniques in order to foster intercultural understanding and critical cultural awareness in learners, such as exposing them to various texts and cultural representations (Perry and Southwell 2011; Ware and Kramsch 2005), but these classroom-based activities would be more effective if supported by direct contact with other cultures, which would provide "experiential learning" experience (Byram et al. 2002; Byram and Feng 2004; Laskaridou and Sercu 2005). Staying abroad, for academic or leisure reasons, appears to be a particularly apt way of fostering an openness to other cultures. Even short visits appear to have beneficial effects on promoting intercultural sensitivity (Anderson et al. 2006; Behrnd and Porzelt 2012; Cadd 2012).

Since staying abroad is not always possible for a variety of reasons, another way of bringing L2 learners closer to other cultures is to provide cultural information in order to stimulate interest in them (Belz 2007). According to Levy (2009), technology makes it possible to become familiar with other cultures and deepen intercultural awareness in foreign language learners through both receptive and productive means. In terms of receptive means, various web sites give learners access to information about other cultures and provide them with relevant, authentic and up to date data. In terms of productive means, technology opens up numerous possibilities for learners to engage in CMC through informal online interactions, or intercultural collaboration projects. Furstenberg (2010: 329) makes the point that the use of the Internet has contributed to refreshed, more innovative ways of incorporating cultural elements in the teaching of foreign languages, "as it has brought the outside world right into our students' homes and into our classrooms, providing students with direct and equal access to the complex, rich, and multifaceted world of the target culture via an abundance of texts, images, and videos". As stressed by Thorne (2005: 2), the main power of Internet-mediated intercultural foreign language education lies in that it makes it possible to support an exchange of ideas, opinions, and collaboration among learners who live in different cultures and in various locations on the globe. Similarly, O'Dowd (2007: 18) observes that since the Internet "is clearly becoming a setting for a great deal of intercultural contact and exchange", the opportunities offered by engaging in CMC (as a form of "online intercultural exchange") with other CMC users from various cultural backgrounds make it an authentic and relevant way of learning an L2 and its culture, and of realizing that L2 communication involves expressing one's cultural identity as well as opening up to other cultures. Leppänen et al. (2009: 1080) emphasize that in an increasingly multicultural world, new technologies create possibilities for young people to transcend their local identities and look for what is common to their generation, and, as a result, "[n]ational identity and language may have less significance here than shared interests, values, and ways of life".

Within a sociocultural approach to CMC research, researchers have focused on how CMC enhances L2 learners' intercultural competence and awareness. In Zeiss and Isabelli-García's (2005) study, American-Mexican CMC participation was found to influence learners' knowledge of the target language culture and to enhance their cultural awareness of several culture-related topics (such as current events, daily life, and educational systems); moreover, it positively influenced their willingness to study abroad. Schuetze (2008) investigated factors influencing the level of engagement in CMC dialogs between groups of Canadian and German students and the extent to which this engagement led to the development of intercultural communicative competence. It was found that those learners who asked wh-questions, shared personal information, provided examples, and were ready to look for materials that were not a part of the course, were most willing to learn by getting into contact with another culture and were most successful in online intercultural communication. Lee (2009) described a Spanish-American project based on social networking tools, the aim of which was to enhance learners' intercultural communication and awareness. The findings revealed the participants' positive attitudes toward online cultural exchange, enhanced levels of cross-cultural understanding and increased communication skills due to personal engagement. Similarly, Elola and Oskoz (2008) found cross-cultural blogging to have a very positive effect on the knowledge of the target language culture and perceptions about the target-language population. However, as noticed by many researchers (Blake 2008; van Compernolle and Williams 2009), intercultural CMC may also bring about communicative breakdowns resulting from insufficient cultural understanding. For example, Ware and Kramsch (2005) described a miscommunication episode in a classroom-based telecollaboration project between learners of German in the US and learners of English in Germany. According to the researchers, this example shows how much "culture is inescapably part of language as discourse, in other words, language is social semiotic practice" (Ware and Kramsch 2005: 202). It also sheds light on the fact that online participation in a multicultural community might pose a great challenge to L2 learners and their teachers, who are expected to function as cultural mediators.

3 The Aims of the Study

This study differed considerably from the other studies reported in the previous section, as it concentrated on learners' engagement in CMC in their free time, out of class, and not as part of classroom-based contact with L2 or any formally organized activity. Consequently, it did not focus on a single predetermined mode of CMC; since the learners' Internet use was not monitored by their teachers, the study focused on CMC in the general sense, with the underlying assumption that the learners used a variety of its modes and tools.

Generally, the study aimed to explore the potential benefits of CMC for stimulating the development of L2 learners' intercultural competence. The elements of intercultural competence within the scope of this study are understood as both the cultural knowledge dimension of becoming interculturally competent, and the attitudinal dimension of the process, i.e. pursuing interest in other cultures, seeking opportunities to interact online with other L2 users, and becoming more open and sensitive to cultural differences. Investigating these dimensions within a cross-cultural perspective, across two groups of participants from different cultures, for both of whom English was a foreign language, was considered a relevant factor in the study.

The particular aims of the study were formulated in order to contribute to a more comprehensive picture of the participants' development of intercultural competence as supported by intercultural use of computer-enhanced technology. One of the initial aims was to evaluate the intensity of the participants' (English majors) engaging in various forms of CMC in English. Moreover, the study aimed to investigate their declared use of Internet resources in order to explore their knowledge of the culture of English-speaking countries. Another aim was to investigate their perceptions of CMC as useful in developing intercultural competence; in other words, to see whether, according to the participants' own estimations, engagement in CMC helped them gain knowledge about and arouse interest in other cultures. Finally, the study's aim was to see whether there were differences in Internet-use habits and perceptions about its usefulness for developing intercultural competence between Polish and Romanian students.

4 Method

A total of 195 participants took part in the study, among them 167 females and 28 males. The participants were university students majoring in English in the 1st through 3rd years of a BA program. The mean age of the whole sample was 21.2, while the median age was 21 (min. 19, max. 31). The group of participants consisted of two subgroups: a group of Polish students from Adam Mickiewicz University in Poznań (n = 149), and a group of Romanian students from Vasile Alecsandri University in Bacau (n = 46). The participants' level of English was upper-intermediate/advanced, and their mean length of learning the language was 12 years for the Polish students and 10 years for the Romanian students.

The tool used for data elicitation was a questionnaire administered to participants in pen-and-paper form. Apart from questions aimed at eliciting demographic information, the questionnaire comprised 11 questions which focused on eliciting data concerning the participants' contact with the culture of English-speaking countries and intercultural interactions with other users of English. Most of the questions, apart from the final one, which asked for additional comments, were closed-ended (either of a multiple choice or a ranking scale format). A *t*-test was applied to calculate the differences between the groups' responses. The questionnaire is enclosed in the Appendix.

5 Results

The first two questions concerned the participants' experiences visiting foreign countries. Figure 1 presents the number of countries the Polish and Romanian participants had visited in general, and Fig. 2 focuses on the number of times they had visited English-speaking countries. As can be seen from the figures, Polish students had traveled abroad more widely, as the most frequent answer, marked by 41 % of them, pointed to the range "more than 5 countries", while among the Romanian group, the most frequently chosen answer (by 44 %) was "between 1 and 2 countries".

Similarly, although in both groups the most frequent answer about the number of times the participants had visited English-speaking countries was "none" (55 % of the Polish and 76 % of the Romanian students), considerably more Polish than Romanian students ticked other answers.

In addressing the following questions, two participants in each group stated that they did not have steady access to the Internet, while the others did. All the

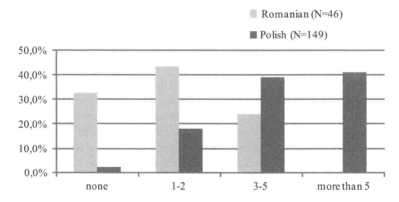

Fig. 1 The number of foreign countries the participants had visited

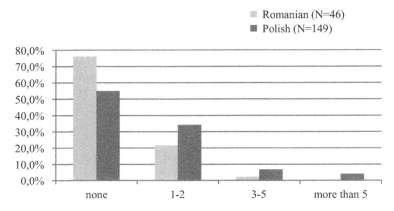

Fig. 2 The number of times the participants had been to English-speaking countries

participants said they used the Internet mainly at home. The Polish participants declared using the Internet on average for 2.3 h on weekdays and 3.2 h at weekends, while in the Romanian group the estimated average time spent surfing the Internet was slightly higher: 3.1 h on weekdays and 3.8 h at weekends.

Next, the participants were asked about the frequency of taking part in CMC in general, and in English. The most frequent answer concerning CMC use indicated by the sample as a whole was "every day", with 60 % of the Polish and 46 % of the Romanian students providing this answer. In terms of the frequency of using English in CMC, the most frequent answer in both groups was "sometimes" (42 % of the Polish and 37 % of the Romanian students indicated this answer), while the total for the "often" and "very often" answers in both groups was 44 %. In terms of the particular forms of CMC the participants engaged in using English, a similar pattern was revealed in both groups, as the same three forms were ticked as the most frequently used: email (85 % Polish and 61 % Romanian students declared writing emails in English), instant messaging (indicated by 42 % of Polish and 44 % of Romanian students), and social networking sites (the use of which included English for 68 % of the Polish and 57 % of the Romanian students).

Figure 3 presents the mean scores of the participants' declared frequency of engaging in online activities through which they could broaden their knowledge of the culture of English speaking countries. Here, the participants ticked their answers on a 5-point scale, in which 1 denoted never, 2—rarely, 3—sometimes, 4—often, and 5—very often. As can be seen from Fig. 3, watching movies in English was the activity in which most of the participants in both groups engaged most frequently, as the mean score for each of the groups oscillated between "often" and "very often". Reading literature was next on the list, with the declared frequency falling between "sometimes" and "often". Interacting with other users in English, both native and non-native speakers, appeared to be less frequently undertaken by the study participants, although the mean scores were around 3, which denoted the "sometimes" option.

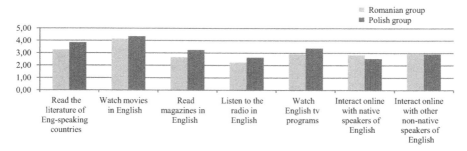

Fig. 3 The participants' declared frequency of engaging in online activities (1—never, 2—rarely, 3—sometimes, 4—often, 5—very often)

Table 1 Descriptive statistics and *t*-test results for contacts with foreigners through CMC (where 1—strongly agree, 2—disagree, 3—no opinion, 4—agree, 5—strongly agree)

Statement	Group	M	SD	t	sig (2-tailed)
Through CMC I seek contact with people from other cultures	Polish	3.17	1.13	1.365	0.174
	Romanian	3.43	1.10		
I have made friends with foreigners through CMC	Polish	2.74	1.28	3.250	0.001
	Romanian	3.43	1.16		
I find interacting with people from other cultures interesting	Polish	4.26	0.86	−0.308	0.758
	Romanian	4.22	0.81		

Table 2 Descriptive statistics and *t*-test results for statements concerning openness to other cultures through CMC experience (where 1—strongly agree, 2—disagree, 3—no opinion, 4—agree, 5—strongly agree)

Statement	Group	M	SD	t	sig (2-tailed)
My attitudes toward other cultures are more positive thanks to CMC	Polish	3.47	0.94	1.682	0.094
	Romanian	3.74	0.97		
CMC helps me understand other cultures	Polish	3.50	0.94	1.642	0.102
	Romanian	3.76	0.97		
Through CMC I become more open to other cultures	Polish	3.58	0.94	0.593	0.554
	Romanian	3.67	1.03		
Through CMC I notice differences between people from different cultures	Polish	3.55	0.96	3.164	0.002
	Romanian	4.04	0.78		

In Tables 1, 2, and 3 descriptive statistics and statistical significance levels for participants' answers to Likert-type statements which focused on their perceptions of intercultural experience through CMC are presented.

The mean values for the participants' declared answers indicate that the Romanian students expressed more positive opinions about seeking contacts with people

Table 3 Descriptive statistics and *t*-test results for statements concerning the cultural and language knowledge dimension in CMC (where 1—strongly agree, 2—disagree, 3—no opinion, 4—agree, 5—strongly agree)

Statement	Group	M	SD	t	sig (2-tailed)
CMC helps me gain information about other cultures	Polish	3.95	0.86	2.286	0.023
	Romanian	4.26	0.64		
Through CMC I learn how people live in other countries	Polish	3.80	0.86	1.412	0.160
	Romanian	4.00	0.78		
CMC is a source of authentic English, which has high cultural value	Polish	3.74	1.01	-1.513	0.132
	Romanian	3.48	1.02		
My English improves through CMC	Polish	3.87	0.94	1.139	0.256
	Romanian	4.04	0.84		
In CMC I share information about my own country	Polish	3.27	1.03	3.497	0.001
	Romanian	3.87	0.95		

from other cultures or even having established intercultural friendships through CMC (for this statement, statistically significant differences between the groups were recorded, $p = 0.001$). The high standard deviation levels, however, point to considerable variation among the participants. Both groups appeared to agree or strongly agree that interacting with people from different cultural background was an interesting experience for them.

As shown in Table 2, although for most of the statements, the between-group differences were not statistically significant, the Romanian students expressed more agreement with the statement concerning the positive influence of CMC on their attitudes toward other cultures, and agreed more with the statements that engaging in CMC contributes to a better understanding of and more openness to other cultures. The Romanian students also marked more positive answers indicating that while communicating online, they noticed cultural differences.

As the data in Table 3 show, while both groups indicated CMC as a vital source of information about other cultures, the Romanian students agreed more with this statement. The difference between the two groups is statistically significant ($p = 0.023$), and the Romanian group's lower standard deviation level points to a greater uniformity within this group. Similarly, the participants seemed to agree that through CMC they learn about lifestyles in other cultures, with the differences between the groups being minimal. The Polish group seemed to agree more with the statement that encountering authentic English through CMC has a cultural value, while the Romanians appeared to appreciate the positive influence of CMC on their proficiency in English more. Finally, the Romanian students admitted to sharing information about their own country more than the Polish students.

In the final section of the questionnaire, the participants were invited to provide their own comments on the usefulness of the Internet as a source of cultural information and as a scene of intercultural exchanges. Only 15 comments were made, nine by the Romanian students and six by the Polish ones. All of the comments expressed positive opinions about the benefits of the Internet for their linguistic and intercultural development.

Some of the students stressed the value of the Internet as a source of cultural information through its offering interesting websites, access to online media, and intercultural interaction opportunities. The following quotations illustrate this point: "When using the Internet, I gain knowledge about other cultures (through literature, films, games and interaction) to a large extent. Moreover, I gain knowledge about other topics connected with my subject of study, although to a lesser degree"; "I rarely interact with people, I do, however, enjoy reading the remarks that they leave. I think in this way I learn a lot about foreign cultures"; "I appreciate the fact that I learn so many things about other countries, e.g. their traditions, food, clothes, etc. I learn a lot from watching English and American t.v. series".

Another group of comments stressed the nature of their interpersonal contacts through CMC, as in this example: "I initiate a lot of contacts with native speakers of English by playing games and connecting with them on their kinds of sites. Later, I chat with some of them through other media (Facebook, IM, email). In this away, I get closer to their culture". One Romanian student wrote, "I'm not sure if I learn something about other cultures because what people say in CMC may not be true. They may pretend to be completely different". Another student emphasized that CMC was more suitable for maintaining old relationships rather than making new friends: "I don't really seek new contacts with foreigners through CMC, but it helps me maintain contacts with the people I already know". Some students also highlighted the relevance of the topics discussed with other Internet users: "I have managed to talk to students from other countries and thanks to it I know how studies are organized there".

Some of the comments underscored the dimension of developing a deeper intercultural understanding through engaging in online interactions, for example, the following ones: "Through the Internet I am connected to other cultures. CMC helps me to better understand other cultures and become more open to them"; "With the help of the Internet you can connect to people from different countries and learn about their cultures. For example, I have spoken to a teacher from Egypt and this helped me to understand more their culture, habits, their deep appreciation of every aspect of life. We talk about the nature of relationships, such as friendship and family relationships, in our countries".

Other comments concerned the additional value of engaging in intercultural CMC for their linguistic development, as highlighted in these examples: "For me, the Internet is a great source of authentic English, which I don't have a chance to encounter otherwise"; "Through Internet conversations with foreigners I'm able to practice my English and to expand my knowledge about other ways of living"; "Thanks to CMC I practice so many different skills, such as writing and speaking in English (e.g. through Skype), but I also get closer to other cultures"; "It's interesting to notice that on the Internet native speakers use a lot of slang and do not pay attention to mistakes. Their grammar is very often incorrect".

6 Discussion

The participants of the study, Polish and Romanian students of English, reported frequently engaging in CMC in English, the most popular forms being emails, instant messaging and social networking sites. Such an intensive and, as one may assume, relevant and meaning-oriented beyond-the-class contact with the target language offers considerable potential in terms of language learning by providing both exposure to language and opportunities for intercultural interaction. Moreover, technology may have the power to stimulate in young people the urge to develop life-long learning skills, which "develop a global mind and intercultural skills in a self-managed and goal-directed process" (Sercu 2010: 21). Generally, the participants expressed openness toward intercultural online exchanges, indicating that interacting with foreigners was interesting to them, which can be interpreted as an indicator of the potential for developing intercultural competence and of intercultural awareness being stimulated through engagement in CMC.

However, although both groups of study participants indicated positive attitudes toward other cultures and enhanced intercultural understanding as a result of engaging in CMC, the Romanian students' attitudes toward intercultural online interactions were consistently more positive. In light of other study findings, which indicated considerably less visit-abroad experience by the Romanian students, perhaps their greater appreciation of intercultural contacts online may be interpreted as some form of compensation for their more limited opportunities for direct intercultural contact.

The results of the study, both the answers to the closed-ended questions and the open-ended comments provided by the participants, point to the value of the Internet as a source of cultural information. The participants declared discovering information about how people live in other countries, and about the values and beliefs expressed by foreigners. Although this dimension of becoming interculturally competent may appear to be rather superficial, as obviously cultural knowledge alone does not lead to intercultural competence, knowledge about other cultures may lead individuals to explore different worldviews, reflect upon their own culture, and may contribute to a better understanding of culture-related behaviors. It can be argued that for learners of a foreign language who do not have a systematic direct contact with the L2 culture or have never even visited the target language country, knowledge about certain cultural phenomena, lifestyles, values, or family relationships, may be a vital initial step in arousing interest in these and other cultures. In addition to noticing cultural differences, the acquisition of knowledge may also be an important step toward developing intercultural understanding and sensitivity.

Another point highlighted by the study was the linguistic dimension of online intercultural contact. Even if at such a high level of proficiency in English their competence may not visibly improve through CMC contexts, the cultural value of these linguistic experiences appears to be considerable. Online language use is very often specific, as it is adjusted to the specific situation of online interactions. By becoming familiar with or reflecting upon such language use, learners of English as a foreign language become aware of linguistic processes in specific discourse communities—they therefore acquire valuable hands-on experience with the cultural reality of authentic language use. Students gain exposure to certain linguistic and cultural norms and conventions typical of online spaces. Moreover, interacting with others in an L2 on topics of mutual interest (e.g. student life or online gaming) also has the potential to stimulate authentic language use and cultural awareness.

Although the study results shed light on the potential benefits of computer-enhanced technology for intercultural experience, it needs to be noted that even if the participants' contact with other cultures was considerably increased through CMC, "intercultural contact in and of itself does not necessarily lead to cultural understanding" (Kern 2011: 207). Intercultural contact needs to be supported by specific skills and predispositions in order to contribute to one's intercultural awareness.

Hence, the study leads to certain practical implications. In order to be effective, beyond-the-class intercultural experience needs to be supported by classroom-based training in the form of discussions, brainstorming, or awareness-raising activities, about what intercultural competence is and why it is important. In this way, learners can conceptualize intercultural competence in a broader sense, and not focus entirely on the cognitive dimension of the concept. Moreover, their valid beyond-the-classroom linguistic and cultural experience may be enhanced by training in metacognitive and cognitive strategies that can be used while interacting online.

Conclusions and Limitations

The study had several limitations. Some of them resulted from the fact that it relied exclusively on self-reported data, in which the reliability of the responses can be questioned. Apart from that, the questionnaire format allowed for limited depth of insight into the reported data. Finally, the study highlighted only the potential of computer-enhanced environments for the development of intercultural awareness, rather than measuring the actual development of intercultural competence.

However, despite these limitations, the study findings allow for the formulation of some conclusions concerning the benefits of CMC for enhancing intercultural contacts and fostering intercultural understanding and sensitivity in advanced learners of English. The results suggest that CMC experience can, at least to a certain extent, compensate for insufficient intercultural experience through direct contact. They also point to a heightened curiosity about other cultures, a better ability to notice cultural differences, and in general, a higher level of intercultural openness and understanding as a result of participating in online environments. These are important elements of foreign language education and valid traits that help prepare learners for the challenges of lifelong learning in the contemporary world.

Appendix

Dear Students, I will be grateful for your filling in the questionnaire below. It serves research purposes and is anonymous. Thanks!

Sex: Male/Female
Age: . . . . years
Nationality: . . . .
How long have you been learning English? . . . . years

1. How many foreign countries have you visited in your life?

    (a)   none
    (b)   1–2
    (c)   3–5
    (d)   more than 5

2. How many times have you been to English-speaking countries?

    (a)   never
    (b)   1–2 times
    (c)   3–5 times
    (d)   more than 5 times

3. Do you have steady access to the Internet? Yes/No
4. Do you mainly use the Internet

    (a)   at home
    (b)   at university
    (c)   at other places (e.g. Internet cafes)

    Note: CMC is "communication between humans that is mediated by computer technology" (Levy and Stockwell 2006: 24)

5. How much time on average do you spend on computer-mediated communication (CMC)?

    . . . . hours a day on weekdays
    . . . . hours a day at weekends

6. Do you use the following forms of computer-mediated communication? If you do, in which language(s) do you communicate in these ways? *Tick the ones that you use and the language of communication*

CMC form	In L1	In English	Another language?
Email			
Blogs			
Discussion forums			
Chats			
Wikis			
Instant messaging			
Social networking sites			
Virtual worlds			
Skype			
Other:			

7. How many times a week do you take part in CMC?

    (a)   less than once a week
    (b)   once a week
    (c)   2–3 times a week
    (d)   more than 3 times a week
    (e)   every day

8. How often do you use English while engaging in CMC?

Never—Rarely—Sometimes—Often—Very often

9. Please choose the best-matching answer to the questions below:

How often do you use the Internet to:	Never	Rarely	Sometimes	Often	Very often
a. read the literature of English-speaking countries (in English)					
b. watch movies in English					
c. read magazines in English					
d. read newspapers in English					
e. listen to the radio in English					
f. watch English tv programs					
g. gain knowledge about works of art from the culture of English-speaking countries					
h. gain knowledge about places of interest in English-speaking countries					
i. interact online with native speakers of English					
j. interact online in English with other non-native speakers of English					

10. Please mark the best-matching answers to the following statements according to the following key:

    1—I strongly disagree, 2—I disagree, 3—I have no opinion, 4—I agree, 5—I strongly agree.

1.	Through CMC I seek contacts with people from other countries	1	2	3	4	5
2.	I have made friends with foreigners through CMC	1	2	3	4	5
3.	My attitudes toward other cultures are more positive thanks to CMC	1	2	3	4	5
4.	I find interacting with people from other cultures interesting	1	2	3	4	5
5.	CMC helps me understand other cultures	1	2	3	4	5
6.	Through CMC I become more open to other cultures	1	2	3	4	5
7.	Through CMC I notice differences between people from different cultures	1	2	3	4	5
8.	CMC helps me gain information about other cultures	1	2	3	4	5
9.	Through CMC I learn about how people live in other countries	1	2	3	4	5
10.	CMC is a source of authentic English, which has high cultural value	1	2	3	4	5
11.	My English improves through CMC	1	2	3	4	5
12.	In CMC I share information about my own country	1	2	3	4	5

11. If you have any comments concerning your Internet contact with the culture of English-speaking countries or CMC contact with people from other cultures, please write them here: ....

References

Anderson, P.H., L. Lawton, R.J. Rexeisen, and A.C. Hubbard. 2006. Short-term study abroad and intercultural sensitivity: A pilot study. *International Journal of Intercultural Relations* 30: 457–469.

Baker, W. 2012. From cultural awareness to intercultural awareness: Culture in ELT. *ELT Journal* 66: 62–70.

Behrnd, V., and S. Porzelt. 2012. Intercultural competence and training outcomes of students with experiences abroad. *International Journal of Intercultural Relations* 36: 213–223.

Belz, J. 2007. The development of intercultural communicative competence in telecollaborative partnerships. In *Online intercultural exchange: An introduction for foreign language teachers*, ed. R. O'Dowd, 127–166. Clevedon: Multilingual Matters.

Blake, R. 2008. *Brave new digital classroom: Technology and foreign language learning.* Washington, DC: Georgetown University Press.

Byram, M., and A. Feng. 2004. Culture and language learning: Teaching, research and scholarship. *Language Teaching* 37: 149–168.

Byram, M., B. Gribkova, and H. Starkey. 2002. *Developing the intercultural dimension in language teaching.* Strasbourg: Council of Europe.

Byrnes, H. 2010. Revisiting the role of culture in the foreign language curriculum. *The Modern Language Journal* 94: 315–317.

Cadd, M. 2012. Encouraging students to engage with native speakers during study abroad. *Foreign Language Annals* 45: 229–245.

Castro, P., and L. Sercu. 2005. Objectives of foreign language teaching and culture teaching time. In *Foreign language teachers and intercultural competence*, ed. L. Sercu, 19–38. Clevedon: Multilingual Matters.

Corbett, J. 2003. *An intercultural approach to English language teaching.* Clevedon: Multilingual Matters.

Council of Europe. 2001. *The Common European Framework of reference for languages: Learning, teaching, assessment.* Cambridge: Cambridge University Press.

Elola, I., and A. Oskoz. 2008. Blogging: Fostering intercultural competence development in foreign language and study abroad contexts. *Foreign Language Annals* 4: 454–477.

Espinar, A., A. Rodriguez, and E. Parra. 2012. ICT for intercultural competence development. *Píxel-Bit Revista de Medios y Educación* 40: 115–124.

Furstenberg, G. 2010. Making culture the core of the language class: Can it be done? *The Modern Language Journal* 94: 329–332.

Kern, R. 2011. Technology and language learning. In *The Routledge handbook of applied linguistics*, ed. J. Simpson, 200–214. London: Routledge.

Korhonen, K. 2010. Interculturally savvy or not? Developing and assessing intercultural competence in the context of learning for business. In *Testing the untestable in language education*, ed. A. Paran and L. Sercu, 35–51. Bristol: Multilingual Matters.

Kramsch, C. 2011. Language and culture. In *The Routledge handbook of applied linguistics*, ed. J. Simpson, 305–317. London: Routledge.

Laskaridou, C., and L. Sercu. 2005. Experiential culture learning activities: School trips and exchange projects. In *Testing the untestable in language education*, ed. A. Paran and L. Sercu, 110–119. Bristol: Multilingual Matters.

Lee, L. 2009. Promoting intercultural exchanges with blogs and podcasting: A study of Spanish-American telecollaboration. *Computer Assisted Language Learning* 22: 425–443.

Leppänen, S., A. Pitkänen-Huhta, A. Piirainen-Marsh, T. Nikula, and S. Peuronen. 2009. Young people's translocal new media uses: A multiperspective analysis of language choice and heteroglossia. *Journal of Computer-Mediated Communication* 14: 1080–1107.

Levy, M. 2009. Technologies in use for second language learning. *The Modern Language Journal* 93: 769–782.

Levy, M., and G. Stockwell. 2006. *CALL dimensions: Options and issues in computer-assisted language learning*. New York: Routledge.

O'Dowd, R. 2007. Foreign language education and the rise of online communication: A review of promises and realities. In *Online intercultural exchange: An introduction for foreign language teachers*, ed. R. O'Dowd, 17–36. Clevedon: Multilingual Matters.

Perry, L.B., and L. Southwell. 2011. Developing intercultural understanding and skills: Models and approaches. *Intercultural Education* 22: 453–466.

Scarino, A. 2010. Assessing intercultural capability in learning languages: A renewed understanding of language, culture, learning, and the nature of assessment. *The Modern Language Journal* 94: 324–329.

Schuetze, U. 2008. Exchanging second language messages online: Developing an intercultural communicative competence? *Foreign Language Annals* 41: 660–673.

Sercu, L. 2005. Teaching foreign languages in an intercultural world. In *Foreign language teachers and intercultural competence*, ed. L. Sercu, 1–18. Clevedon: Multilingual Matters.

Sercu, L. 2010. Assessing intercultural competence: More questions than answers. In *Testing the untestable in language education*, ed. A. Paran and L. Sercu, 17–34. Bristol: Multilingual Matters.

Thorne, S. 2005. Internet-mediated intercultural foreign language education: Approaches, pedagogy, and research. CALPER Working Paper No. 6. Center for Advanced Language Proficiency Education and Research. http://calper.la.psu.edu/publication.php?page=wps6. Accessed 6 Jan 2010.

van Compernolle, R., and L. Williams. 2009. (Re)situating the role(s) of new technologies in world-language teaching and learning. In *Second language teaching and learning in the net generation*, ed. R. Oxford and J. Oxford, 9–21. Honolulu: National Foreign Language Resource Center.

Ware, P., and C. Kramsch. 2005. Toward an intercultural stance: Teaching German and English through telecollaboration. *The Modern Language Journal* 89: 190–205.

Young, T.J., and I. Sachdev. 2011. Intercultural communicative competence: Exploring English language teachers' beliefs and practices. *Language Awareness* 20: 81–98.

Youngs, B., L. Ducate, and N. Arnold. 2011. Linking second language acquisition, CALL, and language pedagogy. In *Present and future promises of CALL: From theory and research to new directions in language teaching*, ed. N. Arnold and L. Ducate, 23–60. San Marcos: Computer Assisted Language Instruction Consortium (CALICO).

Zeiss, E., and C. Isabelli-García. 2005. The role of asynchronous computer mediated communication on enhancing cultural awareness. *Computer Assisted Language Learning* 18: 151–169.

Wikis and New Perspectives for Collaborative Writing

Małgorzata Marzec-Stawiarska

Abstract This paper presents new perspectives wikis offer for collaborative writing in a foreign language. Specifically it discusses the implementation of a wiki for developing academic writing skills in a foreign language. The study described in the article showed participants' positive attitude to collaborative writing on the wiki. They valued the wiki most for the options for error correction and possibility to discuss writing on chats or with comment boxes. The study also revealed that the wiki influenced the process of writing in a positive way as students cared more about the audience, by attempting to create more accurate, more interesting and better structured products. Some problems were also observed, e.g. students were dependent on each other to complete a task, which was problematic when one of team members was late with accomplishment of his/her part. The paper also includes a detailed description of an activity which may be used as a suggestion on how to use a wiki while developing students' writing skills.

Keywords Collaborative writing • Wikis • New technologies • Social software applications

1 Introduction

Social software applications (social technologies) such as wikis, blogs, forum discussions and chats have recently become common tools for everyday communication. As they all are based on written discourse, their potential for developing writing skills in a foreign language has been noticed and put under investigation. One of them, a wiki, is based on the idea of collaborative writing in which a text is created and edited asynchronously by many authors. The research on collaboration in a foreign language classroom, understood as creating texts rather synchronously, in pairs or in groups, "in a traditional way" with a sheet of paper and a pen, has been found to be an efficient way of teaching and learning writing (e.g. Dobao 2012).

M. Marzec-Stawiarska (✉)
Pedagogical University of Cracow, Cracow, Poland
e-mail: m.marzec.stawiarska@gmail.com

© Springer International Publishing Switzerland 2015
L. Piasecka et al. (eds.), *New Media and Perennial Problems in Foreign Language Learning and Teaching*, Second Language Learning and Teaching,
DOI 10.1007/978-3-319-07686-7_3

Therefore, it seems worth analysing what benefits wikis, which allow for using new technologies to promote collaboration on a written product, have to offer in the search for efficient measures of developing writing skills in a foreign language.

2 Literature Review

The following sections present an outline of research results on collaborative writing and on the use of wikis in developing writing skills in a foreign language.

2.1 Collaborative Learning

The idea of collaborative learning can be traced back to social constructivism and Vygotsky's (1978) idea of learning and development, in particular to the zone of proximal development (ZDP) and the role of mediation. ZPD is a potential level of development which can be achieved when a novice observes and imitates an expert. In the context of L1 acquisition it is a child who when assisted by parents can develop her cognitive and linguistic knowledge. A more knowledgeable adult performs a role of a mediator who helps a novice to go beyond an actual developmental level. This experts' assistance which helps novices to develop, called *mediation*, has been also referred to as *scaffolding* (Shehadeh 2011).

In the context of L2 and foreign language learning scaffolding has most often been associated with a situation in which a teacher or any competent user of language helps a noncompetent learner to achieve higher levels of language proficiency. However, scaffolding may be also observed among foreign language students during pair or group work when they may perform a role of both an expert and a novice, depending on a communicative situation and a linguistic structure (when student A does not know the needed phrase, student B may take a role of an expert if he or she is able to recall and use the structure properly). This aspect of scaffolding has been propagated by e.g. Swain (1999, 2006, 2010) together with the notion of a collaborative dialogue. Students engage in a collaborative dialogue when they are to perform some task in a second or foreign language. As they complete their assignment they need to say or write something which gives them a chance to test language hypotheses. A collaborative dialogue also allows students to notice "holes" (Swain 2000:100) in their linguistic knowledge and "fill them by turning to a dictionary or grammar book, by asking their peers or teacher; or by noting to themselves to pay attention to future relevant input" (Swain 2000:100). When students say something aloud they end up with an 'objective product" (Swain 2000:102) that can be responded to by others or by oneself. In a collaborative dialogue students both solve problems and build knowledge. To stress this high learning potential of the process of producing the language while engaging into a collaborative dialogue Swain (2006:97) reintroduced the term *languaging* which, in this context, means using language "in an attempt to understand—to problem solve—to make meaning." Swain (2006:98) also stressed that "languaging about language is one of the ways we learn language" as it makes students engaged cognitively and memorably in a language task. The idea of scaffolding and languaging can be incorporated into collaborative writing. During writing in pairs or in groups students talk, discuss and negotiate linguistic structures which should be used to express the ideas they planned to present in a compositions. They talk about problems and try to deal with them. On many occasions when a student does not know a relevant word the other may act as an expert and suggest the right lexical item. This interaction during the process of writing seems to have many benefits, therefore the next section of the article presents the current research results on the efficiency of collaboration while composing texts in a foreign language.

2.2 Collaborative Writing

Collaborative work in a foreign language classroom is a common practice especially in developing speaking skills. However, the idea of collaboration in teaching writing does not seem to have been investigated to the same extent as only some elements of collaborative writing, namely error correction and peer feedback, have been intensely analysed and found to be of high teaching and learning value (e.g. Cho and MacArthur 2010; Diab 2010).

If collaborative writing is to be understood as cooperation through a whole process of writing in a foreign or second language, from planning to editing, the research in this area is scarce and has just started to develop. Moreover, two trends can be observed in it: the first one investigates collaboration while writing reconstructions of texts read to students by teachers (Kuiken and Vedder 2002a, b; Kim 2008), the other one focuses on the process of writing compositions in a more "traditional" way when students are given a topic and they are supposed to write an essay (Storch 2005; Shehadeh 2011; Dobao 2012).

Kuiken and Vedder's (2002a) research revealed that interaction in groups did not influence acquisition of the passive voice: there were no statistically significant differences between the experimental group, in which students collaboratively reconstructed texts, and the control group, in which students did the same tasks individually. However, the qualitative analysis of interaction revealed that group work stimulated students to notice more passive voice structures.

Kuiken and Vedder (2002b) analysed also the influence of interaction on the quality of a text reconstruction. In detail the correlation between the use of lexical strategies and lexical and grammatical diversity of texts written in groups (of three or four) during a dictogloss task was under study. The qualitative data analysis did not confirm the hypothesis that the use of lexical strategies (noticing) in the interaction while writing a text would result in a better linguistic quality of the written texts. The study also showed how difficult it was to analyse interaction in a foreign language and pointed to many variables, e.g. lexical competence of students, text difficulty group dynamics (interaction between dominating and shy students), which made interaction a highly challenging issue to investigate.

Kim (2008) compared text reconstructions written in groups and individually in order to analyse vocabulary retention. The research showed that there were no differences between the number of language related episodes in interaction of groups and think aloud protocols of students working individually. However, group writing resulted in more efficient vocabulary retention which was supported by results of a post test and a delayed post test.

Storch (2005) compared texts written by pairs with those produced individually and investigated the process of writing by analysing students' interaction recorded while they were performing a task. Collaboratively produced texts were shorter but more accurate, contained more complex linguistic structures and were superior in terms of text organisation. The analysis of the compositions' construction process showed that the participants spent most time on gathering ideas. The interview with the participants revealed their positive attitude to collaborative writing. The possibility of sharing ideas, learning from one's own and others' errors, learning new lexical and grammatical structures were the benefits of group writing students mostly appreciated. There were also some problems detected. Students were afraid to point their partner's errors not to hurt their feelings. Some students were intimidated and scared that their partner would see how little they knew. One participant noticed that collaborative writing did not allow him/her to focus on the task.

Shehadeh (2011) conducted the longest lasting study on comparing the quality of individual and collaborative writing. For 16 weeks the experimental group wrote compositions in pairs (with different partners), and control group did the same assignments individually. The research showed that collaboration positively affected content, organisation and vocabulary of compositions. No statistical differences were observed in the case of grammar and mechanics. It was hypothesised that students' grammatical competence was not sufficient to give proper feedback. The interviews with participants revealed that they appreciated collaborative writing for the possibility of speaking practice, exchanging ideas and error correction. The opinions were different as far as changing partners was concerned: some participants believed it aided learning, some noticed that it made the task more difficult, depending on a partner.

Dobao (2012) compared results of collaborative writing in the most extensive way: she contrasted individual, pair and group writing. The number of language related episodes was comparable in pairs and groups. As far as efficiency of collaboration is concerned, group work was discovered to be the most efficient, especially in the case of language accuracy. Pairs made fewer errors than individual students but the result was not statistically significant. No differences were observed in fluency and linguistic complexity. It was also observed that texts produced individually were longer than those written collaboratively.

The studies presented in this section point to some benefits of collaborative writing, e.g. higher linguistic accuracy, better text organisation, rich content and more diversified vocabulary. Moreover, efficiency of collaboration seems to depend on the proficiency level of participants: it affects accuracy positively if introduced among more advanced students. The answer to the question whether collaboration is more efficient than individual work in the acquisition of structures is negative as the attempts to measure retention of structures after collaboration did not bring any results in favour of either group or pair work. It may be also observed that the researchers frequently did not obtain statistically significant differences, which in most cases resulted from a limited number of participants as the nature of research on collaboration makes it very difficult to organise large scale research. Leaving statistics aside, affective and motivation values of collaborative writing should be stressed as it was found to be an interesting form of writing, in most cases appreciated and liked by students.

2.3 Wiki as a Teaching Aid

Wikis belong to Web 2.0 social software applications. The idea of Web 2.0 appeared for the first time during a conference session between O'Reilly and MediaLive International (O'Reilly 2005). One of its distinctive features is "harnessing collective intelligence" (O'Reilly 2005:37), which stresses an immense role of internet users who are not passive receivers of the web pages any more but active participants and creators of the internet. The Web 2.0 tools allow for and are based on active participation and collaboration of users who are now viewed as "co-developers" (O'Reilly 2005) of internet software. This social aspect of Web 2.0 can be mirrored by a rising popularity of social software applications, for example wikis, blogs, chats, forums, collaborative software, e.g. Moodle, which allow for computer mediated communication.

The first wiki was created by Wart Cunningham in 1995 and it can be defined as "a freely expandable collection of interlinked Web pages, a hypertext system for storing and modifying information—a database where each page is easily editable by any user with a forms-capable Web browser client" (Leuf and Cunningham 2001:14). Its idea is based on a voluntary contribution to a web page which is to be facilitated by an easy access and an intuitive navigation system.

As the use of wikis in teaching and learning foreign languages has just started, the research in this area is scarce at the moment. Wang et al. (2005) analysed the process of edition while writing in a foreign language on a wiki page. They focused on students' page editing behaviour and its correlation to their overall language achievement represented by final examination scores. The researchers observed that students who rarely edited the page achieved better results at an exam than "high usage group". This observation may put in doubt the value of wikis as teaching tools. The authors stipulated that it might be due to poorer students' use of learning strategies. On the other hand, it may be also assumed that more proficient students or better writers did not need to make a lot of corrections or editions in their writing as the quality of their entries/compositions was satisfactory for them at the start.

Mak and Coniam (2008) organised a wiki project among 24 students at secondary 1 level in Hong Kong. In groups of four, the participants were using a wiki to write a part of a school brochure in English which was subsequently printed, after consultation with a teacher, and handed to their parents. The researchers investigated students' engagement in wiki projects and the product. The analysis of t-units, defined by the authors (Mak and Coniam 2008:454) as "the main clause in a sentence with any dependent associated dependent clauses," showed that students' contributions were longer as the project progressed. However, an increased length of t-units resulted in an increased error rate. It was also observed that students grew in confidence as writers as the project continued. Some tendencies were also noticed in students' editing behaviour. They most often added their ideas to the text; attempts to amend, expand and reorganise the text were sporadic (they intensified as the project progressed). Researchers underlined that these text related operations could rarely be observed among Hong Kong students who very often applied a product oriented approach to writing and finished their composition once that had reached a word limit. A wiki also made students write more: though the word limit was 150 words, some of students' contributions (all the writing activities on wiki) amounted to 500 or 1,000 words. Finally, the authors observed that students became more creative as far as content was concerned. They attributed this behaviour to the fact that parents would read their product. However, this benefit seems difficult to attribute exclusively to wiki as traditional group writing which would result in a printed version could also affect a brochure's content quality to the same extent.

Miyazoe and Anderson (2010) investigated effects of three social software applications: forum, blog, and wiki in teaching EFL to students at a university in Tokyo. Students used all three tools for out-of-class writing activities. The research showed that students perceived wikis as the most enjoyable and useful applications. Blogs and forums were next. However, it should be added that while forums and blogs were used to practice writing in English, a wiki was used exclusively to translate a passage and students appreciated it for "mastering reading English, translating English and fostering communication" (Miyazoe and Anderson 2010:191).

Kuteeva (2011) analysed the use of a wiki to develop writing skills as a part of Effective Communication course at Stockholm University. Students reported that writing on a wiki made them pay more attention to grammar and spelling accuracy. They also admitted to focus more on paragraph structure though it should be added that one of the activities was strictly oriented on coherence and cohesion. Moreover, students appreciated the access to texts written by other groups. Kuteeva also analysed the use of interactional metadiscourse resources in the texts on a wiki. The high use of engagement markers (e.g. we, you) and self-mentions (I, me) was observed while writing on a wiki. Finally, students admitted that awareness that someone else would read the text made them make more effort to produce an accurate essay.

As the literature review shows, the use of wikis for collaborative writing has not been investigated in the context of developing exclusively academic writing skills among students whose major specialisation is English. Therefore, the aim of this study is to extend research into this area and analyse the wiki's potential in this context. Academic writing course participants' attitude to wikis will be analysed in detail. Secondly, the impact of a wiki on the process of writing will be investigated as there is only one study in this area. Furthermore, potential benefits of wikis for the development of writing skills will be sought and possible problems one might encounter while using wikis in developing writing will be identified. As a result, the project is to give answers to the following research questions:

- What is academic writing course participant's attitude to the use of a wiki as a tool for developing writing skills?
- What benefits does a wiki offer for the development of writing skills?
- What are students' opinions about the influence of wiki writing on the process of writing?
- What problems may occur while implementing a wiki into developing writing?

Moreover, the project fulfils an additional objective. Practical information on how to use wikis is still scarce: from the studies presented above not much can be inferred on how to plan and organise writing activities in an efficient way. Therefore, this article describes in detail a writing task prepared for the purpose of the study which can be used by trainers interested in implementing wikis into their teaching.

3 Method

In order to find answers to the research questions, a pilot study was conducted. As the author was interested in the process of writing of a small sample of students, the qualitative research was carried out.

3.1 Participants

There were ten participants in the pilot study. They were all daily students of the first year at a teacher training college. Their major specialisation was teaching English as a foreign language. They attended a course on academic writing run by the author of the article. They all passed an extended matura examination and their language competence was B2. There were nine females and one male in the group.

3.2 Instruments

For the purpose of gathering the participants' opinions about the project and the wiki's efficiency, a questionnaire was constructed (see Appendix for details). It consisted of 14 items: 11 Likert scale questions, e.g. "Writing on the wiki made me think about readers of my text more", thee open questions in which respondents were to finish a statement with examples, e.g. "The most problematic with writing on the wiki was that . . .", one closed question with a pool of answers, e.g. "Which aspects of writing with the wiki do you find beneficial? (tick as many items as you want)

- developing writing skills
- learning new vocabulary
- learning new grammar structures
- I observe how others write (. . .)
- other . . ."

The questionnaire was distributed among the students after the wiki assignment was completed and assessed. The students were asked to provide sincere answers and were informed that it was anonymous.

Moreover, the trainer wrote some field notes. Their aim was to note down problems arising during wiki implementation. Later the problems would be analysed and suggestions concerning their possible solutions formulated.

3.3 Procedure

First the author of the article set a wiki page on http://www.wikispaces.com/ and invited students to join it. Once the students had logged in they were invited to have a trial session with the wiki. For this purpose a page was created with a story which comprised some linguistic and structural errors. The students were to correct at least two errors in this text and write a few comments or get engaged in a chat about the text or accuracy of structures. They were given 2 weeks for that and if any problems appeared, they were free to ask for the trainer's help, either during classes or with the use of comments or mail box offered by a wiki engine. No explicit instruction was given about the use of the wiki as wikis' basic feature is that they are supposed to work in an intuitive way.

After this initial stage a special option offered by the wiki, called 'project', was used and students were divided randomly into three groups (2 groups of three, 1 group of four). All the groups were given the same task. They were to describe their favourite place or the place they recommend to see in the area of Rybnik, which was the place the students came from.

Students were given a model text and materials which discussed the features of a description as a genre (Evans 1998:11–17). They had also written a description of a place they recommended to visit during vacation during some previous class. The assignment was 250–300 words long and the students had 2 weeks for completing the task.

As students used the wiki for the first time and at the same time they were to write collaboratively for the first time, they were assigned a specific range of obligations which were placed on the wiki home page. Giving particular students very specific objectives was also to motivate them to participate in the task and to avoid a situation in which only some of the group members would work on a composition. The distribution of roles for Team 1, for example, was as follows:

- Introduction: Student 1
- Main body: 1st paragraph (set the scene, reasons for choosing a particular place) Student 2
- Main body: 2nd paragraph (overall look and particular details) Student 3
- Main body: 3rd paragraph (overall look and particular details) Student 4
- Conclusion: (feelings and final thoughts about the place) Student 1
- Edition: Student 2, Student 3, Student 4, Student 1

The students were also given specific instructions on how to manage the task:

Each of you is responsible for one part of a composition. However, once the last person has added the last element you are supposed to edit the whole composition (add improvements, correct errors, make it more interesting, implement any changes you think would make your composition better). Every member of the team is to do that and here you can find the order of your editions, e.g. 'Edition: Ola, Ania, Marta' means that Ola should check the composition first. If she is ready she needs to send a comment "I'm done with the edition' and then Ania will check the composition. Once she has decided she is ready she will send a comment "I'm done..." and another group member will continue. When the whole team has decided that you are ready you need to send me a message and let me know that you are done with the assignment (before the deadline).

In order to engage students into using comments and chat boxes, they got obliged by the trainer to publish a specific number of contributions. The instructions were as follows:

Before you start writing you should agree together on a place you are going to describe. Discuss it by using comment options or chat boxes on the page of your project. Each student is required to send at least one comment connected with a decision about the place you are going to describe, and do at least two corrections while editing your writing.

4 Results

The following section presents the results of the study. They are based on the questionnaires distributed among the students who experienced collaborative writing on a wiki. The tendencies in students answers were observed by looking at a frequency of choosing a particular answer.

4.1 Students' Attitudes to a Wiki as a Tool for Developing Writing Skills

Course participants seemed to have a positive attitude to writing on the wiki as seven agreed with the statement "I think that collaborative writing on wiki during academic writing course is a good idea", and nine disagreed with the point "I would rather not write on Wiki during the course any more". The research also aimed to check whether students preferred to use the wiki for collaborative writing or for individual writing. Nine participants stated that they preferred using it for collaborative work and one person preferred writing individually with it. There was also an open question which asked the participants to compare efficiency of developing writing skills through collaboration on the wiki with efficiency of individual writing. Seven respondents disagreed with the opinion that "group writing is not as efficient as individual writing". They gave the following justifications: "I like working in a group, it is better for me",[1] "I liked that we did something together", "I cared about corrections not to let my group down", "When I analyse a text written by someone else and when I read comments with corrections of errors I remember more", "Ideas of other students make conclusions easier. The possibility of consulting makes writing easier". "I see what errors others make and by that I learn how to write correctly" "We are careful with our errors and we look for the errors of others". One person said that it was equally efficient and stressed that having had more time to write on the wiki than during classes allowed them to use various sources.

Some problems with wiki writing were also observed. Two students stressed the value of individual writing pointing that while writing on the wiki they paid attention only to a fragment of a text: "We focus only on a part of the text we are responsible for and do not focus on the text as a whole", "Everyone cares only about their own piece and does not engage into correcting so much".

4.2 Wiki and the Process of Writing

The research aimed to investigate the role of the wiki in the process of creating students' texts. It was to assess whether the wiki has any influence on the content of writing, on organising compositions, on editing an essay, and on the choice of lexical and grammatical structures. Eight students agreed (two within this group strongly agreed) that they took greater care to make a composition more interesting, nine participants stated that they paid more attention to correct the structure of paragraphs. All students agreed (two within this group strongly agreed) that they checked compositions more intensely in order to make it more accurate. As far as

---

[1] The statements have been copied verbatim from the questionnaires, only spelling errors were corrected by the author of the article.

lexical structures are concerned, nine students tried to use more varied vocabulary (three strongly agreed, six agreed, one neither agreed nor disagreed). It seems that collaborative writing did not influence the quality of grammatical structures as six respondents did not know whether they tried to use more varied grammar structures, one person did not agree with the point that she/he was looking for more diversified structures and four agreed with the statement. Finally, students were to assess their attitude to the statement "Collaborative writing in wiki made me think more about the audience". It seems that the wiki makes writers more aware of readers of their product as eight students agreed with the statement (one did not agree and some other did not have any opinion).

4.3   Benefits of Wikis Acknowledged by Participants

As far as benefits of writing on the wiki are concerned, the students were given a pool of options from which they could choose. The most beneficial items identified by respondents were the possibility of correcting other students (8 students), being corrected by others (8 students), learning new vocabulary (7 students), observing how other students write (7 students) and of communicating with other students (6 students). There was also an open question in which students were asked what they liked about the wiki and nine students appreciated the options of correcting other students and being corrected by others and seven students valued the possibility of writing comments and chatting with others. Moreover, one respondent wrote "finally, after 14 years at school we are using computers to actually learn something".

4.4   Problems with Wikis' Implementation

The analysis of the answers to open questions in which students were to write about problems with the wiki and point to the things they did not like about it, some tendencies may be observed. The students' first impression of the wiki was that it was quite complicated (4 students), e.g. "at the beginning complicated, after some time easy", "at the beginning it was too complicated and I thought we don't need it".

The second problem seemed to be connected with the organisation of group work. Not everyone was equally involved, especially as far as time was concerned: "some students were responsible for their parts. It was difficult to manage because they did everything in the last moment"; "everyone entered wiki at different time, it was difficult to connect everything"; "we couldn't contact each other, when and what someone is going to write and it was difficult to combine everything in one piece"; "I didn't like it that you depend on other people and have to wait for them"; "when working in a group some people were not engaged into corrections".

The third difficulty was connected with the students' obligation to write comments. Three students complained about it, e.g. "writing comments was difficult. They should be in the form of a chat so it was difficult to make a conversation"; "I didn't like writing comments".

Three students also complained about a technical aspect of text editing, namely about a lack of an indenting option, e.g. "you cannot tab a text" "you cannot start a paragraph properly". One respondent also stressed the issue that correcting someone was problematic: "when you see that someone's piece is not good, it is still very difficult to correct it".

Field notes revealed two technical problems. The first one was students' logging in the wikispaces. It was observed that in some cases the students got the message that they were accepted as wiki members, however, they could not edit the page. The solution suggested by wikispaces administrators was that in this case a student should start his/her own wiki and through his/her wiki he/she should try to edit some page in the wiki whose member he/she wants to become. It did work, but it took some time to deal with this inconvenience and caused some delay. The second problem was that sending invitations collectively did not work as some students did not get them. If every student is to get an invitation, the best option is to send it to each student separately.

The last problem which occurred at the end of the project was the assessment of students for their writing on the wiki as it was visible for the trainer that two students were very passive and kept their activity to a minimum (surprisingly, one was the best and the second the poorest in the group).

5 Discussion

The study revealed the students' positive attitude towards the wiki used as a tool for collaborative writing of academic texts. All students also admitted to be willing to continue writing with wikis. They were satisfied with their collaborative writing which shows wikis' motivational potential in learning to write.

It was observed that wiki influenced the process of writing: the students admitted that they took a greater care of their product as they were thinking more about the audience. They claimed to have paid more attention to linguistic accuracy and paragraph organisation in their essays, which corroborates Kuteeva's (2011) study results. This study additionally revealed that they took greater care to make their composition more interesting. Moreover, unlike Kuteeva's participants, most students were not able to state whether they used more varied grammatical structures, which may suggest that at this level of linguistic proficiency the students had no competence which would allow them to diversify grammatical structures. This opinion may also result from a relative easiness of diversifying vocabulary, either with the help of a monolingual dictionary, or any dictionary of synonyms or collocations. It is more difficult in the case of grammar as students do not have equally convenient tools.

The students praised especially the opportunity that they might correct their peers' errors and that their errors were corrected. Appreciation of this option offered by the wiki might be connected with linguistic competence of the group and their writing skills. They were fully communicative, very creative and they were able to write interesting essays. However, they made numerous lexical and syntactic errors (which they were able to correct without any problems once the errors were coded by the trainer). Once they had faced the requirements of an academic writing course and assessment criteria, accuracy became a big challenge for them. Therefore, this may be the reason why they praised the wiki for the opportunity of being corrected and correcting others. This finding suggests that wikis may be very beneficial for students at a systematic stage of interlanguage development (Brown 2000) because then they need to have their errors pointed out as they are not able to notice them yet.

It was also observed that the students appreciated that they could see how other students wrote (also observed by Kuteeva 2011). Moreover, an additional benefit of wiki was revealed: the participants stressed that in this way they learnt new lexical items.

The students also seemed to value the idea of collaborative writing as such. They believed that writing in a group was easier as they worked on ideas together and they could get feedback from their peers. However, the research showed a negative aspect of collaboration on wiki, which is dependence on other students, problems with procrastination of group members and difficulty in getting everyone to work, which may be frustrating for motivated and diligent students. As stated earlier, the students were assigned very specific tasks in order to help them accomplish the project smoothly and successfully; however, it seems that it was not as efficient as expected. This observation suggests that teachers should use wikis with caution if they know that they have numerous unmotivated students.

This problem also raises the issue of assessing students for their writing on the wiki. Its complexity was acknowledged by Miyazoe and Anderson (2010); however, neither these nor other researchers suggested any specific way of dealing with this problem. In the evaluation process it may be very difficult to come up with a solution that would allow to avoid disappointment for more motivated students who got engaged in the project but could not accomplish it in a satisfactory way due to other students' delay in work. On the one hand, it would be fair to assess students for their participation, and give them different grades dependent on their share of work. On the other hand, it seems to disagree with the idea of collaborative writing, which ends with one product of a certain quality which should be assessed with one grade.

The wiki gives the opportunity to trace each student's contribution to writing and also shows who edited the text, but tracing back and analysing students' contributions would be highly time consuming and tiring for the trainer, and from a practical point of view it would be still very difficult to come up with a fair assessment (e.g. not all contributions are right choices, sometimes students' amendments made a source text of poorer quality, some students corrected a spelling error, some corrected a more complex syntactic structure). As a result, a common grade for an assignment seems to be the most practical solution. In this project the instructor allowed students to decide on their own whether they wanted to have their grade for wiki writing taken into account while giving them a final grade for the course. Two students did not want a grade as it would lower their grade point average. This seems to be a reasonable solution during initial stages of teaching with a wiki; however, it can lower students' motivation if used constantly with wiki writing.

It seems that wikis are not difficult to operate though at the beginning they may be intimidating. That is why the best option at this point would be introducing a wiki to students during a class in a computer lab. The following tasks seem necessary to run a wiki project: set up a wiki page, invite students to your wiki and accept their membership, write a piece of text on it, ask participants to edit it by introducing some changes, e.g. adding some phrases, correcting errors, deleting pieces of a text, and necessarily adding comments and using a chat (the research showed that comments were most problematic for some participants but, on the other hand, they turned out to be most valued by those who were able to use them).

The results of this project show that it is also possible to use a wiki without prior training. However, due to some problems noticed by the students and the trainer, it is not possible to conclude that the wiki worked entirely intuitively. As a result, a trial session with a trainer being present and giving instructions seems to be highly advisable as it would make the process of the wiki implementation more efficient and less discouraging for the participants.

Appointing specific tasks to the students by the trainer was deliberate as the students were using the wiki for the first time and for the first time they were writing in groups. Though this idea seemed to work as the students managed to complete their tasks and were satisfied with the outcome, it also caused some problems. Since the students were to write individually a paragraph of a text and later perform editions on the whole text, some of them complained that they focused only on their own piece and did not care much about the whole text. It seems a bit surprising as they were explicitly informed that they would be assessed for the whole composition; however, this drawback needs to be taken into consideration if the project suggested in the article is to be used in other educational contexts . It is also possible that with next writing projects the students would be more willing to edit and change larger pieces of text. As Mak and Coniam's research (2008) showed, with time and a number of compositions written on a wiki students became more willing to write and more courageous to introduce major changes in the text.

An additional benefit of writing with the wiki was observed, namely the opportunity to practice both formal and informal writing. Informal writing can be developed with comments and chats, as text written there bear some features of "orality" (Montero et al 2007), in other words, they are similar to speech. The seven students who discovered how to use these applications appreciated this option and stressed that it was an efficient way of learning a language.

Conclusions

The results of the pilot study showed that the students who experienced writing with the wiki developed positive attitudes to this form of writing. The most appreciated aspects of this social software application were options for errors correction and a possibility of discussing issues on chats or in comment boxes (though it seems that students might need some explicit instruction on how to use them). The study showed that the wiki influenced the process of writing in a positive way as students cared more about the audience, by attempting to create more accurate, more interesting and better structured products. The major problem with wiki projects was the students' reliance on each other to complete an assignment as some more diligent students were delayed by others less willing to engage in the project. The study also revealed that asking students to write one paragraph of a text may result in students focusing only on their own piece of the text. Finally, it was also noticed that for the participants the wiki did not operate in an intuitive way. Additionally, the article suggests a way of implementing wiki into teaching writing skills. Some practical guidelines on how to distribute obligations and run the wiki project are given and a sample writing task has been presented.

As a final word, it should be added that despite some problems wikis may cause as teaching tools, they seem to be valuable assets in developing writing skills which allow foreign language instructors and students to benefit from what new technologies have to offer.

Appendix

Questionnaire concerning implementing a wiki for the purpose of developing writing skills

1. I have used wikis for writing (any kind) or editing some web pages before.

   * yes
   * no

2. Group writing on the wiki as a part of an academic writing course is a good idea.[2]

Strongly agree	Agree	Neither agree nor disagree	Disagree	Strongly disagree

3. I don't want to write on the wiki any more.
4. The most problematic aspects of writing on the wiki were ....

---

[2] All the questions except for 1, 4, 5 were in this Likert scale format.

5. What I liked about writing on the wiki was ....
6. I am willing to write on the wiki but I would prefer to write individually.
7. Writing on the wiki made me think about the reader more.
8. Writing on the wiki made me use more diversified vocabulary.
9. Writing on the wiki made me use more diversified grammar structures.
10. Writing on the wiki made pay attention to paragraph construction.
11. Writing on the wiki made me think about the content more.
12. Writing on the wiki made me care more about accuracy of my writing.
13. Writing on the wiki is an efficient way of learning academic writing.
14. I am satisfied with what we managed to write on the wiki.

References

Brown, H.D. 2000. *Principles of language learning and teaching*. New York: Pearson and Longman.

Cho, K., and C. MacArthur. 2010. Students revision with peer and expert reviewing. *Language and Instruction* 20: 328–338.

Diab, N.M. 2010. Effects of peer- versus self-editing on students' revision of language errors in revised drafts. *System* 38: 85–95.

Dobao, A.F. 2012. Collaborative writing tasks in the L2 classroom: Comparing group, pair, and individual work. *Journal of Second Language Writing* 21: 40–58.

Evans, V. 1998. *Successful writing upper-intermediate*. Newbury, UK: Express Publishing.

Kim, Y. 2008. The contribution of collaborative and individual tasks to the acquisition of L2 vocabulary. *The Modern Language Journal* 92: 114–130.

Kuiken, F., and I. Vedder. 2002a. The effect of interaction in acquiring the grammar of a second language. *International Journal of Educational Research* 37: 343–358.

Kuiken, F., and I. Vedder. 2002b. Collaborative writing in L2: The effect of group interaction on text quality. In *New directions for research in L2 writing*, ed. G. Rijlaarsdam, S. Ransdell, and M. Barbier, 168–187. Dordrecht: Kluwer.

Kuteeva, M. 2011. Wikis and academic writing: Changing the writer–reader relationship. *English for Specific Purposes* 30: 44–57.

Leuf, B., and W. Cunningham. 2001. *The Wiki way: Quick collaboration on the Web*. Boston: Addison-Wesley.

Mak, B., and D. Coniam. 2008. Using wikis to enhance and develop writing skills among secondary school students in Hong Kong. *System* 36: 437–455.

Miyazoe, T., and T. Anderson. 2010. Learning outcomes and students' perceptions of online writing: Simultaneous implementation of a forum, blog, and wiki in an EFL blended learning setting. *English for Specific Purposes* 30: 44–57.

Montero, B., F. Watts, and A. Garcıa-Carbonell. 2007. Discussion forum interactions: Text and context. *System* 35: 566–582.

O'Reilly, T. 2005. What is Web 2.0? Design patterns and business models for the next generation of software. http://www.oreillynet.com/pub/a/oreilly/tim/news/2005/09/30/what-is-web-20.html. Accessed 1 Nov 2012.

Shehadeh, A. 2011. Effects and student perceptions of collaborative writing in L2. *Journal of Second Language Writing* 20: 286–305.

Storch, N. 2005. Collaborative writing: Product, process and students' reflections. *Journal of Second Language Writing* 14: 153–173.

Swain, M. 1999. Integrating language and content teaching through collaborative tasks. In *Language teaching: New insights for the language teacher*, ed. W.A. Renandya and C.S. Ward, 125–147. Singapore: Regional Language Centre.

Swain, M. 2000. The output hypothesis and beyond: Mediating acquisition through collaborative dialogue. In *Sociocultural theory and second language learning*, ed. J.P. Lantolf, 97–114. Oxford: Oxford University Press.

Swain, M. 2006. Languaging, agency and collaboration in advanced language proficiency. In *Advanced language learning: The contribution of Halliday and Vygotsky*, ed. H. Byrnes, 95–108. London: Continuum.

Swain, M. 2010. Talking-it through: Languaging as a source of learning. In *Sociocognitive perspectives on language use and learning*, ed. R. Batstone, 112–130. Oxford: Oxford University Press.

Vygotsky, L.S. 1978. *Mind in society: The development of higher psychological processes*. Cambridge, MA: Harvard University Press.

Wang, H., C. Lu, J. Yang, H. Hu, G. Chiou, Y. Chiang, and W. Hsu. 2005. An empirical exploration of using Wiki in an English as a second language course. In: *Proceedings of the Fifth IEEE International Conference on Advanced Learning Technologies* (ICALT'05), Kaohsiung, Taiwan, 5–8 July 2005.

The Foreign Language Classroom in the New Media Age: Videoconferencing and Negotiated Interaction Among L2 Learners

Barbara Loranc-Paszylk

Abstract This study aims to explore the capabilities of videoconferencing for providing L2 learners with input modification, feedback, and opportunities to produce output through negotiation. The potential of videoconferencing for language learning has already been discussed in literature. Its greatest advantage might lie in giving learners numerous opportunities to come into authentic contact and to interact in real time with native speakers and speakers of other languages. However, unlike most of the studies on videoconferencing and language learning that have focused on interactive contexts with native speakers or with expert speakers, in the present article I would like to discuss the potential of videoconferencing for negotiated interaction among foreign language learners. The students who participated in this investigation, which resulted from collaboration between the University of Bielsko-Biala (Poland) and the University of León (Spain), were from Poland and Spain, respectively (English majors in both cases). Beside the fact that videoconferenced spoken interactions between the students from two different countries were highly valued by the participants, the findings confirm claims made by Courtney (1996) and suggest that also in this particular context, the quantity of negotiation of meaning seems to depend on the particular type of task.

Keywords Interactional modifications • Videoconferencing • Meaning negotiation

1 Introduction

Interaction in a foreign language is considered a prerequisite for facilitating acquisition. Interactional modifications that contribute to making input more comprehensible and, in particular, corrective adjustments made by native speakers or experts who are more competent than the learners, draw learners' attention to the gaps in their interlanguage (Schmidt 1990), which furthermore leads to

---

B. Loranc-Paszylk (✉)
University of Bielsko-Biała, Bielsko-Biała, Poland
e-mail: bloranc@gmail.com

© Springer International Publishing Switzerland 2015
L. Piasecka et al. (eds.), *New Media and Perennial Problems in Foreign Language Learning and Teaching*, Second Language Learning and Teaching,
DOI 10.1007/978-3-319-07686-7_4

modification of their output in the L2 and its adaptation to the negotiated form (Swain 1985, 2000; Long 1996). Yet, the way L2 learners interact among themselves may differ substantially from the way learners and native or expert speakers interact. Thus, to identify and analyze the negotiation routines among L2 learners, a simple discourse model as described by Varonis and Gass (1985) may perhaps be used. In their model for negotiation of meaning, proposed on the basis of non-native speakers vs. non-native speakers (NNS-NNS) conversations, Varonis and Gass (1985) claim that the horizontal flow of conversation is interrupted when acknowledgement of a communication problem (the indicator) occurs following a source of non-understanding (the trigger); and it is continued until a response, or reaction to the response (optional), is provided; in other words, until the negotiation of meaning ends either with a positive or negative result. The conversation is then resumed to the main line of discourse.

Factors stimulating meaning negotiation and providing more opportunities for meaning negotiation among L2 learners have already been discussed in literature. Studies on negotiation of meaning indicate that it is more likely to occur in groups of NNS than in teacher-led classes (Pica and Doughty 1985), and it is more likely to occur among students with different linguistic backgrounds (Varonis and Gass 1985) as well as within small, working groups (Ellis 1994). Furthermore, interactional modifications are more likely to relate to lexical items than grammatical morphology (Pica et al. 1993). Courtney (1996) suggests that the quantity of negotiation of meaning depends on the particular type of task, hence tasks which require information exchange allow learners to plan their output, and most importantly, have a limited number of possible outcomes, may be more effective with respect to a fuller realization of meaning negotiation potential. Therefore, an information gap task, a jigsaw task, a problem-solving task or a decision-making task may result in increased interaction which facilitates acquisition, whereas a role-play task might be the least encouraging for negotiation of meaning.

Discourse markers play an important role in spoken interaction (Carter and McCarthy 2006). They signal transitions in the process of the interaction, sustain coherence of the conversation and also indicate an interactive relationship between speaker, hearer, and message (Fraser 1999), as well as in the interpersonal and cross-cultural dimension (Wierzbicka 1991). Most important, they constitute an aspect of pragmatic competence that underlies the learners' ability to use language in culturally, socially, and situationally appropriate ways, and they serve as useful interactional units to structure and organize speech on interpersonal, referential, structural and cognitive levels (Fung and Carter 2007). Discourse markers are therefore an essential indicator of discourse management skills.

Interactional modifications in foreigner talk have been classified by Ellis (1994) and divided into discourse repair and discourse management, with the latter involving an amount or type of information conveyed, use of questions, comprehension checks and self-repetition. Interactional modifications aiming at discourse repair may be linked both with repair of communication breakdown (clarification checks, requests for confirmation, self- and other repetitions, relinquishing the topic) and repair of learner error (avoidance of other correction, self-correction).

Unlike most of the studies on meaning negotiation among L2 learners that focus on classroom settings or on interactive contexts with native speakers or with expert speakers (Pica 1987; Long 1996; Foster 1998; Swain 2000) this article aims to discuss the role of videoconferencing in fostering the development of oral production in English among native speakers of Polish and Spanish, in both cases learners of English as a foreign/second language. Furthermore, while exploiting the potential of videoconferencing, it attempts to investigate: how, and to what extent, L2 learners with different L1 backgrounds negotiate meaning while interacting in English via a videoconference; which tasks best allow for interactional modifications among learners of English as a foreign/second language; and what interactional modifications students make.

2 Videoconferencing

Limited opportunities for interaction outside the classroom may be overcome nowadays through the use of new technologies, especially new capabilities for video communication that have emerged lately in educational contexts, and which are particularly useful in realizing language-learning goals (Levy and Stockwell 2006; Wang 2006; Phillips 2010; Lee 2007; O'Dowd 2000; Katz 2001; Kinginer and Belz 2005). Videoconferencing refers to a system where two or more participants in different locations can interact via both audio and visual mode in real time with the help of specialized equipment and a high-speed Internet connection (Smith 2003). Due to its cost-effectiveness, videoconferencing has become more and more popular nowadays, especially in the field of distance learning (Martin 2005; Ozcelik and Zoltay-Paprika 2010; Lawson et al. 2010).

Communication in real time that requires an immediate response along with the audiovisual channel puts the videoconferencing context very close to a real-life authentic situation. Such a claim seems to be supported by a recent study by Kim and Craig (2012) in which experimental tests were carried out with test takers using face-to-face and videoconferenced oral interviews. Findings indicated no significant differences in performance between the two test modes and also evidenced the comparability of the videoconferenced and face-to-face interviews in terms of comfort, computer familiarity, environment, non-verbal linguistic cues, interests, speaking opportunity, and topic effects. In another study, Yanguas (2010), while examining task-based, synchronous oral computer-mediated communication (CMC) among intermediate-level learners of Spanish, found no significant differences in the way video and traditional face-to-face communication groups carried out these negotiations.

As a matter of fact, videoconferencing offers many of the advantages of the traditional face-to-face mode plus the added advantages derived from the use of technological applications, which most importantly allow large distances to be bridged. It is nevertheless important to mention that videoconferencing significantly differs from text-based computer-mediated communication (CMC) since it retains audiovisual channels in the interaction, which preserves such essential elements of the communication process as visual contact, allowing the reception of non-verbal cues, and secondly, immediacy and spontaneity of response (White 2003). In the case of the videoconference, participants can compensate for their linguistic breakdowns with the use of body language to sustain the communication process with their partners. Unlike participants of traditional synchronous communication via text chats, videoconference participants cannot delay their response for too long, as they are under time pressure. As Lee (2007:637) asserts, videoconferencing relies heavily on listening and speaking skills, therefore learners may feel more pressure to process both input and output in real time.

Bearing in mind that innovation through the new technologies takes place only when we use them to provide students with opportunities to experience news way of "collaborative enquiry and construction of knowledge" (Kern et al. 2004:255), it was aimed to design a project that would allow the participants to experience a new dimension of learning: performing interactive tasks with foreign students via videoconferencing may certainly be included into such a category.

3 The Context and Objectives of the Project

The project took place at the University of Bielsko-Biala in November and December 2012. The project was designed in collaboration with Prof. Veronica Colwell O'Callaghan from the University of León, and formed a part of a series of similar projects carried out between the two institutions since March 2011 (cf. Loranc-Paszylk 2011; Colwell O'Callaghan 2012). All the participants were students reading for a BA in English and were native speakers of either Polish or Spanish. The main objective of the project was to provide participants with the opportunity to develop their speaking skills in English by preparing for and participating in a series of oral tasks performed via videoconferencing; the second objective was to investigate the effectiveness of the interactions via videoconferencing with respect to language-learning goals. It was assumed that the results obtained might contribute to establishing a list of recommendations and criteria for effective task design and language learning via videoconferencing.

In this study, while being located within the context of the videoconferencing project, we will seek to answer the following general research questions:

To what extent will the videoconferencing experience be enhanced by the task type and its organization?

Which tasks best allow for interactional modifications among learners of English as a foreign/second language? What interactional modifications do students make?

3.1 The Participants

The group of Polish students from the University of Bielsko-Biala who took part in the project consisted of 39 participants; they were randomly divided into two teams, each team taking part in one of a series of consecutive videoconferencing sessions. They were all BA students, English majors, all between 19 and 22 years old, and residing in the Bielsko-Biala region. Their English language competence could be described as oscillating between B2 and C1 according to the Common European Framework of Reference for Languages (Council of Europe 2001). Based on a pilot pre-treatment background questionnaire, we found that 4 participants stated that they had not yet had any opportunity to communicate with a foreigner in English, and another 14 students described their real life interaction with foreigners as very occasional and involving the exchange of basic information.

The Spanish interlocutors, also working in two teams (one consisting of 10 participants, the other of 15) were BA students from the University of León. They were quite comparable to the Polish students with respect to the profile of their studies and age, although their language level might perhaps have been more differentiated: generally between B1 and C1.

3.2 Technological Tools

The videoconferencing sessions were conducted in a language lab equipped with the Polycom® HDX 7000™ videoconferencing system. The equipment allowed for image transmission at a resolution of $1,280 \times 720$ and a speed of 30 frames/s, (720 p). The quality of the transmission was very good: HD voice, HD video and HD content. The device established the Internet connection directly by dialling to other endpoints (IP address).

3.3 Procedure

Our project was based on a series of videoconferencing sessions—each time with a different group of Polish participants who performed a different task interacting via videoconference with Spanish interlocutors.

Group A (25 participants, the first series of sessions) carried out the videoconferencing sessions based on a mock job application process. Group B (14 participants, the second series of sessions) carried out the videoconferencing sessions based on poster presentations followed by question time and discussions.

In the case of Group A, the project followed a number of steps as described below:

Step 1: Students prepared to play roles of job applicants. Each person needed to choose two job advertisements sent from Spain and apply for the jobs. Once the advertisements were selected, a genre analysis of CVs and covering letters was carried out in class and following brief training, the students had to write and send via e-mail their application packs which included a CV and covering letter for their two chosen job offers. As individual candidates, the students participated in two job interviews via videoconferencing. The time allowed for each interview was 10–13 min.

Step 2: Students prepared to play roles of recruiting team members. The students' roles as members of the recruiting teams involved preparing job advertisements for the Spanish applicants, collecting their applications, selecting suitable candidates on the grounds of received applications, and finally, carrying out a series of job interviews with the candidates.

It might be important to mention that in Bygate's (1987) functional analysis of speaking, the genre of job interview could be classified as an example of an interaction routine (cf. Berkenkotter and Huckin 1995), and it would suggest a certain conversational pattern with typical questions and predictable stages to be expected by the interlocutors. Therefore, it might be classified as a speaking task based on role-play.

In the case of Group B, the project followed the steps described below:

Step 1: Students prepared to play roles of poster presenters. Each participant needed to prepare an abstract for his or her poster presentation. The students were given free choice as to the topics. Once the topics had been selected, a genre analysis of an abstract was carried out in class and after brief training, the students had to write and send their output via e-mail. As individual candidates, the students had to deliver an individual presentation via videoconferencing to the Spanish audience. The time allowed for each presentation was 5–10 min with a subsequent 10–13 min devoted to question time.

Step 2: Students prepared to play roles of audience. The students' roles as members of the audience involved preparing a list of questions for the individual Spanish presenter on the grounds of the abstracts sent beforehand, and finally, asking questions and interacting with the individual presenters. In this part of our project, which was based on more authentic interaction, the students had many opportunities to freely manipulate source materials (via comparing, contrasting and evaluating), (cf. Bloom and Krathwohl 1977), which might have contributed to a more spontaneous and unpredictable flow of interaction.

All the sessions were recorded for further analysis of the students' oral interactions.

We also applied two additional data collection procedures, such as: the teacher's personal observations and the post-session informal interviews with the participants. Both the teacher's attention and the questions asked during the post-session informal interviews with the students were focused on the evaluation criteria for videoconferencing-based tasks identified by Wang (2007:593). Having adjusted the measures for CALL Task Appropriateness formulated by Chapelle (2001), Wang (2007) suggested a modified set of five criteria for evaluating videoconferencing-based tasks, namely:

- practicality (correspondence between the task and the capability of the video-conferencing tool(s) to support task completion);
- language-learning potential (realized best through balancing learners' attention both on the language forms and meaningful task-based activities);
- learner fit (correspondence between the level of the difficulty of the tasks and the level of proficiency of the learners);
- authenticity (correspondence between the videoconferencing activities and target language activities of interest to learners outside the classroom);
- positive effects of the videoconferencing tasks on the participants (e.g., the impact of the video, the impact on learners' confidence in learning, etc.)

The students were thus asked by the teacher how they liked the project, what language gains they could mention, or what personal advantages they could identify.

3.4 Results

In our case study we carried out both a quantitative and qualitative analysis of the data. For transcription and coding of the participants' interactions we used the c-unit system. The c-unit defined by Brock (1986) as an independent utterance providing referential or pragmatic meaning allows for utterances which are meaningful though not necessarily complete. The c-units are considered to be more sensitive to the transmission of meaning and therefore, are a more appropriate measure for an investigation into oral language (Foster 1998). The transcripts were coded for c-units in order to measure the incidence of negotiation routines, discourse markers and self-corrections. While analyzing students' performances, we aimed to identify examples of repairs and negotiation routines as demonstrated in Vargonis and Gass' (1985) model for NNS interactions. The results of the quantitative analysis for the performances of Group A are illustrated in Table 1.

First, let us look at the results of the job application participants as illustrated in Table 1: While the c-units for all student performances totalled 983, the number of negotiation routines equalled 43 instances, which suggests more or less 2 instances of negotiation routine per individual student performance. Among the examples of negotiation routines we identified some *clarification checks*; selected examples of which are provided below (cf. Examples 1–2). To illustrate these routines, we used the following coding: (T) for the trigger, (I) for the indicator, and (R) for response, as suggested by Varonis and Gass (1985).

Table 1 The results of group A (the role play task on job application)

Students' number:25	The number of c-units	Negotiation routines	Discourse markers	Self-corrections
Total	983	43	91	62
Mean	39.32	1.92	3.64	2.48

Example 1

- SS1:[Did you like some of them especially?] (T)
- SS2:[Could you repeat?] (I)
- SS1: [Which..which county did you prefer of all of them?](R)

Example 2

- SS1:[Why have you free time now?] (T)
- SS2:[Excuse me?] (I)
- SS1: [Why are you having free time now?](R)

While the c-units for all student performances totalled 983, the number of self-corrections in this group was 62 instances, which suggests on average 2.48 instances of self-correction per individual student performance. We identified the following examples of *self-correction* in this group's performance (cf. Examples 3–6):

Example 3

- SS1: [Where you.. Where have you travelled in Europe?]

Example 4

- SS2: [..you mentioned working as an assistant .. What is the meaning of it. . .in what sense?]

Example 5

- SS3: [For example, I was in French.. France.]

Example 6

- SS4: [..it is related with doing sth with Poland.. ehm.. Polish people]

We also identified the use of discourse markers in the students' performances; of the total 983 c-units, the total number of discourse marker instances was 91, the most typical discourse markers used by the participants being: *okay, well, yeah, so,* and *all right*. The mean use of discourse markers per participant was 3.64.

Finally, let us look at the results of the poster presentation participants as illustrated in Table 2. While c-units for all the students' individual performances

Table 2 The results of group B (the poster presentation task—students' performances during question time)

Students' number: 14	The number of c-units	Negotiation routines	Discourse markers	Self-corrections
Total	694	63	62	75
Mean	49.57	4.5	4.43	5.36

given during the question time following poster presentation together totalled 694, the number of negotiation routines equalled 63 instances, which suggests an average of 4.5 instances of negotiation routine per individual student performance. Among the examples of negotiation routines we identified some *clarification checks*, selected examples of which are provided below (cf. Examples 7–8):

Example 7

- SS1:[Do you think some students may work satisfied] (T)
- SS2:[You mean are students satisfied?] (I)
- SS1: [Ehm..are the students really satisfied because of the jobs they have?](R)

Example 8

- SS1:[Do you think censorship a necessity nowadays in filmmaking?] (T)
- SS2:[Ehm. . . you mean necessary?] (I)
- SS1: [Yes, is censorship necessary?](R)

While c-units in total equalled 694 for all student performances, the number of self-corrections in this group was 75 instances, which suggests an average of 5.36 instances of self-correction per individual student performance. We identified the following examples of individual *self-correction* in this group's performance (cf. Examples 9–11):

Example 9

- SS1: [Why is it you. . . why did you choose this topic for your presentation?]

Example 10

- SS2: [..you ever worked as a translator? .. I mean.. did you ever work as an translator or interpreter?]

Example 11

- SS3: [I mean language critical period, ehm, critical period in language acquisition.]

We also identified the use of discourse markers in the students' performances: whereas c-units in total equalled 983, the total number of discourse marker instances was 62, the most typical discourse markers being: *okay, well, yeah, so,* and *all right;* the mean use of discourse markers per participant was 4.43.

Discussion and Conclusions

As we can see from the results provided in Tables 1 and 2, the two tasks, namely the job interview based on role-play and the discussion following individual poster presentations, differ with respect to interactional modifications in foreigner talk as classified by Ellis (1994). The following categories of interactional modifications were taken into consideration: repair of communication breakdown (negotiation routines as suggested by Varonis and Gass' (1985) discourse model), repair of learner error (illustrated by a number of self-corrections made by the participants) and discourse management (exemplified by the use of discourse markers).

As regards the first category analyzed—repair of communication breakdown—we observed minor instances of meaning negotiation in the case of Group A whose participants took part in a series of videoconferenced job interviews. The number of meaning negotiation episodes amounted to less than 0.5 % of all c-units that occurred in the students' individual speaking performances. However, the number of interactional modifications made by the students who took part in discussions following poster presentations was significantly higher with respect to the previous group: there were 63 meaning negotiation episodes, which amounts to almost 9 % of all c-units. Such a difference might have resulted from the type of task performed by the students. As the job interview constitutes a highly predictable genre of spoken discourse, both the questions asked and answers given might be expected by the interlocutors and in the case of misunderstandings, they might be assumed or interpreted according to the interview etiquette without interrupting the conversation. Besides, as has been claimed by Foster (1998), any breakdown in communication suggests incompetence, therefore students have a tendency to pretend comprehension rather than clarify misunderstandings . Such an explanation might be particularly applicable in the formal settings of the recruitment process, first of all, because it is usually based on a highly predictable flow of conversation, and secondly, in this context all the details count and the candidates want to sound as professional as they can. On the other hand, post-presentation discussions can be identified as a less threatening setting for interactions—a student having selected the topic for his or her presentation and thus fulfilling the role of an expert is likely to be more self-confident and eager to clarify any possible misunderstandings. Moreover, questions asked after a poster presentation are aimed at clarification and explanation, thus any attempts to solve possible communication problems are more natural and simply essential for continuing the flow of discussion.

We may therefore assume that the episodes of meaning negotiations are more likely to occur during discussions than in the context of a role-play based on a highly predictable interactional pattern. Our findings correlate with the claims already made by Courtney (1996) who suggested that the

(continued)

quantity of negotiation of meaning depends on a particular type of task, with the role-play task being the least encouraging for negotiation of meaning.

The second category of interactional modification occurring during foreigner talk refers to repair of learner error. In our study the repair of learner error was illustrated by a number of self-corrections made by the participants. We observed numerous instances of self-correction in the case of Group A, who took part in a series of videoconferenced job interviews. The number of self-correction episodes was higher than the number of meaning negotiations in both groups and amounted to 62 (mean: 2.38) in the case of Group A and 75 (mean: 5.36) in the case of Group B. Such results correlate with the suggestions made by Schwartz (1980), who observed a general preference for self-correction over other correction in NNS/NNS spoken discourse.

Finally, with respect to the discourse management category we observed a relatively frequent use of discourse markers in the case of the group involved in the job application process (91 episodes in total, which gives on average 3.64 per individual student) and even more frequent use of discourse markers in the case of the group involved in poster presentations (62 instances in total, thus on average 4.43 per individual student). As Fung and Carter (2007:435) claim, discourse markers are useful for both native speakers and learners to structure and organize speech in several categories. On the interpersonal level, they are specifically "useful to serve as solidarity building devices to facilitate and to mark shared knowledge, attitudes, and responses", but on the cognitive level their use reflects the speaker's thinking processes and signals the management of the conversation (Fung and Carter 2007). This might explain the higher number of discourse marker instances among the students who discussed the poster presentations, since their interactions had a more interpersonal dimension and were in some cases focused on signalling the solidarity between interlocutors, or shared knowledge.

The findings suggest that the answer to the first research question—To what extent will the videoconferencing experience be enhanced by the task type and its organization?—might depend on the particular needs of learners. In order to answer this question we might refer to the results of the following data collection methods: the teacher's personal observations and the post-session informal interviews which aimed at investigating if Wang's (2007) evaluation criteria for videoconferencing had been met in this project.

First, *practicality* of the videoconferencing tools to support task completion was achieved. The Internet bandwidth along with the video and audio quality during the sessions was perfect and allowed task completion without any problems. Facial expressions, body movements and voices were clearly received by both parties and were found quite advantageous during the job application process and poster presentations (the posters were sent in advance

(continued)

via e-mail). All participants were very positive about the technological capabilities of the videoconferencing system.

The second criterion: *language-learning potential* was met successfully, especially from the perspective of exposure to spoken language, and individual engagement in interactions. Tasks involved in preparing for the interviews and poster presentations made participants focus on several linguistic forms, whereas performing such oral activities as self-presentation, answering questions asked by job interviewers and overall conversation management, were more focused on meaning and contributed to strategic and discourse competence development and in particular, the job application process might have had a positive effect on the students' level of sociolinguistic or pragmatic competence. However, from the perspective of interactional modifications as factors facilitating language acquisition, the meaning negotiations made during students' speaking performances and the discussions following poster presentations realized the language learning potential in a fuller way.

The tasks were of moderate difficulty, thus fulfilling the *learner fit* criterion; we noted correspondence between the level of the difficulty of the tasks and the level of proficiency of the learners from both Polish and Spanish groups. Moreover, as we mentioned, participants from both groups had a comparable level of proficiency in English.

As for the fourth criterion, *authenticity*—described as correspondence between the videoconferencing activities and target language activities of interest to learners outside the classroom—the results were also positive. Practicing job interviews and, to a larger extent, discussions following poster presentations were an advantage of the project, as it focused on developing skills useful in the real world. Another important aspect constituting authenticity of the project was the interaction with foreigners in English. The combination of interlocutors involved in the project gave the participants the opportunity to become exposed to and familiarize themselves with English spoken with a foreign accent.

Finally, fulfilment of the last criterion: *the positive effects of the videoconferencing tasks on the participants*, can be well illustrated by participants' engagement as reflected in informal interviews. They valued the fact that it was a peer-to-peer international project that had provided them with a unique chance to interact with peers from a different country who had chosen the same profile of studies, as well as the opportunity to try "something new" in learning. At this point it should be mentioned that our results correlate with the findings of the study that focused on the Spanish participants (Colwell O'Callaghan 2012) who were reported to find the videoconferenced interactions with Polish students helpful in enhancing the perceptions of their own and others' strengths, weaknesses and coping strategies and very motivating for further language learning.

(continued)

The second research question—Which task best allows for interactional modifications among learners of English as a foreign/second language?—can be answered in a more conclusive way. The results reported in Tables 1 and 2 suggest that it was the poster presentation discussions that stimulated interactional modifications and allowed more instances of self-correction by participants. The students who took part in the discussions following poster presentations were apparently more engaged in the conversation, making more interactional modifications, self-corrections and using discourse markers more frequently than the students who took part in the job application process. This particular part of our project was based on more authentic interactions due to some apparent affective and motivational advantages which resulted from the fact that the students' presentations concerned their personal interests and opinions—and, as Courtney (1996:321) claims, "the focus on actual meaning and problem solving through language use can provide a powerful stimulus to oral performance."

We hope that the results of the present study will show researchers and educators that we can maximize the potential of videoconferencing through carefully designed and planned tasks, which contribute to raising the learner's interest level and allow him or her to engage into meaningful interactions based on problem solving tasks rather than predictable interactional routines. Moreover, on the basis of the program designed for the videoconferencing sessions we might conclude that organizing the students' interactions according to suitable contents matching their profile of studies, interests and cognitive and emotional needs might contribute to the effectiveness of the interactions. Through this medium, learners could experience authentic interactions which are difficult to replicate using traditional L2 classroom methods.

Although our study has been limited by the small number of participants, and thus the results should not be considered generalizable, it seems quite clear that videoconferencing may offer many of the advantages of the traditional face-to-face mode plus the advantages derived from the use of technological applications, most importantly, allowing interactions of language learners from remote locations in many interesting configurations. It would thus seem reasonable to advocate that videoconferencing could be implemented very successfully in language education.

References

Berkenkotter, C., and T. Huckin. 1995. *Genre knowledge and disciplinary communication: Culture/cognition/power*. Hillsdale, NY: Lawrence Erlbaum.

Bloom, B., and D. Krathwohl. 1977. *Taxonomy of educational objectives: Handbook I: Cognitive domain*. New York: Longman.

Brock, C. 1986. The effect of referential questions on ESL classroom discourse. *TESOL Quarterly* 20: 47–59.

Bygate, M. 1987. *Speaking*. Oxford: Oxford University Press.

Carter, R.A., and M.J. McCarthy. 2006. *Cambridge grammar of English: A comprehensive guide to spoken and written grammar and usage*. Cambridge: Cambridge University Press.

Chapelle, C.A. 2001. *Computer applications in second language acquisition: Foundations for teaching, testing and research*. Cambridge: Cambridge University Press.

Colwell O'Callaghan, V. 2012. Engaging L2 undergraduates in relevant project work and interaction: A role for video conferencing. *Language Learning in Higher Education* 2: 441–461.

Council of Europe. 2001. The common European framework of references for languages: Learning, teaching, assessment. http://www.coe.int/t/dg4/linguistic/Source/Framework_EN.pdf. Accessed 1 Apr 2013.

Courtney, M. 1996. Talking to learn: Selecting and using peer group oral task. *English Language Teaching* 50: 318–326.

Ellis, R. 1994. *The study of second language acquisition*. Oxford: Oxford University Press.

Foster, P. 1998. A classroom perspective on negotiation of meaning. *Applied Linguistics* 19: 1–23.

Fraser, B. 1999. What are discourse markers? *Journal of Pragmatics* 31: 931–52.

Fung, L., and R. Carter. 2007. Discourse markers and spoken English: Native and learner use in pedagogic settings. *Applied Linguistics* 28: 410–439.

Katz, S. 2001. Videoconferencing with the French-speaking world: A user's guide. *Foreign Language Annals* 34: 152–157.

Kern, R., P. Ware, and M. Warschauer. 2004. Crossing frontiers: New directions in online pedagogy and research. *Annual Review of Applied Linguistics* 24: 243–260.

Kim, J., and D. Craig. 2012. Validation of a videoconferenced speaking test. *Computer Assisted Language Learning* 25: 257–275.

Kinginger, C., and J.A. Belz. 2005. Sociocultural perspectives on pragmatic development in foreign language learning: Microgenetic case studies from telecollaboration and residence abroad. *Intercultural Pragmatics* 2: 369–422.

Lawson, T., Ch. Comber, J. Gage, and A. Cullum-Hanshaw. 2010. Images of the future for education? Videoconferencing: A literature review. *Technology, Pedagogy and Education* 19: 295–314.

Lee, Y. 2007. Fostering second language oral communication through constructivist interaction in desktop videoconferencing. *Foreign Language Annals* 40: 635–649.

Levy, M., and G. Stockwell. 2006. *CALL dimensions: Options and issues in computer assisted language learning*. Mahwah, NY: Lawrence Erlbaum.

Long, M. 1996. The role of linguistic environment in second language acquisition. In *Handbook of second language acquisition*, vol. 2, ed. W. Ritchie and T. Bhatia, 413–478. San Diego, CA: Academic.

Loranc-Paszylk, B. 2011. Exploring the potential of videoconferencing in foreign language teaching for speaking skills development: evidence from a case study. *Scientific Bulletin - Education Sciences Series* 2: 37–58.

Martin, M. 2005. Seeing is believing: The role of videoconferencing in distance learning. *British Journal of Educational Technology* 36: 397–405.

O'Dowd, R. 2000. Intercultural learning via videoconferencing: A pilot exchange project. *ReCALL* 12: 49–63.

Ozcelik, H., and Z. Zoltay-Paprika. 2010. Developing emotional awareness in cross-cultural communication: A videoconferencing approach. *Journal of Management Education* 34: 671–699.

Phillips, M. 2010. The perceived value of videoconferencing with primary pupils learning to speak a modern language. *Language Learning Journal* 38: 221–238.

Pica, T. 1987. Interlanguage adjustments as an outcome on NS-NNS negotiated interaction. *Language Learning* 37: 563–593.

Pica, T., and C. Doughty. 1985. Input and interaction in the communicative language classroom: A comparison of teacher-fronted and group activities. In *Input in second language acquisition*, ed. S.M. Gass and C.G. Madden, 115–136. Rowley, MA: Newbury House.

Pica, T., R. Kanagy, and J. Falodun. 1993. Choosing and using communicative tasks for second language instruction. In *Tasks in a pedagogical context*, ed. G. Crookes and S.M. Gass, 9–34. Cleveland, UK: Multilingual Matters.

Schmidt, R. 1990. The role of consciousness in Second Language Learning. *Applied Linguistics* 11: 129–158.

Schwartz, J. 1980. Error correction as an interactional resource. In *Discourse analysis in second language research*, ed. D. Larsen-Freeman, 138–153. Rowley, MA: Newbury House.

Smith, S. 2003. Online videoconferencing: An application to teacher education. *JSTE E Journal* 18: 62–65.

Swain, M. 1985. Communicative competence: Some roles of comprehensible input and comprehensible output in its development. In *Input in second language acquisition*, ed. S.M. Gass and C. Madden, 235–256. New York: Newbury House.

Swain, M. 2000. The output hypothesis and beyond: Mediating acquisition through collaborative dialogue. In *Sociocultural theory and second language learning*, ed. J.P. Lantolf, 97–114. Oxford: Oxford University Press.

Varonis, E., and S. Gass. 1985. Non-native/non-native conversations: A model for negotiation of meaning. *Applied Linguistics* 6: 71–90.

Wang, Y. 2006. Negotiation of meaning in desktop videoconferencing-supported distance language learning. *ReCALL* 18: 122–145.

Wang, Y. 2007. Task design in videoconferencing-supported distance language learning. *CALICO Journal* 24: 590–630.

White, C. 2003. *Language learning in distance education*. Cambridge: Cambridge University Press.

Wierzbicka, A. 1991. *Cross-cultural pragmatics: The semantics of human interaction*. Berlin: Mouton de Gruyter.

Yanguas, I. 2010. Oral computer-mediated interaction between L2 learners: It's about time! *Language Learning and Technology* 14: 72–93.

E-mail, Facebook, and Mobile Phones as Essential Tools for Lower Secondary School Students' Communication

Anna Kozioł

Abstract The process of communication in the contemporary world and classroom has changed due to the Internet becoming more popular as an important means of exchanging information among young people. The Internet has also influenced relations and modes of communication between students and teachers. In consequence, the social distance between teachers and students has shortened and their relations have become less strict and formal. The following study concerns teacher–student, student–student classroom practices in lower secondary school, and addresses the issue of students' preferences in communication and teacher–student communication satisfaction. The participants were 16-year-olds from two village schools (located in the south-west of Poland about 50 km from the capital of the province). The study's purpose was to determine whether teacher–student communication at schools is satisfying for third-grade, lower secondary school students, and to evaluate teacher–student relationships, which appear to be satisfying and important to students. The survey revealed that students spend plenty of time in front of their computers, and most of them have mobile phones and stay in touch with teachers and classmates outside the classroom. According to the results, most students appreciate personal, face-to-face contact more than virtual or mobile phone contact, and believe that face-to-face contact can never be replaced.

Keywords Social media • Teacher–student relations • Communication satisfaction

1 Introduction

The process of communication in the contemporary world and classroom has undergone a significant change. The Internet has widened its range and become more popular, and in consequence, in every school and almost every home learners have Internet access. The Internet, with its social networks and messengers, has become an important and popular means of exchanging information among young people. Technology has become an everyday tool in the teaching profession, and is

---

A. Kozioł (✉)
Opole University, Opole, Poland
e-mail: koziolanna@interia.eu

© Springer International Publishing Switzerland 2015
L. Piasecka et al. (eds.), *New Media and Perennial Problems in Foreign Language Learning and Teaching*, Second Language Learning and Teaching,
DOI 10.1007/978-3-319-07686-7_5

used for creating materials and communicating with colleagues and learners. Technology can certainly improve input and make its quality more varied thanks to authentic materials available on the Internet. By means of technology, learners can be provided with relevant feedback, and have a chance to contact other people. Geographical distance, then, becomes unimportant. What is more, incorporating technology into teaching and learning trains students in its use—one of the fundamental skills in everyday life. Technology has also influenced relations and ways of communication between learners and teachers. As a result, the social distance between teachers and students has lessened and their relationships have become less strict and formal. However, questions arise as to whether both students and teachers accept these changes, and which type of contact—personal or virtual—is more important to learners. To address this issue, the results of a survey concerning teacher–student, student–student classroom communication practices are discussed. The study focuses on the quality of communication at local schools, students' communication preferences, and the ways teenagers use the Internet.

2 Previous Research

The following section deals with two topics—the importance of relations between teachers and students, and the new use of media in foreign language learning and teaching. The first question has been of researchers' interest for many years, and its importance has already been proven (cf. Pianta 1999). The second one, however, is still under investigation, as technology is constantly developing and its impact on teaching, and hence its educational value, is hard to grasp.

2.1 The Importance of Teacher–Student Relations

Hurt et al. (1987) emphasize that the primary difference between knowing and teaching is communication. Scientific publications provide arguments, evidence, and information that the role of the teacher has a vital impact on student performance. The teacher's communication skills, together with good teacher–student relationships, are the factors that affect the results of teaching. Moreover, Nussbaum (1992) points to other important factors such as timing, context, content, and student ability, which teachers have to deal with and adapt to in order to achieve success at work, or put another way, teach effectively.

Being a teacher is not an easy job. The teacher's task is to form, educate, and prepare young people to live their adult lives on their own in a constantly changing world. Teaching is not only connected with passing down important information, facts, and data, but also showing and indicating how to behave, form social bonds, respect, be respected by others—and ultimately, how to use knowledge gained in practice. There is no question that teachers and students are under steadily growing pressure because of rising demands and expectations (Pianta 1999). Schools are thoroughly assessed and evaluated on various bases, such as student achievement on standardized tests, additional initiatives, or documents, all of which are frequently not strictly connected with the teaching process. In Poland, teachers have numerous other duties to fulfill connected with paperwork, explanations, reports, and plans. In consequence, less and less time is left for teaching.

Teacher–student relationships have been described by Hinde (1987) as a dyadic system because every relationship is determined by the individual features of both parties, such as developmental histories, biological factors, or information exchange processes. However, the teacher–student relationship is a very special one because it is asymmetrical—as there are "differential levels of responsibility for interaction and quality that are a function of the discrepancy in roles and maturity of the adult and the child" (Pianta 1999: 73).

Students' relationships with teachers (who are non-parental adults) are emotional experiences, and for the learners provide opportunities to learn social skills. Relationships with teachers often mirror the relationships between children and their parents (Pianta 1999). Following this line of reasoning, this fact can have serious consequences, especially when these relations are disturbed by different factors in the child's home, or when children do not have good relationships with their parents. Teachers then face a serious problem, as these learners happen to be problematic, and do not know how to behave in various situations with adults or peers. In these cases the teacher's efforts might not be effective because the attitudes they support are not reinforced by parents at home, or because at home the children are inculcated with values that oppose those taught at school. Such a dichotomy may lead to confusion in the learner's mind and cause further disorders.

At every school, every learner has the opportunity to develop a relationship with a teacher (who is a qualified pedagogue), which can be a resource for development. However, some believe that computers will replace teachers in the future (Kern 2011). To justify this belief, they claim that the teacher's role is merely to familiarize learners with information, and computers can do so in a better, more interesting and creative way. Those who do not agree with this point of view state that teachers are essential in helping students understand language, culture, and the world, which means that teachers play a significant role in child development (Kern 2011). They teach learners how to live, behave, and use their knowledge and talents. Teachers spend a lot of time with learners, observe their problems and progress, then react in a way that is suited to their needs, abilities, and personalities. Computers are unable to personalize their actions to the learner, and cannot support, motivate, help, or stay with a child when they need it.

Teacher–student relationships develop during the school year through interaction. Forming strong and supportive relationships with teachers allows students to feel safer and more secure in the school setting, enter into positive interpersonal relationships with peers, and achieve greater academic success. Noddings (1992) observes that students who have good relationships with friends and teachers make learning a higher priority and thus work harder for teachers, whom they care about, since these teachers value the effort they invest in their learning. Howes et al. (1994) state that the child's relations with the mother influence relationships with teachers, and these relationships with teachers are also predictors of behavior with friends and of social adjustment. According to Hamre and Pianta (2006), positive student–teacher relationships are characterized by open communication, as well as by emotional and academic support. They are important in kindergarten and primary school, where students need to feel safe and secure in order to develop fundamental skills, abilities, and functions. Alexander and Entwisle (1988) and later Alexander et al. (1994) claim that the learner's future success or failure at school can be predicted by the end of the third grade. That is why the early school years might be described as a sensitive and very important period. Student–teacher relationships are not less meaningful during early adolescence, when students have moved from the supportive environment of the elementary school to the more disjointed atmosphere of lower secondary school. Wentzel (2002) points out that relationships that feature open communication and a sense of closeness are the most beneficial for teenage students.

Resnick et al. (1997) conducted a survey on adult health status and the role of adolescents' social context in their risk behaviors. It showed that supportive relations with adults were vital to the respondents when they were teenagers. In addition, which is of higher importance here, they mentioned teachers and school personnel most frequently as those they relied on.

In order to avoid boredom and monotony, as well as to follow current methodological trends, teachers spend numerous hours preparing lessons, searching for ideas and materials. More and more frequently they incorporate technology and new media as teaching tools in order to interest students and to show them how to use these resources in a profitable way. The additional reason for this trend is the growing popularity of technology, as its development has revolutionized communication, which has become fast and cheap and thus accessible to almost everyone. Information, photographs, and messages can now be sent all over the world in a few seconds. Nowadays, people join social networks, stay in contact, and renew their friendships on a regular basis. In consequence, these changes have reached schools. It seems justified, then, to take advantage of these media and use them in teaching.

2.2   New Media and Foreign Language Learning and Teaching

With the flow of time, computers have changed from a tool supporting individual learning to a machine engaging participants in an authentic discourse with other users, facilitating interpersonal communication (Brett and Gonzalez-Lloret 2009). Kern (2011: 200) claims that "a unique and defining feature of digital technology is that it combines previous media which were traditionally displayed in their own specific format (...) and represents text, image, sound and video with a common underlying data structure." This technology has also become popular in language learning and teaching areas. According to Brett and Gonzalez-Lloret (2009: 353), "technology is not just a tool for individual language learning, but a skill for independent language use and effective daily communication in an increasingly digital world." It is no longer a single tool but a set of tools involving various types of equipment that are used for educational purposes. Due to this fact, it is impossible to discuss all the available technological inventions and solutions incorporated in the process of teaching and evaluate their utility holistically. In this paper, attention is focused on social media such as *Facebook*, which seems to be most popular among Polish teenagers (Poland Facebook Statistics 2012), and its usefulness in teaching.

Social media is defined as "a group of Internet based applications that built on the ideological foundations of web 2.0, which allows the creation and exchange of user-generated content" (Kaplan and Haenlein 2010: 61). Boyd and Ellison (2007) distinguish three features of Social Network Sites (SNSs), which allow users to:

1. Construct a profile
2. Choose other users to connect with
3. Have access and insight into other users' connection lists and activity logs.

Hutchby (2001) focuses on technologies from another angle, claiming that they have 'design features' and 'features in use,' as they relate to the function that they were designed to serve and to the function they are appointed to serve by the user—these two are not necessarily interconnected. This situation can be observed when using social media in foreign language teaching/learning. The learners take advantage of their flexibility and accessibility and use them for educational and self-development purposes (Ota 2011). The very popular *Facebook* (with more than 10 million active users in Poland and more than 900 million world-wide: Poland Facebook Statistics 2012) has been applied as a second language learning tool by teachers during classes and by learners after school. Skon et al. (1981) suggest that peer assistance, which is involved in learning through social media, influences higher achievement more than individual effort. Because social media give the learners a chance to cooperate, it may be assumed that they are a valuable teaching aid. Blood (2002) states that through social networks learners are able to improve their literacy, receive stimuli from different backgrounds, and be encouraged by practice and active learning. Additionally, students fulfill their social needs while acquiring language, which is an additional gratification. Kern (1998) emphasizes that learners who communicate and learn through the Internet become to some extent anonymous on the web—a fact that enhances language production, especially in the case of students who are otherwise inhibited. They do not have face-to-face contact with their interlocutor, so the fear of embarrassing themselves by making a mistake diminishes. Then, they are more confident and eager to communicate, and they can check on the spot whether they were understood and if their communication was effective. This situation not only lowers the learner's stress level but also motivates him or her to learn and practice. Through social media learners have an opportunity to access native speakers and practice their skills with native users of a language, as well as to encounter authentic materials that appear in the target language and concern everyday issues (Goertler 2009).

It must not be forgotten that communication through the Internet is very distinctive in its form, especially informal communication, which involves written content but imitates oral communication. This has both advantages and disadvantages. Thurlow (2001: 288) uses the terms 'netlingo' and 'netspeak,' both referring to the language used on the Internet to describe a phenomenon of language that is a "hybrid of speech and writing in terms of format, grammar and style."

Simpson (2012) emphasizes that very few teachers share their experiences with social media use in academic journals, and there is not enough empirical evidence on the effectiveness and usefulness of this tool. However, in the light of all the above-mentioned arguments and the results of the survey presented below, it is worthwhile considering how to incorporate new media into the FL teaching process for the benefit of learners. Thus, the most popular way of communication and the opportunities that social media offer together with successful language teaching and language practice could be combined. Language learning is a complex process that requires loads of exposure, negotiation, and practice, and new media provide another chance to improve language skills.

3 The Study

The following section discusses the results of a survey on teacher–student, student–student classroom communication practices in lower secondary schools.

3.1 Aim and Hypothesis

The purpose of conducting this survey was to determine whether teacher–student communication at schools is satisfying for third-grade, lower secondary school students. Its objectives were to evaluate teacher–student relationships, which are a very important factor in the teaching process, and to gather some information about the ways of communication in the lower secondary schools of a small community.

For this study the hypothesis states that in small communities face-to-face communication dominates in educational and private contexts.

3.2 Method

The following part presents how the study was conducted. It describes in detail the participants and materials used in the study, and the procedures used to achieve the goal.

3.2.1 Participants

The participants were 46 third-grade students attending two lower secondary schools in two villages (located in the south-west of Poland about 50 km from the province capital). There were 22 students from one village and 24 students from another, all aged 16. They attended the same school and were in the same school environment for 9 years. In those villages people know one another and meet in everyday situations at local shops and the church, where they talk and exchange opinions. The adults live in a traditional community, communicating face-to-face or by telephone.

As far as their level of English is concerned, they are a varied group. Final exams are designed for two levels: A2 as the basic level and B1 as the extended level. The learners are supposed to take both parts. They all have been learning English for 9 years however, their competence varies. Their final certificate grades are between 2 and 6, which gives the mean score of 3.56 (in Poland, the lowest positive grade is 2, the highest is 6, for the outstanding students). In the case of the basic level English language exam, their mean score is 69.08 % (minimum score 28 %, maximum 100 %). At the extended level exam, their scores are lower, and the mean equals 45.48 % (minimum score 5 %, maximum 98 %).

3.2.2 Instruments

The instrument used to verify the hypothesis was a survey that consisted of 14 - forced-choice questions, e.g. How do you communicate with your teachers? After the questions a checklist of various possibilities followed, which learners marked *yes* or *no*. In some cases the participants were asked to justify or explain their choice by giving the reason for their answer. Generally, the questions in the survey were connected with the students' activities during the lesson, the quality of communication, the learners' confidence, and the preferred means of communication with the teacher and peers. The survey was in the students' mother tongue, that is, Polish. The participants' answers were analyzed by means of frequency counts.

3.3 Procedure

The survey was conducted in June 2012, 1 week before the summer holiday break. It was the participants' last week at schools before graduation. They had spent 9 years in their schools and were taught by the same teachers during that time. The participants received the surveys, which they were asked to complete. They were informed that the results would be used only for research purposes. They were ensured of the safety of personal information and encouraged to give honest answers.

3.4 Results

The survey shed light on and gave insights into lower secondary school learners' preferences in communication and ways of using the Internet and mobile phones in everyday situations. What is more, students were asked about their relationships with their teachers and about their general satisfaction with the quality of communication with the teachers, as well as about their feelings about being a student at their particular school.

The first question addressed the issue of how frequently students ask teachers questions during the lessons when they need additional explanation. Five students out of forty-six (11 %) answered that they often ask questions when something is unclear or when they need additional explanation, 29 students (63 %) asked sometimes, and 26 % asked rarely or never. They claimed that they did not need to ask because everything was clear, they were not interested in the topic, or they were afraid of being embarrassed in front of their classmates. Most of them were self-centered and lacked confidence. They worried that their peers could perceive asking for clarification as a sign of lack of possibly obvious knowledge. Consequently, such behavior would not be accepted and could result in being laughed at. Fortunately, there were not many students with this attitude towards school and learning.

Talking with students after lessons about their lives is a way that teachers can show an interest in students. Adults at schools can provide an important resource for students who are having difficulties or need to talk to someone (Pianta 1999), so the learners were asked whether they stay in touch with teachers after lessons. Their answers are illustrated in Fig. 1.

As the data show, 11 % of students never talk to their teachers after classes, during school parties, teachers' afternoon office hours at school, or through new media—their contact is restricted only to lessons and breaks. 42 % of learners rarely talk to their teachers after lessons, but 48 % do so sometimes, often, and very often. Students talk to their teachers not only during the lesson time but also afterwards, which seems to be an optimistic result, as it influences their relationship and allows teachers to find out more about the pupils.

Students were asked about their feelings while talking to their teachers. As it appeared, most students felt natural (52 %), 26 % of students had problems defining their feelings while talking to teachers, and 22 % of students felt tense or very tense. The learners implied that it depends on the circumstances and the situation in which the conversation takes place. Furthermore, both students and teachers have different personalities and some are more extroverted and outgoing than others. In addition, the question was general; it concerned all the schoolteachers, not individual ones.

Normally, being helpful, kind, and supportive regarding students is a part of the teacher's job, as creating good relationships and a friendly atmosphere makes for a more effective teaching environment, allowing teachers to be perceived as trustworthy by the learners (Hamre and Pianta 2006). The fourth question asked students

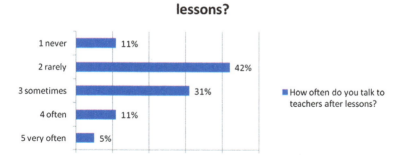

Fig. 1 Students' answers to the question: How often do you talk to teachers after lessons?

whether they expected they would get help when they told the teacher about their problems. The students' answers are presented in Fig. 2.

For some of the students it was difficult to give a precise answer and they chose the "I don't know" option. For 33 % of the students it was possibly a hypothetical situation, because students are probably not aware how often teachers help them to solve their problems. However, 54 % of the students thought that they would be treated seriously and they would get help, while only 11 % believed that they could rely on teachers. Fortunately, there were more students who trusted teachers and were aware that they were people ready and eager to help them in almost every situation. There is also a possibility that there were learners who perceived problems narrowly as a personal difficulty, mainly connected with their social life, which means that they did not ask teachers for help in such matters.

The next issue that the survey tackled was 16-year-olds' preferences for a means of communication in everyday situations with other classmates and teachers. Figure 3 shows the means by which students communicate with teachers.

Most students communicate only verbally during or after lessons. Some students (9 %) use the Internet to exchange information with teachers. At this point students' inconsistency may be observed because only 9 % of the learners admitted that they used the Internet to communicate with teachers, while 33 % students invited teachers to become their friends on social media. Possibly, students do not consider being friends on social media a way of communication or a way of exchanging information. 13 % of the students communicated with teachers on the phone in matters important to their class. Using new methods and means of communication is not popular among students as a way of communication with teachers. They prefer standard face-to-face communication at school.

As far as communication with friends is concerned, the preferences vary quite a lot compared to the previous example. The answers are illustrated in Fig. 4.

Verbal communication during face-to-face meetings with learners' friends, either at school or after school, is still most popular. Teenagers also use mobile

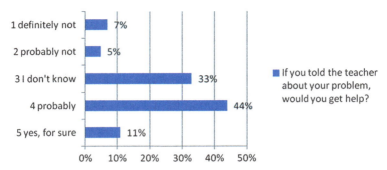

Fig. 2 Students' answers to the question: If you told the teacher about your problem, would you get help?

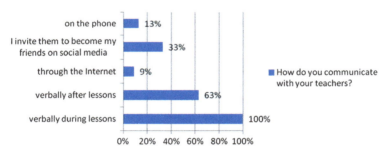

Fig. 3 Means by which students communicate with their teachers

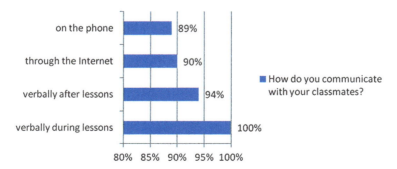

Fig. 4 Means by which students communicate with their friends

phones (mostly to send messages) as well as the Internet. As can be observed, in this case the use of new media is quite popular and appears quite frequently.

This survey also investigated communication through the Internet and the frequency of using this tool. 70 % of the students used the Internet every day in order to communicate with the classmates. *Facebook*, *Nasza-Klasa* (a Polish equivalent of *Facebook*), *gadu-gadu*, *Skype* and email were the most popular among teenagers. 8 % of the students used the Internet a few times a week, 11 % did so rarely, and 11 % did not use it to communicate with classmates at all.

Teenagers were also asked what factors they take into consideration when they choose a means of communication. They answered that their decision depended on the situation and the place they were in, or the amount of money they had in their mobile account. The survey showed that 7 students out of 46 (15 %) did not have a mobile phone and what is more, some of the learners in the group investigated did not have Internet access at home.

The 16-year-olds were asked how much time they spent with their classmates after school (face-to-face or virtually). All the students stayed in touch with their classmates and very frequently the classmates were their best friends. It is worth mentioning that there were various reasons for this situation, and one of them was the fact that these were rural communities where children live in close proximity to one another and most school children know one another not only from school. Youngsters preferred face-to-face meetings (27 students—59 %). However, mobile phones and the Internet also seemed very important tools to them.

Because the Internet and social media are very popular among teenagers, the next question was connected with preferences and habits of using them. The results are presented in Fig. 5.

Six teenagers (13 %) did not use social networks and did not have an account on any of them. The rest of the students were very active users. They shared links to interesting songs, pictures, movies, websites, exchanged information, added pictures and commented on friends' pictures. The smallest group—12 students (26 %)—admitted that they updated information about themselves, their location,

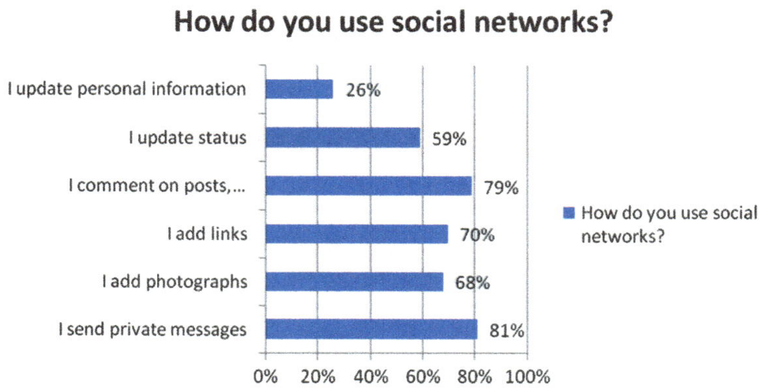

Fig. 5 How do you use social networks?

'single' or 'in a relationship' status, and private life events. Some of the youngsters admitted that social networks such as *Nasza-Klasa* and *Facebook* have become part of their everyday lives and they checked their profile at least once a day.

The last two questions concerned face-to-face and virtual contact. As regards the question "What way of communication do you prefer?"—98 % of the students answered that they preferred face-to-face communication. Only one person preferred contact by means of new media. However, they also admitted (46 %) that they spent most of their spare time after school in virtual contact with their friends. Bearing this in mind, it is interesting that when students were asked whether face-to-face communication would be replaced by new media communication in the future, their opinions were divided. Most of them claimed that new media would never replace personal, face-to-face communication (67 %), but 33 % of the students believed it would happen one day.

The last part of the survey, and the most important to the schools at the same time, concerned student satisfaction with the quality of communication between them and their teachers. Here the answers from both schools are presented separately because showing them together would not be useful, as the results come from two different schools with different teachers and different students. Figure 6 depicts student satisfaction with their relationships with teachers.

Firstly, Village A will be discussed. At this school, 20 students out of 22 (91 %) considered the quality of communication between the teacher and the students satisfying. They emphasized their teachers' openness, friendliness, individual approach to every student, the ability to listen to others' problems, and respect for the student as a person. Two students did not agree with this opinion, claiming that they were stressed and tense while talking to their teachers, and that their teachers did not treat them as partners in the conversation, but emphasized their superiority instead.

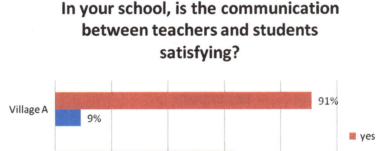

Fig. 6 Student satisfaction with their relationships with teachers

However, in Village B the results were less optimistic. Only 15 out of 24 (63 %) considered the quality of communication between the teacher and students satisfying. Those students emphasized the teachers' friendliness and individual approach to every student. Unfortunately, 9 students (37 %) did not agree with this opinion, claiming that they were stressed and tense while talking to their teachers. In these students' opinion, negative feelings were also the result of a lack of trust toward the teachers and their lack of interest in the students' problems.

On the basis of the data presented, satisfaction with good communication at school was higher in Village A than in Village B. Although most students in Village B were satisfied, the negative opinions should be taken into consideration and the situation should be carefully observed and explained. It may be the case that other factors not strictly connected with teachers, but resulting from the opinion that it is not 'cool' to have good relationships with teachers, might have influenced these teenagers' answers.

The next part presents the assumptions, explanations, interpretation, and possible reasons for the results presented above.

3.5 Discussion

The aim of this survey was to identify the preferred means of communication among classmates and teachers used by third-graders of lower secondary schools in the new media age. Additionally, the survey focused on the nature of student–teacher relations, which are crucial in the educational process, as good relationships have many advantages for both teachers and students. Generally, good relationships produce a good environment within the classroom, which is vital to the success of both the teacher and the student.

As far as the results are concerned, the survey showed that most of the students have mobile phones. They reply that if they had to choose between a mobile phone and a computer, they would prefer smart phones, by means of which they have both Internet access with all its functions, and the possibility to make phone calls and write messages. Teenagers use new media in everyday relations with peers and teachers. However, their communication with teachers is more limited when compared to their communication with peers. Actually, teacher–student relations are formal, sometimes becoming semi-formal, and their contact is mostly limited to school. This has both advantages and disadvantages, as it is not the teacher's duty to be available to the students all the time. This way of after school communication via new media happens in some important and urgent matters, but teachers have a right to privacy and students have to respect that.

Teachers at both schools are considered to be trustworthy, helpful, and ready to give advice and support. The majority of the students at both schools are satisfied with the quality of teacher–student communication in their schools. Generally, students are not stressed out and feel comfortable while talking to teachers. They easily present their different points of view, which is a perfect example of learners' being treated seriously and perceived as partners in a discussion. Hamre and Pianta (2006) mention all these issues as characteristics of positive student–teacher relationships, which are influential in forming social bonds and friendships, and important in learners' functioning in a peer group.

A slightly worrying situation appears in Village B, where the students admit they spend plenty of time talking to teachers even after lessons, they usually feel natural and comfortable in such situations and in spite of this fact more than a third is not satisfied with teacher–student relations. They feel they are not treated seriously enough and do not trust the teachers. This situation should definitely be carefully observed, checked, and explained because the teenagers might be rebellious at this age, and their answers could be the result of their way of thinking or other similar factors, such as their image—having good relations with teachers might be perceived by their friends as disloyal behavior and may weaken their position in the group—especially in the case of learners who lack self-confidence. Obviously, it might also be a sign that there is a worrying and problematic situation in teacher–students relations. In that case some actions should be taken to solve the problem and improve those relationships.

Having the results in mind and the fact that students speak more to teachers and spend more time with them in Village B than in Village A, it might be assumed that the teenagers do not want to have such a close contact with their educators. Maybe they do not expect it and do not need it, and some social distance must exist to have good relationships and a greater satisfaction in terms of relationships. Additionally, students' age must be taken into consideration because the teenagers (the 16-year-olds who took part in this survey) happen to be rebellious and it might be hard to explain their point of view due to their inconsistency.

At their age, friendship is very important. Friends give teenagers support, and make them feel needed. The participants' closest friends are very frequently their classmates, because they spend long hours together at school and afterwards their contact continues outside the school. Teenagers prefer personal, face-to-face meetings with friends, however, 46 % of students questioned admit that they spend more time staying in a virtual touch with classmates. According to that finding the statement that technology opens a door to opportunities but also closes the door to real-world encounters seems true. Learners use *Facebook*, *gadu-gadu*, *Skype*, *Nasza Klasa* (Polish equivalent of *Facebook*) and email to communicate with one another. Poland is in 23rd place in the world as far as *Facebook* popularity is concerned (the number of Polish active users is still rising) and most users come from the following age groups: 18–24, 25–34; 13–15 age group comes third (Poland Facebook Statistics 2012).

The participants spend 1–3 h every day in front of the computer. Communication through the Internet is so popular mostly because it does not restrict learners to doing only one thing. They can tidy their room, eat dinner, or do other duties while talking to a friend, without leaving home or their room. Some students even say that the greatest advantage of new media communication is that it takes less time than visiting or meeting someone.

The study showed that there are no differences as far as English language comprehension is concerned between the users of social media and students who do not use them. It might be the consequence of using them only for non-educational, leisure activities. It appeared that learners do not know the range of possibilities that such applications offer and how to use them in the way that would be profitable for their foreign language competence.

The 16-year-olds are active users of social utilities, but they are not aware of the extent to which they compromise their privacy and how far the information reaches. Only one third of the learners admit to inviting teachers to become their friends on social networks; however, according to the teachers' opinions and observations, the number of such students is higher. Accepting an invitation has its consequences, because afterwards teachers become the receivers of the information posted by youngsters. Frequently, the posts are connected with the private, social, and informal aspects of students' lives, which, in other circumstances, would not reach the teacher. This situation has both advantages and disadvantages, because in some cases it might be helpful (e.g. it might give the teacher information when a student encounters a problem or something bad happens), but more often the information is simply irrelevant to the teachers, as they are not the target receivers. There is also evidence that they do not know how to use the settings bookmark, where the group of receivers who have access to one's activities, or subscriptions, can be defined. Bearing in mind this conclusion, it would be worth considering how to make students more aware of using new technologies and social networks to be safe on the Internet, and in this way help them become conscientious users.

The hypothesis of the study was confirmed. Face-to-face communication dominates in educational and private contexts, however, the virtual one has got its supporters and is frequently chosen especially in an after school contacts.

Conclusions and Implications for the FL Classroom

To sum up, the survey revealed that the students spend plenty of time in front of their computers, and most of them have mobile phones and stay in touch with teachers and classmates outside school. According to the results, most students appreciate personal, face-to-face contact more than the virtual contact through the Internet or mobile phones. They also believe that personal contact will never be replaced.

It is obvious that essential social skills, some social nuances and unspoken rules of another culture, can only be learnt by face-to-face encounters and face-to-face communication. But bearing the results in mind, it might be worth taking advantage of social networks as an English teaching supplement. Giving an example of Internet forums, Kern (2011: 210) notes that "some of the richest learning environments may not be at all 'pedagogical' in purpose." A similar situation concerns social networks: they may be useful in foreign language learning, although it is not their target function. As far as

(continued)

technology is concerned, it is the teacher's choice to select "those tools that are the most appropriate for implementing their pedagogical approach and/or to help develop those skills that best fit to their teaching philosophy" (Brett and Gonzalez-Lloret 2009: 353).

There are numerous ideas about how teachers can incorporate new media in foreign language teaching. They can utilize *Facebook* or other social networks for class projects or for enhancing communication where students are able to continue exchanging information and continue their discussion even after FL classes. Students can connect with native speakers or keep up with the news through English-language websites which are a source of authentic English and topics concerning current affairs. Learners frequently are familiar with them in their native language that is why comprehension of authentic texts becomes easier as they can refer to their background knowledge. Learners can be shown how to join interest user groups or how to create such groups. Participation in such a group supports language learning because it takes place in a group and concerns various topics. Every post or comment can be stimulating and can be a source of knowledge as well. *Facebook*, as a new medium, allows not only receiving information but also its verification or its correction if such a need appears. Every user can comment and moderate the discussion and this way it becomes a source of knowledge in a real time.

Posting homework after English classes through *Facebook* may be an interesting routine breaker for learners. It definitely promotes collaboration and social interchange, as students can help one another. Students may be asked to create a profile of their favorite film or literary character, fan page of their favourite actor or singer, or to post an interesting photo with a comment. The additional advantage of this kind of tasks is its continuance. The profile will exist and learners can update, modify, or extend it, which is an additional language practice. However, it is advisable for teachers to create a separate teacher's account, different from their personal one. Some teachers may find it useful as a means facilitating communication, reminding students of important events, tests, or celebrations. It may be a chance for shy students who may not want to approach the teacher to communicate.

Research indicates positive effects of technology on education, as students learn more in less time when they receive computer-based instruction, and the use of technology results in a higher level of reasoning and problem solving abilities. To be effective, however, its usage must be related to the foreign language curriculum, adjusted to the learner's needs and abilities, and consistent with methodological and pedagogical principles of language teaching. Combining the popular leisure time activity with language learning purposes might be a profitable experience for learners, enhancing their motivation and skills. The last advantage, not mentioned before, is that learners are taught

(continued)

how to use such networks responsibly and how to profit from their use—as Internet literacy is now an important life skill.

Although the present study sheds some light on teenagers' preferences for means of communication, the size of the sample in the study was small, the participants came from rural communities only, and the study was descriptive in its approach. Further research involving a larger number of participants from urban communities is necessary. Additionally, conducting experiments connected with incorporating new media in the FL classroom would also be advisable in order to empirically verify the effectiveness and usefulness of social media in language teaching. It is a fact that the number of users is still rising and more and more learners are joining social media, so perhaps implementation of the most popular way of communication, which happens to be a favorite spare time activity, would contribute to successful language teaching. Therefore, researchers should direct their attention to new media and investigate their effect on language acquisition.

In this study, face-to-face communication, often associated with small communities, dominates in educational and private situations. However, it is also a fact that new media are becoming more and more popular in small communities, and very frequently are chosen as a means of communication by teenagers. The choice depends on the situation and the purpose of communication. New media are essential tools for 16-year-olds' broadly understood communication, and, bearing this in mind, its incorporation into the foreign language classroom might be a profitable routine breaker.

In closing, the purpose of the study was achieved. The findings provided some important information about teenagers' communication preferences, which are certainly worth applying in teaching foreign languages.

References

Alexander, K.L., and D.R. Entwisle. 1988. Achievement in the first two years of school: Patterns and processes. *Monographs of the Society for Research in Child Development* 53: 1–157.

Alexander, K.L., D.R. Entwisle, and S.L. Dauber. 1994. *On the success of failure: A reassessment of the effects of retention in the primary grades*. Cambridge: Cambridge University Press.

Blood, R. 2002. *The weblog handbook: Practical advice on creating and maintaining your BLOG*. Cambridge: Perseus.

Boyd, D., and N.B. Ellison. 2007. Social network sites: Definition, history, and scholarship. *Journal of Computer-Mediated Communication* 13. http://jcmc.indiana.edu/vol13/issue1/boyd.ellison.html. Accessed 25 Aug 2012.

Brett, D., and M. Gonzalez-Lloret. 2009. Technology-enhanced materials. In *The handbook of language teaching*, ed. M. Long and C. Doughty, 351–369. Oxford: Blackwell.

Goertler, S. 2009. Using computer-mediated communication (CMC) in language teaching. *Die Unterrichtspraxis* 42: 74–84.

Hamre, B.K., and R.C. Pianta. 2006. Student-teacher relationships as a source of support and risk in schools. In *Children's needs III: Development, prevention, and intervention*, ed. G. Bear and K. Minke, 59–71. Bethesda: National Association of School Psychologists.

Hinde, R. 1987. *Individuals, relationships and culture*. New York: Cambridge University Press.

Howes, C., C.E. Hamilton, and C.C. Matheson. 1994. Children's relationships with peers: Differential associations with aspects of the teacher-child relationship. *Child Development* 65: 253–263.

Hurt, H.T., M.D. Scott, and J.C. McCroskey. 1987. *Communication in the classroom*. Reading, MA: Addison Wesley.

Hutchby, I. 2001. *Conversation and technology: From the telephone to the Internet*. Cambridge: Polity Press.

Kaplan, A.M., and M. Haenlein. 2010. Users of the world, unite! The challenges and opportunities of social media. *Business Horizons* 53: 59–68.

Kern, R. 1998. Technology, social interaction and FL literacy. In *New ways of learning and teaching: Focus on technology and foreign language education*, ed. J. Muyskens, 57–92. Boston, MA: Heinle & Heinle Publishers.

Kern, R. 2011. Technology and language learning. In *Routledge handbook of applied linguistics*, ed. J. Simpson, 202–217. New York: Taylor & Francis.

Noddings, N. 1992. *The challenge to care in schools: An alternative approach to education*. New York: Teachers College Press.

Nussbaum, J.F. 1992. Effective teacher behaviours. *Communication Education* 41: 158–168.

Ota, F. 2011. A study of social networking sites for learners of Japanese. *New Voices* 4: 144–167.

Pianta, R.C. 1999. *Enhancing relationships between children and teachers*. Washington, DC: American Psychological Association.

Poland Facebook Statistics. 2012. Socialbakers.com. http://www.socialbakers.com/facebook-statistics/poland. Assessed 20 Dec 2012.

Resnick, M.D., P.S. Bearman, R.W. Blum, K. Bauman, K.M. Harris, J. Jones, J. Tabor, T. Beuhring, R.E. Sieving, M. Shew, M. Ireland, L.H. Behringer, and J.R. Udry. 1997. Protecting adolescents from harm: Findings from the National Longitudinal Study of Adolescent Health. *Journal of the American Medical Association* 278: 823–832.

Simpson, M. 2012. ESL Facebook a teacher's diary of using Facebook. *Teaching English with Technology* 12: 36–48. http://www.tewtjournal.org/VOL%2012/ISSUE3/ARTICLE3.pdf. Assessed 20 Dec 2012.

Skon, L., D.W. Johnson, and R.T. Johnson. 1981. Cooperative peer interaction versus individual competition and individualistic efforts: Effects on the acquisition of cognitive reasoning strategies. *Journal of Education Psychology* 73: 83–92.

Thurlow, C. 2001. Language and the Internet. In *The concise encyclopedia of sociolinguistics*, ed. R. Mesthrie and R. Asher, 287–289. London: Pergamon.

Wentzel, K. 2002. Are effective teachers like good parents? Teaching styles and student adjustment in early adolescence. *Child Development* 73: 287–301.

Facebook to *Facebook* Encounters in Japan: How an Online Social Network Promotes Autonomous L2 Production

Johnny George

Abstract Norton (2000, 2001), and Kanno and Norton (2003) launched an ongoing discussion on L2 use motivated through imagined communities of practice across various domains; however, there is a lack of investigation of this framework in relation to new media such as social networking services (SNSs). This study supports the primacy of the relationship between affinity with a larger international community of English users and communication through L2 English on a social network. Online social networking has become international for the first time with the recent global expansion of *Facebook*. This new domain of social networkers across physical and linguistic borders has greatly fueled the dominance of English as a lingua franca for online communication. Although most of my students, English majors in a Japanese university, communicate using exclusively their L1 (Japanese) on *Facebook*, a number of my students also actively use their L2 (English). This study examines the type of English used on the *Facebook* status update pages of 50 Japanese university English majors. About three-quarters of those students completed a survey about their use of English on social networking services (SNSs), and a small subgroup was interviewed. The study results show that students who use *Facebook* and *Twitter* increase their L2 use, even in communication with Japanese peers. Although these students felt comfortable using the L2 on *Facebook* or *Twitter*, they generally failed to use the L2 in face-to-face communication. *Facebook's* association with English along with the informality of the medium contributed to the students' desire to use their L2.

Keywords TESOL • English • Social network service • SNS • Language practice

---

J. George (✉)
University of Tokyo, Tokyo, Japan
e-mail: jeg.727@gmail.com

© Springer International Publishing Switzerland 2015
L. Piasecka et al. (eds.), *New Media and Perennial Problems in Foreign Language Learning and Teaching*, Second Language Learning and Teaching,
DOI 10.1007/978-3-319-07686-7_6

1 Introduction: An International Community of Online Social Networkers

When considering communication in the new media age, it is natural to think about the ubiquity of interaction on social network services, such as *Facebook* or *Twitter*; this study examines the use of L2 English by learners in this natural communicative context, which provides access to various languages and people of diverse social backgrounds. This qualitative study aims to: see what effect online social networking has on the choice between the use of L1 (native language) or an L2 (non-native language); to recognize strategies that foster independent language use by L2 learners, and to identify common characteristics of active L2 users. This study examines a group of students who form part of a community of users who communicate with each other via the internet. An online social network prototypically requires the use of a social networking service, hereafter referred to as an SNS. An SNS is an internet site where a user can create a personal account with a profile publically visible to other members of the site. Users post pictures or send messages to individuals or groups of users. The leading SNSs in Japan include: *Facebook* with about 20 million users; *Twitter* with about 10 million users; *Mixi* with about 25 million users; and *Line* with about 20 million users (Akimoto 2012).

New media such as *Facebook* offer a way to linguistically investigate L2 use in relatively natural language communicative contexts. Online social networking has become international for the first time with the recent global expansion of *Facebook*. This new domain of social networkers across physical and linguistic borders has greatly fueled the dominance of English as a lingua franca for online communication. Although most of my students, English majors in a Japanese university, exclusively communicate using their L1 (Japanese) on *Facebook*, a number of them also actively use their L2 (usually English).

My study investigates how an SNS may act as a gateway for language learners to develop a habit of L2 language use. For the participants in this study, the use of *Facebook* encourages the use of L2 with peers, although they may share the same L1 Japanese. This "*Facebook* effect" may allow users to more readily imagine themselves as part of an international English speaking community. Positioning themselves as L2 users in a global context allows them to expand their practice of communicating in English with international friends to include communication in English to L1 speaking peers. Such language users engage in an imaginative community of practice (Norton 2000, 2001; Kanno and Norton 2003) since they choose to use their L2 although they could successfully apply their L1 for peer-to-peer communication.

This study contributes to the growing literature on L2 use on social networks by determining to what degree the social practice of using a social network fosters L2 use. A large body of work investigates the potential educational benefits of the integration of SNS activity with L2 coursework. Kabilan et al. (2010) surveyed a group of Malaysian university students about the benefits of *Facebook* in respect to language learning. The students in the survey responded that *Facebook* interaction, supported and reinforced with coursework by the instructor, could be an effective tool for learning English. Blattner and Fiori (2011) discuss how a social network such as *Facebook* may be exploited to promote L2 development. Other research considers how the use of *Facebook* can support L2 development. For instance, Mills (2011) looks at how the situated learning environment of *Facebook* promotes pragmatic L2 language skills.

What makes this current study unique is the focus on how participation on particular SNSs can increase language learners' use of an L2. This work acts as a case study of Japanese language learners' strategies to increase their use of L2 English. In most Japanese social contexts, few Japanese people have the opportunity to immerse themselves in natural English language contexts. The use of an SNS offers a readily available, and relatively inexpensive means for English language learners in Japan to access an English speaking community. In other English as Foreign Language contexts similar to Japan, students and educators alike can benefit from an increased awareness of how a SNS can promote L2 communication.

1.1 The Imagined Community of Practice Framework

This section gives a brief overview of the imagined community of practice framework. Norton (2000, 2001) coined and elaborated the term *imagined community of practice* to emphasize the fact that L2 learners rely on both their physical communities and conceptual communities in order to develop their language competencies. Kanno and Norton (2003) reintroduce Norton's framework and Kanno (2003) further elaborates the relationship between L2 use and institutional aims influenced by imagined communities through an ethnographic study of bilingual schools in Japan. Norton (2000, 2001) combines the notion of *situated learning* and *community of practice* as developed by Lave and Wenger (1991) with *imagined communities* as outlined by Anderson (1983/2006).

The roots of *communities of practice* lie in variations of practice theory. Lave and Wenger (1991) focus on how novices learn informally from experts in various work settings. They apply notions of social practice developed from social theorists such as Bourdieu (1977) and Giddens (1984) to show how the process of information exchange takes place among people who participate together to complete tasks in a community—loosely defined as a group connected by some common role. Lave and Wenger (1991) emphasize the key role of situated learning, or the informal process of learning while performing tasks, in supporting the process of making a novice into a successful member of a given community. Experience rather than overt instruction allows for competent performance of tasks. For L2 learners, a community of practice would consist of any L2 speaking members of their communities whom they regularly interact with. Performance of L2 in social contexts contrasts with overt language instruction in a classroom in that L2 learners can actively apply their new language in real life contexts. Li et al. (2009) provide an extensive examination of how Lave and Wenger's community of practice framework has evolved and branched out for applications in many fields over time.

Anderson (1983/2006) developed imagined community as a concept to account for nationalism while Norton (2001) expands Anderson's concept to describe how individual L2 language learners gain motivation through the imagination of their future community memberships. As described by Anderson (1983/2006: 6), an imagined political community "is imagined because the members of even the smallest nations will never know most of their fellow-members, meet them, or even hear of them, yet in the minds of each lives the image of their communion." Similarly, Norton (2001) goes on to show for L2 learners that not only physical communities, but also conceptual communities may influence their language learning and use.

1.2   An SNS as an Imagined Community of Practice

On an SNS such as *Facebook*, an imagined community is presumably operative when an L2 English user identifies as a speaker of English, especially in the absence of L1 English speakers. When placed in a social context in which the learner may routinely connect to a community of speakers of that L2, we should see more pronounced effects of a community of practice in the form of increased L2 production. On *Facebook* the students applied their L2 toward an audience of users with the same L1, so the use of that SNS provides support for the operation of an imagined community of practice.

This work treats *Facebook* as an imagined community of practice. *Facebook* has a mixed audience, but those who post publicly on *Facebook* do not know who will read a given post. The language choice will depend on who the imagined audience is and also the image that the writer would like to project. Those who identify a particular SNS such as *Facebook* with a multilingual community may be more inclined to use L2 English.

Facebook in and of itself serves as a community of practice; users interact with one another and acclimate themselves to the practices of others who communicate via that medium. For instance, public chats tend to involve short, informal exchanges with content suitable for their audience of friends. The users of public posts also have an audience of specific interlocutors, and additionally a potential audience of onlookers. Those who post convey not only a message but also an image of who they are to the potential audience. *Facebook,* which originated as primarily a network of English speakers, now acts as a multilingual platform; however, Japanese users, who used *Facebook* before its expansion to Japan, likely carry on their English using practices and expose their typically non-English using Japanese friends to English on *Facebook*. The community of mixed English-Japanese users can fuel the conceptualization of *Facebook* as an English friendly medium for those who typically would not use their L2 English.

2 The *Facebook* Study

This study examines *Facebook* posts and surveys use habits of a group of non-native English speaking university students to determine to what extent an SNS can foster L2 English communication. The research on imagined communities of practice suggests that learners who associate their current or future identities with an English language community will increase their efforts to learn the language. As *Facebook* represents a language community with a strong English language affiliation, this study predicts that students will use more English on *Facebook* than on other SNSs. Student language proficiency, language experience and personal background is also examined to see what other factors influence the degree of L2 use. Students with more exposure to English and English speakers are expected to use more English than students with less exposure.

2.1 Participants

Participants in the study are Japanese native speakers who are English communication majors at a private business university in Japan. Most of the students in the study have been in the program for at least 3 years and are aged between 19 and 22 years of age. The students generally have intermediate proficiency in English and regularly study in a variety of TESOL courses. Over half of the students surveyed were 4th year students, while there were eight 3rd year, eight 2nd year and two 1st year students who completed the survey.

2.2 Method

This research involved the following stages:

- Examination of the public *Facebook* posts of 50 students
- A survey on background and social networking completed by 37 students
- Informal interviews with three female and two male students

2.2.1 Examination and Classification of Public *Facebook* Posts

In the first stage, I investigated the extent of students' use of English on *Facebook* and who their intended audiences were. The English department is relatively small with roughly 300 students so teachers are familiar with most of the English majors. Many students "friend" teachers on *Facebook,* so as a result, I had an existing network of students available on *Facebook* and could examine their public posts. I took a convenience sample of 27 female and 23 male students based on existing

Fig. 1 Example of a *Facebook* post

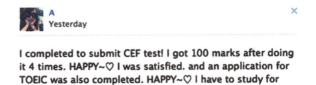

Facebook friends who consented to my use of their posts for this examination. I then classified the patterns of L2 use by the students. The language classifications allowed for identification of students' levels of L2 proficiency and examination of the extent to which they used strategies such as code switching to facilitate English communication. This preliminary investigation also provided information about the intended audiences for their posts. Above is an example of a single post by one of the students along with responses from other students (see Fig. 1).

One post consists of a communication on the "timeline" or public bulletin board of the user's account. In this case, student "A" has created a new post by putting a message on her bulletin board. Other users have the ability to comment on the post, and the creator may also add comments to contribute to a longer conversation. The collection in this study has an average of about 20 posts from each student participant. Each post has an average of about five exchanges although the length of the conversation in a post can range from one to roughly 30 conversation turns. The extent and type of English used varies greatly; therefore, a classification system was created to distinguish among the types of English used. The classification of the type of English produced in the *Facebook* posts reflects the L2 ability of the students in the study. Students with greater proficiency in English are predicted to use more English than students with less ability or experience with English.

2.2.2 Survey on Student Backgrounds and Social Network Activity

I sent surveys via the online survey site *Survey Monkey* to the 50 students who had their *Facebook* posts examined. The survey allowed me to ask questions about their general life history and language background, and see if these served as factors in the type and extent of L2 English communication. About three-quarters of the students completed the survey, which had 37 respondents—23 female and 14 male.

The complete ten-question survey appears in the Appendix. The first seven questions ask for general background information including: place of birth, early education and exposure to English, parental employment as an indirect measure of socio-economic background, and international experience. The final three questions directly ask about their language choices and interlocutors on SNSs. The SNSs specifically listed in the survey are: *Facebook*; the Japanese SNS phone application *Line*; short message service (sms), also known as text messaging; and *Twitter*, the American origin short message service. One of the most popular SNSs in Japan, *Mixi*, was not included in the survey, so most of the responses to "other network" probably reflect participation on *Mixi*.

When designing the survey, the following factors were considered as possible influences on the use of L2: socioeconomic status, proficiency in the L2, the online social network audience, and the choice of online social network technology.

The survey uses parental employment as an indirect measure of economic status as there is support for the relationship between social economic status and educational achievement. Labov (2001) discusses the correlation between social prestige and indices such as income and education level. Those with greater financial resources may have more motivation to study English as an index of social status. Additionally, such language learners can potentially devote more money to support their study of English through private lessons or to study overseas.

The online network audience, whether consisting of Japanese or non-Japanese peers, should influence the choice of language used by the students. The final two questions in the survey ask students to identify their intended audience and language choices for several SNSs. Clearly, if part of their intended audience does not know Japanese, the students would have to use English, or another language, for some of their *Facebook* posts.

The study additionally takes into consideration the fact that the specific choice of SNS may influence the language choices of the students. The SNS may affect the number of Japanese and English speaking peers in a given student's network. For instance, many students started using *Facebook* before it became popular in Japan and initially interacted with overseas friends whom they used English with; therefore, students who have been abroad may have non-Japanese proficient correspondents. The smart phone SNS *Line* began as a Japanese SNS and gradually started expanding overseas. In the case of *Line*, students are expected to have almost exclusively Japanese speaking correspondents made up of local friends. The SNS history affects the dominant language of the SNS and the likely audience for communication.

One expectation is that students who identify themselves as members of an international English speaking community will likely increase their effort to use their L2 English. As an indirect measure of language identity, the survey asks questions about whether the students studied abroad or in Japanese international schools, which would have a mix of Japanese and non-Japanese students. Direct experience with using English with non-Japanese people should have a positive effect on students' self-perception as international users of English. Students' international experience should facilitate belonging in an imagined community of practice that allows students to see themselves as part of an international community of English speakers and validate their use of English with any other English speaker, regardless of shared nationality.

2.2.3 Selected Interviews About Decisions to Use L1 and/or L2

Three female and two male students were given unstructured interviews in order to collect more data about their motivations for language choice. I asked questions such as what languages they used with Japanese and non-Japanese friends and acquaintances, and about their motivations for their language choices. The unstructured interviews allowed for some preliminary insight into student reflections on L2 use and their feelings about their language selection on SNSs. In the unstructured interviews, students were asked about why they chose between the use of Japanese and English for different peers and different SNS platforms.

3 Results

3.1 Classifications of the English Used in the Facebook Posts

This study uses a classification system to distinguish the range of L2 English use in the *Facebook* posts. The students' English skill varied in terms of length of expression and grammatical accuracy; in addition, students frequently code switched between English and Japanese.

Classifications of L2 (English) use:

- R1—L1 primary language with the addition of an L2 word or expression
- R2—L2 primary language with the addition of an L1 word or expression
- R3—Basic L2 expressions
- R4—Complex, "natural," or extended L2 expressions

The classifications represent a rating system with R1 meaning "rating 1," R2 meaning "rating 2" and so on. The progression from R1 to R4 represents the increase in complexity of English used in a given post. The categories of R1 and R2 refer to interactions that involve code switching between L1 (Japanese) and L2 (English). Code switching represents the most common use of English for all of the posts collected for this study. R1 involves the use of L1 clauses or sentences with the addition of L2 words or canonical expressions, such as "good luck!" R2 posts have the L2 as the primary clause or sentence with the addition of L1 words or expressions. The R3 and R4 categories represent posts composed in the L2, with no or very little mixing of L1. Examples of the classifications follow below.

3.1.1 R1: L1 Primary Language with the Addition of an L2 Word or Expression

One of the most common uses of English across all posts is the occasional use of English words or expressions with Japanese. In the following example (see Example 1), the writer refers to going out with her sister.

Example 1 今日は昼からsister's day だったよー!久々に妹とあった♡相変わらず!またあそぼーね!パイとがんばろー(^^)

She has not seen her sister for a long time, so she calls spending the day with her sister "sister's day." She uses English words within a Japanese sentence. In another example (see Example 2), a student uses English in a Japanese statement.

Example 2 今日は halloween party で、コスプレだしわくわく!

The writer expresses excitement about dressing up for a Halloween party. In both R1 examples, the L2 expressions are those that their friends would likely understand, even if they had little English ability. Code-switched English in these types of expressions frequently carries strong associations with foreign culture, as in the use of "Halloween party" above.

3.1.2 R2: L2 Primary Language with the Addition of an L1 Word or Expression

Another common use of English involves the integration of Japanese words or expressions with English phrases. In the following example (see Example 3), a student refers to a picture of a dish with a layer of melted cheese on top.

Example 3 Sounds DEBU!haha—えりも説明後日、やまがたかえるよ!今日はきえと会うんだー

This post starts with a phrase that mixes English and Japanese, "Sounds debu!" *Debu* means "fat," so the writer basically wants to communicate the idea that the food in the picture that accompanies the post looks fattening. The sentence follows the grammatical conventions of English, so although the use of "sounds" instead of "looks" is not accurate, the first sentence categorizes as an R2 use. The next example (see Example 4) represents a more unambiguous addition of a Japanese word into an English sentence.

Example 4 台風is coming soon.

The word台風 means "typhoon." The writer chooses to use Japanese characters rather than roman letters as in the previous example which has *debu* written in roman letters.

3.1.3 R3: Basic L2 Expressions

The third classification of posts consists of simple phrases or sentences. In the following example (see Example 5), the student posts a joke.

Example 5 Oh my god!—Oh my budda! (Japanese ver)

The writer takes a simple English expression and makes a parallel statement to reflect a "Japanese version" of an English expression.

Although expressions from the R3 category exclusively use the L2, some are in direct response to interlocutors who do not fluently read in the L1 language (Japanese), while other expressions are targeted at L2 (English) users who have command of Japanese natively. The next example (see Example 6) illustrates L2 use in response to a person who is not a native Japanese user.

Example 6 Yusuke: 今日は非常に充実した一日でした。いやー。石井さんに感謝です!

Kristy: Looking great in a suit Yusuke! What was your presentation about?

Yusuke: Thanks Kristy!! My presentation about job hunting for 3 years students:)

Yusuke created a post below a picture of himself with two other students giving a classroom presentation. The picture has a Japanese caption that reads, "I had a very satisfying day today. I am grateful to Mr. Ishida!" Kristy, a non-Japanese heritage interlocutor, asks a question in English and prompts an English answer from Yusuke. Yusuke, like many other students in the NUCB language program, had the opportunity to stay abroad for a few months and develop relationships with English users from outside of Japan. Such relationships meaningfully increased the use of English by students on *Facebook* as they developed mixed audiences of users and non-users of Japanese.

In contrast to the use of English towards non-Japanese interlocutors, students also used English directly with other Japanese students. In the next example (see Example 7), a student directly addresses another student from the university.

Example 7 Hey!! Keisuke! You should put your picture on "*Facebook*"!!!!!!!! I'm looking forward to your picture^^

Both of these students have attended at least one of my classes for the last 2 years and although they are friends with each other, I have only seen them have non-classroom lesson related conversations in their L1 (Japanese); however, in the *Facebook* environment there appears some willingness to try out English. As the study results will reflect later, students who share the same L1 will sometimes use the L2 with each other on *Facebook*, despite not using English in casual face-to-face communication.

3.1.4 R4: Complex, "Natural," or Extended L2 Expressions

The final category includes the use of English expressions with subordination or otherwise complex English structure. This category also includes the use of extensive English posts or relatively more "natural" English expression. In the next example (see Example 8) a student talks about going out the prior evening.

Example 8 I really enjoyed yesterday!! Thank you^^ But I was drunk so I had no memory after finished drinking at 昭和食堂 Lol Why didn't Ayaka take me to Karaoke!!!!

The writer uses three English sentences and the second sentence has a coordinating clause beginning with "so"; therefore, this post was classified as an R4. The only use of Japanese 昭和食堂 *Showa Shokudo* refers to the name of a restaurant so it reflects a minor code switch. The writer's intended audience consists of only other L1 users of Japanese who went out with her the previous evening.

The four categories for this study are very broad but are adequate for capturing meaningful distinctions among the types of *Facebook* posts reviewed in this study.

3.2 The Survey Results

The survey, which appears at the beginning of the appendix, asked students questions about their backgrounds, language experience and social network experience. Section 3.2 covers the results of the survey.

3.2.1 Student Background

Although the most advanced students were in their 3rd or 4th year of study in the department, their year of study did not appear to act as a significant factor in students' language choices. The regions where they were born and raised, and social class as indexed through parental occupation also did not appear as significant factors. The lack of significance of English study history and social class may reflect the lack of data available to produce significant results.

3.2.2 International School and Experience Overseas

Attendance at an international school or at least a year of study abroad before university appear to have significant effects on L2 use and performance. Of the 37 students surveyed, five students commonly posted R4 rated English posts; this made up the strongest group of English users. The five students who frequently used R4 rated expressions, before university, either attended international school (2 students) or had at least 1 year of experience studying overseas (4 students). The survey questions focus on potential environments where students may have increased exposure to English or English users. Study in an international school or abroad would insure that students would have a greater opportunity to interact with English speaking peers. Also attending such schools may have a positive effect on a student's self-perception as an English user.

Studying abroad for at least 3 months or more after beginning university seemed to have a positive impact on the degree and type of English use. All students who frequently had posts rated as R4 (5 students) or R3 (4 students) had studied abroad for at least 3 months. A period of immersion in English would account for the increased use of L2 English for these respondents. Additionally, their time abroad allowed the forming of relationships with English speakers who they later corresponded with on *Facebook* and other SNSs.

3.2.3 Choice of SNS

Results of the survey appear in the appendix, *Response to social network use questions*. The responses to survey question eight, frequency of SNS use, and question nine which asks whom students communicate with on SNSs appear in Tables 1 and 2 respectively. Percentages calculated in Tables 1 and 2 represent the percentage out of all 37 respondents in order to prevent the inflation of affirmative responses. Responses to question ten appear in Tables 3, 4, 5, 6, and 7 and ask for language choices for various interlocutors based on the SNS used. The percentage values in these tables are calculated by subtracting the number of "not applicable" responses from the number of "total responses", and then using the difference to calculate the percentage distribution; this calculation shows the language distribution based only on declared users of each SNS.

Table 1 shows that all 37 of the students surveyed use *Facebook* and the Japan originated *Line* SNS; these were the most popular SNSs chosen by the students as 95 % of the students use *Facebook* everyday and 89 % of the students use *Line* everyday. Almost all students indicated that they use *Twitter* or sms. 30 students indicated that they use another SNS network, which is likely to be *Mixi*, a very popular Japanese SNS.

Table 2 shows that students predominately communicate on SNSs with either Japanese or foreign peers. In the case of Japanese peers, *Facebook* and *Line* dominate the other SNSs with 95 % of the students frequenting those sites. *Twitter* and sms represent around 70 % of the users and other network, including *Mixi*, represent only about half the users. The other significant result is that most students use *Facebook* with non-Japanese interlocutors with 92 % for foreign friends and 59 % for foreign teachers and staff members. *Twitter* also stands out with over half of the students communicating to family members via that SNS. Based on these results, communication with peers will likely represent the largest share of SNS time, so peer-to-peer communication acts as an important influence on the students' communicative practices.

Table 3 shows that the SNSs *Facebook* and *Twitter* have a significant effect on increasing L2 communication with Japanese peers. Roughly half the students use a mix of English and Japanese with Japanese peers on *Facebook* and *Twitter*—53 % on *Twitter* and 46 % on *Facebook*. The Japanese origin SNSs have far less mix between the two languages with a majority of students using Japanese exclusively on *Line* at 72 %, sms at 82 % and other networks, largely *Mixi*, at 80 % and mixing

Facebook to Facebook Encounters in Japan: How an Online Social... 103

between English and Japanese no more than 26 % of the time on any of these other SNSs.

Tables 4 and 7 show the results for language choice towards Japanese teachers and staff, and towards family members. In both cases, students use Japanese exclusively for all SNSs between 82 % and 94 % of the time. Choice of SNS does not appear to be a significant factor in language choice when communicating with non-peer Japanese interlocutors.

Table 5 shows that students typically communicate with non-Japanese peers exclusively in English across all SNSs. Students use English exclusively with foreign peers on *Facebook* and *Twitter* 77 % of the time, the highest of all the SNSs; however, the other SNSs show large English-only use at 64 % for *Line* and other networks, including *Mixi*, and 50 % for sms. Another way of viewing the data is exclusive use of any language other than Japanese, which yields distributions of 80 % for *Facebook*, 78 % for *Line*, 70 % for sms, 92 % for *Twitter* and 73 % for other networks. *Twitter* serves as the most dominant network for non-Japanese use with foreign peers.

Table 6 shows that students typically communicate with non-Japanese teachers and staff exclusively in English across all SNSs. Choice of SNS does not appear to be a significant factor in language choice when communicating with non-peer Japanese teachers and staff.

3.3 Interview Results

I did individual, unstructured interviews with three female and three male students about their language choices on SNSs and in face-to-face communication. One of the respondents to the interview discussed how he uses English or Japanese on *Facebook* and *Line* depending on the language chosen by his interlocutor. For one Japanese peer he always uses English on *Facebook* but Japanese on *Line*. In contrast, for another Japanese peer he uses English on *Line*. When I asked him how he chooses which language to use, he said that he was not certain, but it depended on the language initiated by his peer. He felt the need to accommodate the language initiated by the other person. Such an outcome reflects the nature of communication as described in the communication accommodation theory of Giles and Smith (1979), which states that people will adjust their speech, vocal patterns or gestures to accommodate other speakers. Accommodation likely serves as a factor that fosters their use of L2 on SNSs.

I also asked the students about their language choices in face-to-face communication. One female student responded that it would be odd to talk to her peer in English face-to-face but communicating in English on an SNS was different somehow. Another student related that she tries to use English with one of her Japanese peers in face-to-face communication as well as on an SNS. Part of her motivation came from participating in a study abroad program with other students; she and her friend wanted to mutually support each other and maintain the habit of using English, which they developed overseas. Overall, the interviews were inconclusive with regards to face-to-face language choice due to the limited nature of the interviews and small sample.

4 Discussion of Three Factors that Positively Influenced L2 Use on SNSs

Based on the results of the survey and the interviews, there were three factors that reflected some relationship with the extent of English use by the students, namely, the use of the SNSs *Facebook* or *Twitter*, English education background and experience, and peers via language accommodation. The survey results and the type of English used by the students in *Facebook* posts were used to determine which factors best corresponded with the use of L2. The survey also included questions that reflected social class and education level such as, place of birth and residence, years of study at the university and parental occupation; however, the responses to these questions were inconclusive in relation to the respondents' L2 use or performance. The positive influences on the use of L2 on SNSs are explained in more detail in this section.

4.1 The Use of Facebook and Twitter and the Concomitant Increase L2 Production

The results for the survey, displayed in Tables 3 and 5 of the appendix, show that when the students communicate with Japanese or foreign friends, the choice of SNS affects their language choice. Most of the students use Japanese exclusively on SNSs when communicating with Japanese peers; however, on *Twitter* and *Facebook* twice as many students report the use of both English in Japanese in contrast to half that number on the other SNSs. In communication with foreign friends on SNSs the students largely use English but *Twitter* at 92 % has the largest number of students who use languages other than Japanese with this group. As Table 2 of the appendix shows, the students primarily use SNSs to interact with peers, therefore, their peer group has a tremendous influence on the amount of L2 they will use.

The most interesting result of the study is that *Facebook* does not simply affect *who* students communicate with, but more interestingly, it affects *what language* the students use. As expected, students' SNSs provide them with opportunities to communicate with non-Japanese speakers, and most of them use languages other than Japanese with such peers. More surprisingly, according to the survey and evidence from the *Facebook* posts, the use of L2 towards Japanese *peers* can increase because the students use *Facebook* or *Twitter*, SNSs associated with international audiences. A similar claim for the increase in L2 use can be made for *Twitter*, another SNS associated with international users, but the same cannot be said for other types of SNSs, which do not particularly have international associations. Based on the interviews, SNSs also contrast with face-to-face interactions in that some interviewees indicated that they sometimes use L2 English with Japanese peers on SNSs, while almost exclusively using L1 Japanese with Japanese speaking peers in face-to-face interaction.

The positive effect of SNS communication on L2 use may be due to several reasons. One is that SNSs such as *Facebook* and *Twitter* are associated with international communities of speakers; therefore, they facilitate an imagined community of English users. Additionally, while the social network existed only outside of Japan, early adaptors of *Facebook* may have initially posted primarily in L2. As a result, such users continued to associate *Facebook* with L2 use even after its introduction to Japan with a Japanese interface in 2011. The association of *Facebook* or *Twitter* with international peers can then even bleed over and affect the choice of language used with other L1 Japanese interlocutors, and thus license the use of English in interactions where the L1 could otherwise be used without a problem.

The medium and informality of an SNS may also facilitate L2 use. *Facebook* and *Twitter* involve largely communication on public posts; such contexts encourage students to consider not only their Japanese speaking audience, but also their non-Japanese speaking audience. Even though students code switch between English and Japanese in ways non-Japanese speakers cannot understand, just the perception of a mixed audience may prime the students to include English as part of their posts.

Communication on an SNS licenses the use of short phrases in interactions; even native users of English write short posts; therefore, L2 English users can create and respond to posts with short statements legitimately as such communication remains consistent with the norms of an SNS community. This lack of formality allows proficient L2 users to interact with native users on a nearly equal language level. Although there may be errors in production, in so far as a given message is clear, SNS interaction can result in positive feedback in the form of meaningful responses and conversations.

Finally, SNSs such as *Facebook* serve as safe spaces for L2 learners to test their burgeoning language ability. Communicators can avoid the embarrassment of mistakes and misunderstandings in face-to-face interaction. The pressure to perform in real time can be avoided and L2 users can take as much time as needed to create suitable posts or responses to other posts. Users can also target the conversations that they can understand.

Another interesting effect is that there may be L2 "spillover" from *Facebook* into other SNSs. The use of L2 towards other native Japanese speakers on *Twitter* may be due to the association of *Twitter* with an international platform; however, on *Line*, a native Japanese SNS, about a quarter of the respondents indicated that they use Japanese and English with Japanese peers. Since their peers on *Line* are largely Japanese, 95 % as shown in Table 2, it may be the case that the use of English on

Facebook has encouraged a broader use of L2 on other SNS platforms. Since groups of friends my overlap between both *Facebook* and *Line* platforms, students might transplant their English use with particular friends on *Facebook* to *Line* when communicating with those same peers.

4.2 English Education Background and Identity with Community of English Speakers

Ultimately, English experience and language use context both appear to influence the use of L2. Specifically in the case of SNSs, the ability to envision oneself as part of a larger community of English users, consistent with the Norton (2001) and Kanno and Norton (2003) sense of an imagined community of practice, can foster L2 use. For students who study abroad, direct association with peers in an immersive English environment produces an experience that has an effect on their perception as language users. They can see that the world of English speakers extends to a large population of speakers who use English as an L2 lingua franca. Students abroad experience some of the practical functionality of English so they can understand English as a communicative medium rather than merely an area of study. Upon their return from experiences abroad, some of the students interviewed noted that they felt more motivated to try to use English upon returning to Japan. An SNS network not only connects such students to new acquaintances and friends from abroad, but also provides a safe avenue to practice or even showcase some of the new L2 language skills honed abroad. Additionally, for English majors in a university program, an SNS provides an avenue to practice and skills acquired in the university.

4.3 Language Accommodation and the Peer Effect

Language accommodation (Giles and Smith 1979), or the adjustment of speech to accommodate the interlocutor, significantly affects the students' language choice. Despite the fact that the students largely interact in a Japanese language dominant environment with their Japanese peers, they will use English on *Facebook* or *Twitter* with those peers. Japanese friends who use L2 English persistently encourage other Japanese peers to use L2 through example. As a result, particular students can reinforce *Facebook* as a safe environment for L2 English use and bolster the presence of L2 in even L1 dominant communities. The presence of peer groups internationally also encourages the use of L2 English, since the students want to make their public posts accessible to their potentially international audience.

5 The Study Limitations

This study on *Facebook* use has a number of limitations. The sample of students surveyed and *Facebook* posts examined reflect only a convenience sample with a very limited number of participants. A future study would involve a greater number of students and random sampling. The restrictive, small population investigated also means that the results of the investigation may not be representative, so further studies are necessary to test the results of this work. The survey neglects to single out the Japanese dominant SNS *Mixi*, so direct comparison with the English dominant SNSs *Facebook* and *Twitter* was not possible. The survey also fails to ask users about their language choices in face-to-face communication, especially in a way that would determine if they otherwise spoke L1 Japanese to peers they communicated to via an L2 on SNSs. The survey also failed to include open-ended questions related to their motivations for choosing between the use of Japanese or an L2. The survey and interview data consist of self-reported responses from the students, so the results may reflect biases that do not accurately reflect the students' actual L1 and L2 language uses. Any future study would address these concerns.

> **Conclusion**
> This study examines the use of L2 by English learners in an actual communicative and social context. It shows that a group of active L2 users on *Facebook* and *Twitter* increase their L2 production when communicating with Japanese and non-Japanese peers. The users of more advanced English typically had early experiences abroad that may have reinforced their identities as international English users. Additionally, international experience provided a basis for the perception of the students' *Facebook* audience as comprised of an international and Japanese community of English users.
>
> The key stage in a student's use of English comes when the students recognize that their own Japanese peers indeed belong to their English using community. The recognition of their peers as English users, at least in the *Facebook* or *Twitter* context, briefly delinks the strong association between the language of communication and nationality.
>
> This work demonstrates that the medium of an SNS affects the choice of language used. When students use an SNS associated with English speaking communities such as *Facebook* or *Twitter*, they feel more inclined to try using their L2 English. On Japanese origin networks, they use significantly less English. Participation of an international audience drives the increased use of English on *Facebook* and *Twitter* by the students; however, since English use extends to other Japanese peers, the perception of themselves as international users of English appears also to be affected by the choice of SNS community. This result supports the relevance of an imagined community of practice (Norton 2001; Kanno and Norton 2003) when using an L2.

(continued)

Finally, this study recognizes strategies that foster independent language use by L2 learners. Provision of a relatively safe language use environment such as an SNS can encourage an L2 user to test out his or her ability in that L2. The ability to participate and respond according to one's own ability level on an SNS ensures a safe communication environment. The presence of English written by other L2 users not only creates a safe language use environment, but also promotes accommodation, whereby other English L2 users may feel more obliged to respond in English if another peer writes a post using English.

In the case of SNSs such as *Facebook*, sometimes it is not the message, but the messenger that is important. Both *Facebook* and *Twitter* bring together a number of elements that encourage the use of L2: a mixed international audience which requires a shared lingua franca; a modality that licenses communication via short informal phrases; and a platform with origins grounded in the use of English. While L2 use on SNSs does not necessarily entail the use of the L2 in face-to-face interactions, it still facilitates the natural use of L2 English on a regular basis in informal writing.

Social networking opens a new avenue for second language users. Although one may expect the language use in a social networking space to parallel the use in face-to-face encounters, in fact it does not. Factors that influence the degree of second language use on *Facebook* are peer presence in the network, topics discussed and an "image" factor—the decision of how to present oneself in a public social forum. In his study on L2 English use by a group of Taiwanese students, Seilhamer (2010) similarly finds that his students use English on *Facebook* with peers they otherwise would speak to in their L1. Seilhamer's students express a number of motivations for their desire to use English on *Facebook*. They wish to use English in a less face-threatening context and distinguish themselves from peers who do not interact in English on *Facebook* (Seilhamer 2010: 333). Additionally, their choice of language has a strong association with participation on SNSs that they associate with discourse communities of English speakers. Some of the key factors that support L2 use in the *Facebook* environment are that it is public and provides a way to project, represent and promote a desired image or identity.

English novices may use an SNS, such as *Facebook*, as a gateway community to use English even though they lack a native English speaking audience. If a given SNS were to simply increase the amount of English used with native speakers, it would represent a community of practice; however, students increased their use of English toward their peers on *Facebook* and *Twitter*. On those SNSs, English is not used simply because there are English speakers but because one's identity becomes, in a sense, transnational.

Facebook to *Facebook* Encounters in Japan: How an Online Social...

Appendix

Social Network Survey

1. What is your name? 名前はなんですか。
2. What year are you at NUCB? 名商大の安然生ですか。
3. What city were you born in? 生まれた都市はどこですか。
4. What city did you grow up in? 育った都市はどこですか。
5. Did you ever study at an international school in Japan? If yes, where and for how long?
6. Parent's occupations:

   (a) What is your father's occupation? お父さんの仕事はなんですか。
   (b) What is your mother's occupation? お母さんの仕事はなんですか。

7. List your experience overseas. (Where? What year? How long? Purpose?) 海外の経験を例挙してください。(どこ?なんねん?どんなぐらい?目的?)
8. How often do you use...? どんなぐらいの頻度でそれぞれのソーシャルネットワークを使いますか。

	Everyday 毎日	Once a week 週に一度	Once a month 月ごと	Rarely めったにない	Never 使わない
Facebook					
LINE					
sms					
Twitter					
Other network 他のネットワーク					

9. Who do you communicate with on social networks? 誰と会話しますか。

	Japanese friends 日本人の友達	Japanese teachers/staff 日本人と先生と職員	Foreign friends 外国人の友達	Foreign teachers/staff 外国人先生と職員	Family members 家族や親戚
Facebook					
LINE					
sms					
Twitter					
Other network 他のネットワーク					

10. What languages do you often use? To whom? よく使う言語は何ですか。だれに?

	Japanese friends 日本人の友達	Japanese teachers/staff 日本人と先生と職員	Foreign friends 外国人の友達	Foreign teachers/staff 外国人先生と職員	Family members 家族や親戚
Facebook					
LINE					
sms					
Twitter					
Other network 他のネットワーク					

The respondent can select English 英語, Japanese 日本語, English & Japanese 英語と日本語, Other 他, or I do not use 使わない

Responses to Social Network Use Questions

Table 1 Question 8: How often do you use...?

Social Network	Everyday	Once a week	Once a month	Rarely	Never	Total responses
Facebook	35 (95 %)	1 (3 %)	0	1 (3 %)	0	37
LINE	33 (89 %)	1 (3 %)	0	1 (3 %)	2 (5 %)	37
sms	20 (54 %)	3 (8 %)	4 (11 %)	5 (14 %)	3 (8 %)	35
Twitter	22 (59 %)	5 (14 %)	0	3 (8 %)	6 (16 %)	36
Other network	12 (32 %)	9 (24 %)	1 (3 %)	3 (8 %)	5 (14 %)	30

All percentages calculated based on total survey pool of 37 respondents to prevent the inflation of positive responses

Table 2 Question 9: Who do you communicate with on social networks?

Social Network	English	Japanese	English and Japanese	Other	Not applicable	Total responses
Facebook	35 (95 %)	11 (30 %)	34 (92 %)	22 (59 %)	9 (24 %)	37
LINE	35 (95 %)	0	4 (11 %)	3 (8 %)	14 (38 %)	35
sms	26 (70 %)	1 (3 %)	6 (16 %)	4 (11 %)	11 (30 %)	29
Twitter	27 (73 %)	1 (3 %)	6 (16 %)	1 (3 %)	2 (54 %)	29
Other network	20 (54 %)	1 (3 %)	6 (16 %)	1 (3 %)	4 (11 %)	22

All percentages calculated based on total survey pool of 37 respondents to prevent the inflation of positive responses

Responses to Question10

Table 3 What languages do you use toward Japanese friends? *Facebook* effect seen here

Social Network	English	Japanese	English and Japanese	Other	Not applicable	Total responses
Facebook	0	19 (54 %)	16 (46 %)	0	2	37
LINE	1 (3 %)	26 (72 %)	9 (26 %)	0	1	37
sms	1 (4 %)	23 (82 %)	4 (14 %)	0	8	36
Twitter	0	13 (43 %)	16 (53 %)	1 (3 %)	7	37
Other network	0	16 (80 %)	3 (15 %)	1 (5 %)	13	33

Table 4 What languages do you use toward Japanese teachers and staff? *Facebook* effect marginal at best

Social network	English	Japanese	English and Japanese	Other	Not applicable	Total responses
Facebook	2 (9 %)	18 (82 %)	1 (5 %)	1 (5 %)	15	37
LINE	0	8 (89 %)	0	1 (11 %)	22	31
sms	0	9 (90 %)	0	1 (10 %)	21	31
Twitter	0	6 (86 %)	0	1 (14 %)	25	32
Other network	0	5 (83 %)	0	1 (17 %)	25	31

Table 5 What languages do you use toward foreign friends? *Facebook* and Twitter win out slightly here

Social network	English	Japanese	English and Japanese	Other	Not applicable	Total responses
Facebook	27 (77 %)	0	8 (22 %)	1 (3 %)	1	37
LINE	9 (64 %)	1 (7 %)	2 (14 %)	2 (14 %)	19	33
sms	5 (50 %)	0	3 (30 %)	2 (20 %)	23	33
Twitter	10 (77 %)	0	1 (8 %)	2 (15 %)	20	33
Other network	7 (64 %)	1 (9 %)	2 (18 %)	1 (9 %)	22	33

Table 6 What languages do you use toward foreign teachers and staff? No winners here

Social network	English	Japanese	English and Japanese	Other	Not applicable	Total responses
Facebook	23 (79 %)	0	6 (21 %)	0	8	37
LINE	7 (70 %)	0	2 (20 %)	1 (10 %)	23	33
sms	7 (78 %)	0	1 (11 %)	1 (11 %)	23	32
Twitter	6 (86 %)	0	0	1 (14 %)	25	32
Other network	5 (71 %)	1 (14 %)	0	1 (14 %)	24	31

112 J. George

Table 7 What languages do you use toward Family members? Slight edge for *Facebook* here

Social network	English	Japanese	English and Japanese	Other	Not applicable	Total responses
Facebook	1 (6 %)	16 (89 %)	1 (6 %)	0	19	37
LINE	0	18 (90 %)	2 (10 %)	0	15	35
sms	0	15 (94 %)	1 (6 %)	0	17	33
Twitter	0	6 (86 %)	1 (14 %)	0	25	32
Other network	0	8 (89 %)	1 (11 %)	0	22	31

Percentages based on "Total responses" minus "Not applicable" to show language distribution for declared users of each social network.

References

Akimoto, A. 2012. Japan's LINE social network could challenge global competitors. *The Japan Times Online*, July 18. http://www.japantimes.co.jp/life/2012/07/18/life/japans-line-social-network-could-challenge-global-competitors/#.UQvkmr9QhR5. Accessed 10 Oct 2012.

Anderson, B. 1983/2006. *Imagined communities*. London: Verso.

Blattner, G., and M. Fiori. 2011. Virtual social network communities: An investigation of language learners' development of sociopragmatic awareness and multiliteracy skills. *CALICO Journal* 29: 24–43.

Bourdieu, P. 1977. *Outline of a theory of practice*. Cambridge: Cambridge University Press.

Giddens, A. 1984. *The constitution of society: Outline of the theory of structuration*. Berkeley: University of California Press.

Giles, H., and P. Smith. 1979. Accommodation theory: Optimal levels of convergence. In *Language and social psychology*, ed. H. Giles and R. St. Clair, 45–65. Baltimore: University Park Press.

Kabilan, M.K., N. Ahmad, and M.J.Z. Abidin. 2010. *Facebook*: An online environment for learning of English in institutions of higher education? *Internet and Higher Education* 13: 179–187.

Kanno, Y. 2003. Imagined communities, school visions, and the education of bilingual students in Japan. *Journal of Language, Identity, and Education* 2: 285–300.

Kanno, Y., and B. Norton. 2003. Imagined communities and educational possibilities: Introduction. *Journal of Language, Identity, and Education* 2: 241–249.

Labov, W. 2001. *Principles of linguistic change*, Social factors, vol. 2. Oxford: Blackwell.

Lave, J., and E. Wenger. 1991. *Situated learning: Legitimate peripheral participation*. Cambridge: Cambridge University Press.

Li, L., J.M. Grimshaw, C. Nielsen, M. Judd, P.C. Coyte, and I.D. Graham. 2009. Evolution of Wenger's concept of community of practice. *Implementation Science* 4: 11. doi:10.1186/1748-5908-4-11.

Mills, N. 2011. Situated learning through social networking communities: The development of joint enterprise, mutual engagement, and a shared repertoire. *CALICO Journal* 28: 345–368.

Norton, B. 2000. *Identity and language learning: Gender, ethnicity and educational change*. Harlow: Pearson Education.

Norton, B. 2001. Non-participation, imagined communities, and the language classroom. In *Learner contributions to language learning: New directions in research*, ed. M. Breen, 159–171. Harlow: Pearson Education.

Seilhamer, M.F. 2010. Linguistic abilities and identity in a globalizing world: Perspectives from proficient Taiwanese English users. Ph.D. thesis, Department of Language and Literature, National University of Singapore.

Part II
Perennial Issues in Foreign Language Development

Communicating with Oneself: On the Phenomenon of Private/Inner Speech in Language Acquisition

Danuta Gabryś-Barker

Abstract The aim of this paper is first of all to introduce the construct of private/inner speech according to Vygotsky and demonstrate its applicability to research in second/foreign language learning processes. The functions that private speech/inner speech perform in L2 use seem to be fundamental to intentional language processing and are most visibly expressed in learners' editing their language before performing it. Private speech seems to function in a similar fashion in foreign language use to L1 language processing, especially in the case of communicative tasks. In L2 adults, it is observed that private speech performs the role of an instrument in gaining control over one's performance. The paper will demonstrate how the concept of private/inner speech is employed in SLA studies. The main method of data collection, that is, simultaneous introspection, will be elaborated on and also illustrated with examples of think aloud protocols as representative samples of private speech. The discussion will focus on the context of third language acquisition to show how the learning process is commented on by a learner in a dialogue with himself/herself. The empirical data that will serve as the basis for this discussion comes from verbal reports of language learners produced simultaneously with the performance of a language task, in this case translation.

Keywords Private speech • Inner speech • Simultaneous introspection • Dialogue with oneself

1 Introduction

The theme of the present volume is the role of new media in a foreign language classroom. Undeniably technological development has enhanced and offered new possibilities for foreign language learning. However, language learning, like all learning processes, takes place in the learner's head through thinking.

D. Gabryś-Barker (✉)
University of Silesia, Katowice, Poland
e-mail: danuta.gabrys@gmail.com

© Springer International Publishing Switzerland 2015
L. Piasecka et al. (eds.), *New Media and Perennial Problems in Foreign Language Learning and Teaching*, Second Language Learning and Teaching,
DOI 10.1007/978-3-319-07686-7_7

Thus, thinking itself and its verbalized form, private speech, should still remain at the core of studying language learning and development.

Inner speech or private speech (these two terms are used interchangeably in this article) is a commonly observed phenomenon. However, as many researchers claim, it has not been paid enough attention to so far, despite its familiarity (Morin 2004). Each of us to some extent performs some variation of a sub-vocal monologue (or dialogue with oneself) in the mother tongue. The same occurs when using other languages we know, not only when we find ourselves in learning contexts, but also privately. Myers (2001: 138) writes:

> Thinking is both private and public. We solve problems with interaction with others as well as on our own. Thinking alone and thinking with others are, in fact, strikingly analogous situations. In both cases we tend to engage in dialogues, whether real or virtual. (. . .) overt monologues while thinking are not uncommon, and they are even uncontrollable for many.

Why study inner/private speech (IS/PS) in an L2 acquisition context? It is because IS/PS expresses verbally thinking processes in a sub-vocal manner (to oneself) and functions as a preparatory stage for performing external speech. In a bi/multilingual person who has two and more languages at his/her disposal, it may be expected that these languages will be activated to different degrees in his/her thinking and will contribute to the intentional processing of language before the actual performance occurs. The choice of language for thinking and the different types of comment made in selected languages give evidence of crosslinguistic consultations and the status of each language in a multilingual mind. It also demonstrates learning, the recall and production strategies a multilingual uses in language processing before articulating it vocally (external speech). Longitudinally, following the development of one's inner speech will demonstrate the language progress of the learner. The way a learner employs inner speech can also inform research on the affective dimension of language acquisition/use. It is virtually every aspect of mono/bi/multilingual language acquisition that can become the focus of studying inner speech.

2 Defining and Characterising the Language of Thought

When introducing the concept of inner speech, Little (2010: 30) says:

> Our L1 is both an instrument of communication and the tool we use for discursive thinking. Inner speech—the act of silently talking to ourselves—takes many different forms, ranging from fragmentary to fully elaborated, and we use it for many different purposes, for example, to access and shape our memories, to plan utterances, to guide ourselves through complex tasks, to regulate our behaviour, and to solve problems.

Private and inner speech phenomena give evidence of language processing. It was the Russian psychologist Vygotsky (1987) who first asserted the now generally held belief that all our thinking is done via language. All the mental processing of our thoughts and ideas involves language use. Sometimes we voice our thoughts, which is considered to be a facilitating factor in organising our thinking into coherent sequences. Thus language has to be seen as helping us to conceptualize the world around us and to serve as a mechanism for the acquisition of knowledge, not only as a vehicle of communication with others. According to Vygotsky

> children use egocentric speech initially to accompany problem-solving strategies but later to direct problem-solving strategies. With the evolution of inner speech—using attenuated and often silent language—the learner uses language to direct problem-solving strategies. (quoted in Lee 2000: 192)

These instances of verbalisations called private speech are in fact quite commonly observed in young children, who act as if carrying out a dialogue with themselves. However, this quality of speaking aloud our thoughts seems to disappear with age—with our cognitive and language development. However, it does not disappear altogether; it turns into so-called inner speech, which is still grounded in language but is not vocalized (Gabryś-Barker 2005).

Vygotsky (1987) believed that inner speech is developmental and proceeds "through a long cumulative series of functional and structural changes" (119) which ultimately "becomes the basic structure of his thinking" (120). The role of inner speech for speech production was expressed by Vygotsky (1987) in Wertsch (2000: 24–25) as

> a microgenetic process of moving from motive and thought to external speech. (. . .) speech production involves a series of genetic transformations from condensed, abbreviated forms of representation involving sense, psychological predicates, and so forth to an explicit form of social speech with all its expanded phonetic and auditory aspects, meaning, and so forth.

Following Vygotsky's views on IS, Ehrich (2006: 15) sees it

> as a product of higher thought, arises through the series of developmental stages, going from the external world and travelling inwards, its genesis a result of an initial need to solve problems. This inner speech constitutes a separate language function that is centred on word sense and meaning and has its own syntactic structure.

It was also Vygotsky who made this distinction between two opposing concepts of thought and word as expressed by *meaning* (Russ. *znachenie*) and *sense* (Russ. *smysl*), emphasizing that it is sense which is expressed by inner speech, while meaning is expressed by external speech (Table 1).

The differences between inner and external speech are not only observable in their context of use, but also in the linguistic characteristics of each. IS is described by Vygotsky (1986 in Ehrich 2006: 14) as characterised by:

1. dominance of word sense over word meaning (word sense changes through contexts, whereas word meaning remains stable);
2. individual words merging into a single word expressing a complex new idea (so-called agglutination);
3. senses of words combining and flowing into one another and influencing each other.

Syntactic differences between the inner speech (IS) and external speech (ES) are also expressed in the presence of predicate structures in IS, whereas it is both

Table 1 Meaning vs. sense

Meaning	Sense
Explicit, systematically organized form	Implicit, condensed, abbreviated form
Language	Thought
External social speech	Inner speech
Written speech	Inner speech
Phonetic/auditory aspect of speech	Semantic aspect of speech
Grammatical subject and predicate	Psychological subject and predicate

Source Wertsch (2000: 23)

predicates and subjects that constitute the language of ES. To summarise his discussion of inner versus external speech, Vygotsky (1987: 257) contextualizes them by saying that "Inner speech is for oneself. External speech for others".

3 Inner/Private Speech in L2

When discussing the concept of private/inner speech in the context of L2 use, McCafferty (1998: 73) assumes that it "seems to function in foreign language processing similarly to L1 language processing, which can be observed for instance in communicative tasks". He describes private speech as: "vocalised forms of speech for the self that function metacognitively to help the learner plan, guide, and monitor a course of activity" (73).

One of the major researchers investigating IS in L2 contexts is de Guerrero (2004), who observed longitudinally the development of L2 inner speech of her learners. The study was carried out by means of learner diaries. De Guerrero focused on the different types of IS she observed in the learner data:

1. language heard or read was being processed in IS sequences
2. recall of words that were heard, read or used was observed
3. rehearsal of speech (a written text) was performed before actual speaking (writing)

De Guerrero (2004 quoted in Little 2010) also concluded that "the capacity for inner speech develops in L2: first as an instrument of 'shadowing', then as an instrument of recall, then as a support for speaking and writing, and finally as a medium of discursive thinking" (Little 2010: 33)

The functions that inner/private speech performs in L2 use seem to be fundamental to intentional language processing, which is most visibly expressed in learners' editing their language before performing it. Frawley and Lantolf (1985) point to the similarity of private speech in L1 children and L2 adults. In L2 adults, it is observed that PS performs the role of an instrument in gaining control over one's performance (self-direction). Especially during the early stages of learning a language, it is a consciously employed form of mediation, which with growing language competence becomes more automatic and subconscious, an observation I made earlier (Gabryś-Barker 2005). PS, described as an expression of the self-regulatory function, operates at various stages of language processing and focuses on different aspects of language performance: object-regulation, other-regulation and self-regulation:

- object-regulation refers to the learners' reflections on the task performed and comments on language processed conceptualisation
- other-regulation is the expression of the need for cooperation with the "knower" and dialogical aspects of asking questions ("how to say..." conceptualisation/formulation)
- self-regulation demonstrates showing understanding, arriving at the solution, evaluating the solutions/one's performance and articulation (Frawley and Lantolf 1985).

It could be concluded therefore that different sequences of IS/PS use can be understood as different sequences (stages) of language processing. In the object-regulation sequence of language processing, the task and its language are being reflected upon, conceptual demands are being considered (macro-planning) as well as a focus on form (micro-planning) being sought. The other-regulation sequence can exemplify the phase of searching for linguistic solutions, such as lexical search or grammatical information, by asking questions of "the knower", as if consulting oneself with a "How can I say this?"-type of question. The self-regulation sequence constitutes the articulation stage when final solutions (linguistic choices) are being made, and evaluated and the task itself is being performed (Gabryś-Barker 2005).

We may assume that the use of inner speech by L2/Ln learners is determined by language proficiency in a given language. Following other researchers (de Guerrero 1994, 1999; Pavlenko and Lantolf 2000), Dewaele suggests that

> proficient L2 learners are capable of developing a rich and functional inner voice, as complex and useful as its L1 counterpart, at the same time believing that although the amount of inner speech produced by low proficiency level is smaller, it performs different functions, such as mental rehearsal or rehearsing speech before producing it. (personal communication 2012)

4 Language Choice in Thinking

As was emphasized earlier, samples of inner speech, which can be recovered as verbalizations of inner speech allow the researcher to observe the different stages of language processing as they occur and various specific aspects of the process itself. Also, in the case of bi- or multilingual subjects, their choice of language for private speech can be uncovered as deriving from either the language of input, output or any other language known by a subject. The choice of languages activated in the process of verbalization may vary between different levels of processing. It may be different at the level of conceptualisation, at the level of the formulator when encoding occurs (i.e. selection of syntactic, lexical or morphological information) and at the articulation stage when the final language choices are made (Gabryś-Barker 2003). In other words, a multilingual language user performs his/her language processing on a certain language mode continuum, as Grosjean (2001) calls it. Language selection choices depend on a wide variety of factors ranging from age of arrival (AOA) and length of stay in the L2 country (in the context of L2 and not FL) to proficiency in a given language, attitudes, status of languages and also on the content of the message and mode of interaction with the language. A multilingual language user may select the most active language at one stage, thus impeding the activation of other ones, but also he/she may go back to other languages depending on the context, task or instructions. This is best exemplified by both conscious and unconscious code-switching data. Language activation/inhibition is a complex process and research results so far do not yet allow us to create a model for it. Competing models of language activation are discussed in Dewaele (2001) and Dijkstra and van Hell (2001).

Generally, the languages involved in processing can be described as active (involved in the processing of the language sample when performing a task), selected (controlling the language of output) and dormant (passive and not activated in the process) (Gabryś-Barker 2005). Languages (L1, L2 or L3) may be activated intentionally, when for instance the language user perceives a similarity between two languages and finds it to be a facilitative factor. Also unintentional switches may occur in automatic processing of the language, thus no verbalisation can explain the language choice made (Gabryś-Barker 2003). The major factor determining language choices is the learners' language proficiency in L1, L2 and L3. Thus the decrease or even elimination of inner speech in L1 can be seen as occurring due, for example, to high language competence in the other languages (L2, L3). However, it is not that straightforward, as different studies (e.g. Macaro 2000) additionally point to the facilitative role L1 performs in verbalizations. L1 proficiency allows a learner to express verbally what is happening at the moment of language processing more extensively and with more precision.

Among the factors enumerated above, the choice of the language of inner speech may be determined by a type of comment made at a given moment of thinking/processing and how natural the language choice seems to the learner. A good example would be language choices made in expressing feelings when doing a task when L1 would seem more natural than any language learnt (L2, L3). For instance, it may seem more natural for the learner to comment on his or her feelings when performing a language task in his/her mother tongue. On the other hand, it may not be L1, as the learners/language users may consider the use of L2 as safer in expressing emotions since a FL will always be a distancing language (Gabryś-Barker 2003).

5 Types of Comment in Inner/Private Speech

The language of IS can express learners' cognition of the task, his/her metacognitive awareness and the affectivity involved in language processing at the sub-vocal level of thinking. Thus various types of comments can be classified as cognitive, metacognitive and affective ones (Gabryś-Barker 2005). They perform different functions in language processing. Cognitive comments express cognitive processes occurring at a given moment of language performance, they refer directly to language processing in terms of, for example, lexical search, whereas the presence of non-comments, i.e. *pauses* (filled—such as "uh", "um, "well", and unfilled ones) or *hesitation* (evidence of a prolonged search) give evidence of automatic processing. Metacognitive comments are verbalizations of the learner's awareness of language structure and thus his/her declarative knowledge and/or metalinguistic awareness, they demonstrate one's strategic and procedural knowledge (e.g. learner's strategic competence and the ability to self-repair), they express the learner's evaluation of the effectiveness of the strategies used, they also show the learner's approach to the language and task itself. Additionally they may reflect the domain knowledge and show how it contributes to language solutions chosen. Affective comments show the learner's assessment of his or her language performance, they may express self-confidence, self-esteem and belief in success or failure.

The above types of comment reoccur in the course of language processing at its different stages: conceptualisation, formulation, articulation, and in different sequences: object-regulation, other-regulation and self-regulation. Each of them constitutes a piece of interactive discourse with oneself.

6 Studies on Inner/Private Speech

6.1 Methodology

Research methods used in studying inner/private speech embrace the whole spectrum of retrospective methods, from simultaneous introspection (verbal protocols) to retrospection in the form of reflective comments (diaries and journals). However, it is my strong belief that it is simultaneous introspection that most closely reflects the phenomenon of Vygotsky's inner/private speech. Simultaneous introspection was first described and used as data by Ericsson and Simon (1984), who describe levels of verbalizations as vocalization, description and/or explication of content and explanation of thoughts (Table 2).

Verbalizations as presented in think aloud protocols (TAPs) reflect a dialogue a language user performs in interaction with him/herself to reach the ascribed goal.

Also reflective journals and their different forms (diaries, logs) are considered a fairly reliable sources of evidence of this inner dialogue with oneself; however done

Table 2 Levels of verbalization

Level of verbalization	Description	Comment
1. Vocalization	articulation of oral encodings, where no thinking processes take place. In self-directed verbalizations (e.g. in the case of thinking aloud protocols—TAPs), they are individual and depend on the subject's interpretation of the instruction she/he is given or on the semantic content of the task	a direct process in which information encoded is vocalized (articulated), i.e. in a language task a phrase or a sentence is pronounced or read aloud by the subject with no cognitive processes taking place
2. Description and/or explication of content	"labelling" information and recoding it in an idiosyncratic way, characteristic of a subject/informant	encoded verbalizations where the information attended to by the subject (level 1) is modified by recoding processes, i.e. the subject generates a verbal representation of the information she/he has got stored in his/her mind by means of filtering it for the purposes of the task
3. Explanation of thoughts	ideas that rush through the subject's mind or any other, even emotional, reactions to the information (task) she/he is to solve. It involves a process of interpretation	the subject reports his/her ongoing thinking, embracing not only its verbal aspects, i.e. word associations and interferences from L1 and L3 (for example) but also personal, emotional responses to the task

Based on Gabryś-Barker (2011)

in a controlled and deliberate fashion, they often focus solely on selected aspect(s) of interest and thus constitute a less authentic and natural sample of inner/private speech than simultaneous introspection transcribed in the form of think aloud protocols.

6.2 Examples of L1 and L2 Studies

Studying inner/private speech phenomena started with Vygotsky's formulation of the concept and, naturally enough, produced research focusing on child inner/private speech performed in his/her mother tongue (L1). There are relatively few studies that focus on the L2/Ln context. de Guerrero (2005) offers a comprehensive overview of the latter. Table 3 presents sample studies of I/PS.

Table 3 Sample studies on IS/PS

I/P speech	Research
Characteristics of inner speech	Vygotsky (1986)
The role of IS in problem-solving	Frawley and Lantolf (1985) Appel and Lantolf (1994) Anton and DiCammilla (1999)
The developmental stages of IS	Beggs and Howarth (1985) de Guerrero (1994, 1999, 2004, 2005) Pavlenko and Lantolf (2000)
IS as a language acquisition tool	Ushakova (1994) Upton and Lee-Thomson (2001) de Guerrero (2004)
Neural studies on brain activation in IS	McGuire et al. (1996)
Reading processes	Pollatsek et al. (1992) Abramson and Goldinger (1997) Flavell et al. (1996) Ehrich (2006)
IS as an effective tool in generating language	Coltheart (1999)
Language choice in IS	Gabryś-Barker (2003, 2005) Dewaele (2012)

7 An Example of an Inner/Private Speech Study of Multilingual Language Processing

7.1 Research Focus

The major focus of interest in my study on IS in multilingual language processing (Gabryś-Barker 2005) was on the following:

- the influence of the language of input on language processing when performing the task,
- the languages activated in both tasks at different stages of linguistic processing,
- language choice in different types of comments.

In the present exposition of the study, I would like to add one more dimension to its interpretation, namely observations concerning dialogical aspects of inner speech as they occurred in verbalizations.

I hypothesized that the language of input would influence the way language processing develops by either promoting or inhibiting this processing. Secondly, it was believed that not all the three languages would be equally accessible for processing at its different stages of the object-regulation versus other-regulation versus self-regulation sequences. Thirdly, it was anticipated that different languages would be used for different types of comment. For example, it was believed that affective comments will be made in the subjects' L1 more frequently than in their L2, whereas cognitive comments will draw more upon L3 knowledge (Gabryś-Barker 2005). It was also assumed that looking at the dialogical aspects of verbalizations collected in the form of think aloud protocols (TAPs) would allow to interpret IS as a problem-solving strategy, which according to Vygotsky and others is the main function IS performs.

The group of 48 informants involved in the study consisted of trilingual language users with the following constellation of languages: L1—Portuguese, L2—English and L3—German. All the informants were students at a foreign language department of a Portuguese university, studying English as their L2 and possessing an advanced level of competence in this language (C1/C2). All of them were also involved in German instruction, however at a lower level, which could be described as pre-intermediate to intermediate (B1/B2).

The inner speech data collected consists of the verbalizations produced by the subjects when performing the translation tasks. When processing the texts, they were asked to think aloud, i.e. to verbalise all the processes they were involved in when translating the text, as well as their own evaluative and affective comments. The verbalizations were taped and transcribed following a set transcription code. When verbalizing, the subjects worked individually in closed laboratory booths, but with the possibility of contacting the researcher in the case of doubts. Before the data collection, the informants were exposed to sample TAPs for the purposes of training.

7.2 Sample Data

Table 4 offers examples of verbalizations produced by the subjects as inner/private speech instances when performing a translation of a text from Portuguese to German (L1 input) and from English to German (L2 input).

7.3 Findings

The major findings of the study are presented here in relation to the three major research areas: levels of verbalization at different stages of processing in L1 and L2 input tasks, the influence of the language of input on language processing, languages activated during different processing sequences and language choices in the different types of comment.

Comparing the levels of verbalization in L1 input and L2 input tasks at different stages of language processing, it is evident that verbalization in the L1 task is higher by 22 % than in the L2 task because L1 competence allows the subjects to express their thoughts more easily. In the case of both tasks, the highest verbalization occurred in the object-regulation sequences, which can be explained by the fact that it is then that direct attention is paid to language itself, its comprehension and analysis, and that it seems to be particularly focused. At the same time, this very sequence is rich in pauses (unfilled and filled), as evidence of automatic processing

Table 4 Selected examples of inner speech at different stages of self-regulation

Stage	L1 input	L2 input
The object-regulation	*"das—die- der Industrie"* (subject 10, focus on articles) *"Neue kommission—den Dão Wein—den Dão Wein—in der Wein von Dão" (s. 9)* *"Ich wiess nicht (.1) CVDR hat gestern—gestern—die—den Chef"* (s. 4)	*"Não deve ser nada disso"* (Can't be like that) (s. 6) *"Pergunto—pergunto"* (I wonder... I wonder...) (s. 14) *"Passa a frente"* (Skip and go on) (s. 27) *"Falta outra vez"* (Missing again) (s. 29) *"Needs to develop—über **das**—uber **der Entwiklung"** (C)* (s. 1) *"speech—speech –speech—let's try that—A. de Figueira delivered a speech—why not—it is the same thing" (lexical search in L2)* (s. 3) *"Markt—Markte—Marketen **plural**"* *"von Jorge Teixeira als—als— **dative**—no—**accusative**"* (s. 4) *"Als neue—President—Dão Geberg"* (direct translation into German) (s. 2) *"neuer Wein Gruppe—Ich weiss nicht wie Man commission auf Deutsch sagt"* (s. 5) *"Deklination—den Sekretar des Staates"* (s. 8) *"mit einem agressiven—dativ— agressiven Marketing"* (s. 11) *"für Agriculture—und Essen—das Essen—und das Essen"* (s. 26) *"Mein Gott—this is kein Deutsch"* (Oh, God—this is no German) (s. 1) *"Oh—mein name ist Christina"* (s.11) *"Ach Gott—das liert so komisch"*(Oh, God—this is funny) (s. 28)
The other-regulation	*Como é que se diz Comissão?"* (s. 1) *"Como é que se diz alimento?"* (s. 6)	*"Como é que se diz vinho"* (How do you say wine) (s. 1) *"Como é que se diz Governo"* (How do you say government) (s. 6) *"Como que traduziste ísto"* (How do you translate it) (s. 7) *"Komission é com dois emes"* (Commission is with two "m"s?) (s.10) *"food é Essen"* (s. 30) *"Wie sagt Man das—wollte- oh Gott"* (How does one say—oh God) (s. 1) *"es ist sehr schwierig—wie sagt Man auf Deutsch ..."* (This is so difficult—how does one say in German ...) (s. 20)

(continued)

Table 4 (continued)

Stage	L1 input	L2 input
The self-regulation	*"Não sei se traduzir—e super-difícil"* ("I don't know how to translate—it is very difficult", s. 1) *"Não sei- não sou capaz de traduzir mais—não sei mesmo"* ("I don't know—am not capable of translating more—I really don't know", s. 5).	*"Attention-nein (...) pass-nein-hm-hm"* (s. 3) *"This cold is not helping"* (s. 5, a comment made on the conditions in the room) *"I don't know again"* (s. 8) *"es gibt kein Ubersetzung"* (This is bad translation) (s. 11)

Based on Gabryś-Barker (2005)
s subject

which is inaccessible to verbalization at that very moment. There is a significant difference in the self-regulation sequence where the L1 task produces almost twice as many comments compared with the L2 task. As mentioned above, the affective-evaluative comments found most frequently here are easily expressed in L1, which is the language of affect/emotion (see Gabryś-Barker 2005 for more detailed data and analysis).

It was observed that the language of input (task 1: L1 Portuguese, task 2: L2 English) in a non-immediate production task such as translation influences language processing in the task performed. Both a greater variety and a greater number of comments were observed in the L2 input task. This can be interpreted as the result of transfer of training/learning and perception of the task as a learning task. Exposure to the L2 as the language of input of the task required first its analysis (comprehension) before the actual process of translation could occur. At the same time, comments not directly related to language processing are made in L1 (mainly affective ones). Secondly, it is mainly the surface languages (the source and the target ones in each of the tasks) that are selected for processing at its different stages:

- when the language is being comprehended (the stage of conceptualisation),
- manipulated (the stage of formulation) and
- the final output produced (the stage of articulation).

Even though learner' competence in the dormant and not activated language is higher (for example L2 in task 1) than that of the target language (L3), it is not accessed in the course of processing the L1 input text, even when it might have facilitated task performance.

The inner speech data demonstrated that languages activated are different in different processing sequences. In the object-regulation sequences (focus on the task): L2 and particularly L3 are significantly more frequent than L1, which may be assumed to demonstrate the learners' treatment of the task as a learning experience—hence processing is only carried out in the learnt languages. It shows lack of metacognitive awareness of L1 and its possible contribution to language processing of the L1 text—such as was observed in the L2 input task (with reference to L2 awareness). This lack of awareness frequently results in incomplete translations or direct code-switching from L1. At the other-regulation stage (expressing dialogical aspects of inner speech) i.e. asking "oneself" for help when a problem occurs, in L1 input, both L1 and L3 (the output language) are activated for comments, whereas in L2 input, the language of input remains dormant (un-activated) and only L1 and L3 comments occur. L1 seems to be the most natural language choice for expressing the need for consultation, as is commonly observed in a learning situation when the learner asks the teacher or when one consults a reference source such as a dictionary. On the other hand, the use of L3 here might indicate the intentional use of the target language to reinforce or facilitate the activation of for example the lexical item searched for (thinking in L3 when looking for solutions) and at the same time expressing the intention to exclude other languages as possible sources of interference. In the self-regulation sequences (final language decisions): at the level of articulation and evaluation (self-regulation), all the languages are activated, however, affective comments of self-evaluation are expressed either in L1 (negative) or L2 (positive), while cognitive ones focusing on the final articulatory language decisions rely on L2 and even more significantly on L3 expression. The language choice for comments made at this stage might reflect the learners' approach to the task and their strategic competence, such as their ability to manipulate the text in L2 by using either L2-based strategies, such as paraphrasing or word-coinage, or L3-based strategies such as overgeneralization.

As far as language choices made in different types of comment are concerned, they were as follows:

- L1 was activated for affective comments in both tasks because the mother tongue is the intimate language of affect/emotion, and for cognitive comments in the L1 input task because greater fluency in L1 than in L2 and L3 facilitates explicit verbalizations;
- L2 was used predominantly for affective comments and expressing positive aspects of one's performance (L2 is a distancing language) and for cognitive comments in the L2 input task only, for the purposes of strategic text manipulation. As has already been mentioned, it is dormant in the L1 task;
- L3 was activated for all types of comment in both tasks where the focus was on the target language itself and on task performance. It showed the greatest variety and activation—especially in the context of another learnt language, L2.

The three main dimensions of dialogical aspects of inner speech recognized in verbalizations related to:

- asking "oneself" for help when a problem occurred: here L1 seems to be the most natural language choice for expressing the need for consultation, as is commonly observed in a learning situation when the learner asks the teacher or when one consults a reference source such as a dictionary;
- evaluation of one's performance: expressed as affective comments which are verbalized in either L1 in the case of negative judgements or in L2 when the comment is positive;

- searching for final language solutions: the learner's approach to the task and his/her strategic competence, such as the ability to manipulate the text e.g. in L2 by using either L2-based strategies, such as paraphrasing or word-coinage, or L3-based strategies such as overgeneralization; here private speech best illustrates its problem-solving capacities.

Each of the above examples illustrate a different type of strategy for solving a language problem that the subjects were confronted with and each of these could be evaluated more accurately in terms of its effectiveness in carrying out the translation task. Asking oneself for help refers to cooperative strategy of communication (seen as a problem solving situation), demonstrating the degree of learner autonomy and persistence. Evaluation of one's performance (mostly affective) demonstrates how self-confidence, esteem and attitude can influence the progress of language processing (continuation of or withdrawal from it). Searching for the final language solutions is in fact a stage in processing and task performance that best demonstrates the cognitive strategies employed, such as semantic field search, waiting for the word to come, foreignizing, code-switching or approximation, to name just a few.

Conclusions

It was Jeremy Bruner, someone already known for his humanistic attitude to education and pedagogical theories of meaningful learning, who pointed out that

> Modern pedagogy is moving increasingly to the view that the child should be aware of her own thought processes, and that it is crucial for the pedagogical theorist and teacher alike to help her to become more metacognitive—to be aware of how she goes about her learning and thinking as she is about the subject matter that she is studying. Bruner (1996: 64)

The above emphasis on an individual's awareness of learning and thinking as facilitative aspects in educational processes falls in naturally with the trend of regarding the development of reflectivity, not only teacher reflectivity but also learner reflectivity, as a significant dimension of being autonomous.

This article has focused on one specific aspect of L2 "performance", learner's inner speech in TAP verbalisations. This awareness of verbal aspects of one's thinking processes and IS as a type of problem-solving strategy in language rehearsal and performance are significant for L2/Ln learners/users as tools for more conscious facilitation and at the same time for monitoring language learning progress. At the same time they allow for more effective use of language. The observations made in this paper argue for placing more emphasis on studying the IS of language learners, which can inform research on language processing, language learning, production and

(continued)

communication strategies, as well as individual learner differences. Little (2010: 31) believes that

> the capacity for inner speech is a defining characteristic of the truly proficient L2 user-learner, the challenge facing language pedagogy is twofold: to find a means of activating and feeding those processes that are common to all language learning, but at the same time to turn the intentional nature of L2 learning to positive advantages.

As I myself concluded elsewhere (Gabryś-Barker 2005), IS as evidenced by introspection can also be seen as a form of reflection on one's cognition and affectivity and thus a significant learning tool. It allows learners to become more aware of the idiosyncracies of their own learning process, whereas for teachers it may offer guidance on their learners' cognitive and affective profiles.

References

Abramson, M., and S.D. Goldinger. 1997. What the reader's eye tells the mind's ear: Silent reading activates inner speech. *Perception and Psychophysics* 59: 1059–1068.

Anton, M., and F.J. DiCammilla. 1999. Socio-cognitive functions of L1 collaborative interaction in the L2 classroom. *The Modern Language Journal* 83: 233–247.

Appel, G., and J.P. Lantolf. 1994. Speaking as mediation: A study of L1 and L2 text recall tasks. *The Modern Language Journal* 78: 437–452.

Beggs, W.D.A., and P.N. Howarth. 1985. Inner speech as a learnt skill. *Journal of Experimental Child Psychology* 39: 396–411.

Bruner, J. 1996. *The culture of education*. Cambridge, MA: Harvard University Press.

Coltheart, V. 1999. Phonological codes in reading comprehension. Short-term memory, and memory for rapid sequences. In *Fleeting memories cognition of brief visual stimuli*, ed. V. Coltheart, 181–225. Cambridge, MA: The MIT Press.

de Guerrero, M.C.M. 1994. Form and functions of inner speech in adult second language learning. In *Vygotskyan approaches to second language research*, ed. J.P. Lantolf and G. Appel, 83–115. Norwood, NJ: Alex.

de Guerrero, M.C.M. 1999. Inner speech in mental rehearsal: The case of advanced L2 learners. *Issues in Applied Linguistics* 10: 27–55.

de Guerrero, M.C.M. 2004. Early stages of L2 inner speech development: What verbal reports suggest. *International Journal of Applied Linguistics* 14: 90–112.

de Guerrero, M.C.M. 2005. *Inner speech—L2: Thinking words in a second language*. New York: Springer.

Dewaele, J.M. 2001. Activation or inhibition? The interaction of L1, L2 and L3 on the language mode continuum. In *Cross-linguistic influence in third language acquisition: Psycholinguistic perspectives*, ed. J. Cenoz, B. Hufeisen, and U. Jessner, 69–89. Clevedon: Multilingual Matters.

Dewaele, J.M. 2012. Multilinguals' choice for inner speech. A paper delivered at 19 Sociolinguistic Symposium, Berlin, Aug 2012.

Dijkstra, T., and J. van Hell. 2001. Testing the language mode hypothesis. A paper presented at the 2nd international conference on third language acquisition and trilingualism. Leeuwarden: Fryske Akademy, Sept 2001.

Ehrich, J.F. 2006. Vygotskyan inner speech and the reading process. *Australian Journal of Educational and Developmental Psychology* 6: 12–25.

Ericsson, K.A., and H.A. Simon. 1984. *Protocol analysis: Verbal reports as data*. Cambridge, MA: MIT.

Flavell, J.H., D.R. Beach, and J.M. Chinsky. 1996. Spontaneous verbal rehearsal in a memory task as a function of age. *Child Development* 37: 283–299.

Frawley, W., and J.P. Lantolf. 1985. Second language discourse: A Vygotskyan perspective. *Applied Linguistics* 6: 19–44.

Gabryś-Barker, D. 2003. Language processing by a multilingual language user. Paper delivered at 3rd international conference on trilingualism, Tralee, Ireland, Sept 2003.

Gabryś-Barker, D. 2005. *Aspects of multilingual processing, storage and retrieval*. Katowice: Wydawnictwo Uniwersytetu Śląskiego.

Gabryś-Barker, D. 2011. Introspective methods in researching multilingulism. A plenary talk delivered at Forschung Methodologie—Novembertagung, Leipzig Universität, 11–12 Nov 2011.

Grosjean, F. 2001. The bilingual's language modes. In *One mind, two languages: Bilingual language processing*, ed. J. Nicol, 1–25. Oxford: Blackwell.

Lee, C.D. 2000. Signifying in the zone of proximal development. In *Vygotskyan perspectives on literacy research*, ed. C.D. Lee and P. Smagorinsky, 191–225. Cambridge: Cambridge University Press.

Little, D. 2010. Learner autonomy, inner speech and the European Language Portfolio. *GALA* 2010. www.enl.gr/gala/14th/Paper. Accessed 19 Sept 2012.

Macaro, R. 2000. Learner strategies in foreign language learning: Cross-national factors. *Tuttitalia* 22: 9–18.

McCafferty, S. 1998. Nonverbal expression and L2 private speech. *Applied Linguistics* 19: 73–96.

McGuire, P.K., D.A. Silbersweig, R.M. Murray, A.S. David, R.S.J. Frąckowiak, and C.D. Frith. 1996. Functional anatomy of inner speech and auditory verbal imagery. *Psychological Medicine* 26: 39–58.

Morin, A. 2004. Possible links between self-awareness and inner speech: Theoretical background, underlying mechanisms, and empirical evidence. *Journal of Consciousness Studies* 12: 115–134.

Myers, J.L. 2001. Self-evaluations of the 'stream of thought' in journal writing. *System* 29: 481–488.

Pavlenko, A., and J.P. Lantolf. 2000. Second language learning as participation in the (re) construction of selves. In *Sociocultural theory and second language learning*, ed. J.P. Lantolf, 155–178. Oxford: Oxford University Press.

Pollatsek, A., M. Lesch, R.K. Morris, and K. Rayner. 1992. Phonological codes are used in integrating information access cascades in word identification in reading. *Journal of Experimental Psychology: Human Perception and Performance* 18: 148–162.

Upton, T.A., and L. Lee-Thomson. 2001. The role of the first language in second language reading. *Studies in Second Language Acquisition* 23: 269–295.

Ushakova, T.N. 1994. Inner speech and second language acquisition. In *Vygotskyan approaches to second language research*, ed. J.P. Lantolf and G. Appel, 134–156. Norwood, NJ: Alex.

Vygotsky, L.S. 1986. *Thought and language*, ed. A. Kozulin. Cambridge, MA: The MIT Press.

Vygotsky, L.S. 1987. Thinking and speech. In *L.S. Vygotsky collected works vol.1*, eds. R. Rieber and A. Carton, 39–285 (Trans. N. Minick). New York: Plenum.

Wertsch, J.V. 2000. Vygotsky's two minds on the nature of meaning. In *Vygotskyan perspectives on literacy research*, ed. C.D. Lee and P. Smagorinsky, 19–30. Cambridge: Cambridge University Press.

The Effectiveness of Written Corrective Feedback in the Acquisition of the English Article System by Polish Learners in View of the Counterbalance Hypothesis

Lech Zabor and Agnieszka Rychlewska

Abstract The main aim of this article is to investigate the effectiveness of written error correction based on the principles of the *Counterbalance Hypothesis* [Lyster and Mori (Studies in Second Language Acquisition 28:321–334, 2006)]. The hypothesis assumes that learners' ability to notice the gap between the ill-formed utterance produced in their interlanguage and the target linguistic form is enhanced by the shift in their attentional focus from meaning to form in a meaning-focused context and from form to meaning in in a form-oriented setting. Thus, instructional activities such as corrective feedback should act as a counterbalance to the classroom's predominant orientation and are predicted to be more effective than interactional feedback which is congruent with the predominant foreign language teaching methodology. The study examines the differential effect of two types of written corrective feedback (CF) and the extent to which the type of foreign language instruction mediates the effects of CF on the acquisition of articles by adult intermediate Polish learners of English ($N = 59$). Four research groups were formed: (1) a direct-only correction group taught inductively, (2) a direct-only correction group taught deductively, (3) a direct meta-linguistic correction group taught inductively, and (4) a direct meta-linguistic correction group taught deductively. The study revealed that all the treatment groups outperformed the control group on the immediate post-tests, and the direct meta-linguistic group taught inductively performed significantly better than the remaining research groups. The results also showed that written CF targeting a single linguistic feature improved the learners' accuracy, especially when meta-linguistic feedback was provided and the learners received the inductive type of formal instruction (FI).

Keywords Corrective feedback • The counterbalance hypothesis • Writing in a foreign language

---

L. Zabor (✉) • A. Rychlewska
Wroclaw University, Wroclaw, Poland
e-mail: l.r.zabor@uni.wroc.pl; rychlewska.agnieszka@gmail.com

© Springer International Publishing Switzerland 2015
L. Piasecka et al. (eds.), *New Media and Perennial Problems in Foreign Language Learning and Teaching*, Second Language Learning and Teaching,
DOI 10.1007/978-3-319-07686-7_8

1 Introduction

The research on corrective feedback (CF) has recently gained prominence in the field of second language acquisition (SLA). The role of the teacher's reaction to learners' errors has been investigated from the linguistic, pedagogical, psychological and social perspectives. For more than three decades theories of first and second language acquisition have taken different positions regarding the importance of CF. The significance assigned to error correction varied with disciplinary orientation of researchers. For example, under the influence of the behaviourist theory of learning based on the principle of habit-formation, errors were viewed as damaging to learning and needed immediate correction. Brooks (1960), for example, compared a language error to a sin that needs to be eradicated and avoided at all cost. In the 1970s and 1980s, in accordance with nativist views of language learning, acquisition was seen as a process based on *positive evidence*, i.e. primary linguistic data were processed by means of language acquisition device, and CF was considered as playing no or a marginal role. For example, linguists such as Chomsky (1975) depreciated the role of corrective feedback and its influence on the first and second language learning process. Similarly, Krashen (1982: 74) argued against the role of CF in second language (L2) and called the correction process 'a serious mistake'.

More recently, under the influence of interactionist theories of language learning, errors were viewed as 'treatable' through corrective feedback in both naturally occurring interactions and classroom practice. For instance, Long (1996) advocated the position that underlined the effectiveness of CF based on the *focus-on-form* approach. He claimed that CF arose from negotiations for meaning and provided a learner with an opportunity to attend to new linguistic forms. Similarly, other theories of SLA such as *The Output Hypothesis* (Swain 1995) and *The Noticing Hypothesis* (Schmidt 2001) maintained that CF helped learners to notice the gap between interlanguage (IL) forms and target language forms (TL) and then enabled a learner to correct his or her errors.

A number of definitions of corrective feedback can be found in the literature on SLA and in the field of foreign language teaching (FLT). Chaudron (1977: 31), for example describes CF as "any reaction of the teacher which clearly transforms, disapprovingly refers to, or demands improvement of the learner utterance". The reaction in question was not only limited to verbal behaviour but it also concerned any kind of reaction to pinpoint an incorrect form and force a learner to respond. Lightbown and Spada (1999: 171–172) expanded the former definition and distinguished between explicit versus implicit feedback. They described CF as:

> any indication to a learner that his or her use of the target language is incorrect. This includes a variety of responses that a language learner receives. When a language learner says, 'He go to school every day', corrective feedback can be explicit, for example, 'No, you should say goes, not go' or implicit 'Yes, he goes to school every day', and may or may not include meta-linguistic information, for example, 'Don't forget to make the verb agree with the subject'.

Similarly, in one of the most recent publications Ellis (2008: 958) defines this concept as "information given to learners which they can use to revise their interlanguage", emphasising that CF can be explicit or implicit. All those definitions of CF assume that any kind of the teacher's reaction to learners' errors encourages them to reflect and has a beneficial effect on learners' production.

2 Approaches to Writing

Before we analyse the types and the effectiveness of written corrective feedback in SLA and language teaching, let us briefly analyze the views of the process of L2 writing from the pedagogical perspective. Whereas SLA researchers are concerned mainly with how CF can influence the process of L2 acquisition, writing experts, ELT methodologists and language teachers have been more concerned with how CF influences writing development. The key issue in this respect is the approach to the writing process. We can distinguish the three main viewpoints that will be discussed below.

The Structural Approach It presents the development of L2 writing as the construction of the orthographic representation of lexical and syntactic features of L2 speech. This approach reflects behaviourist views of L2 learning, which involve producing correct grammatical patterns in controlled exercises. Corrective feedback is provided whenever an incorrect structure occurs since the aim of teaching is to minimize the number of errors. According to the approach the process of acquiring the writing skill involves the four necessary stages (Hyland 2003: 4):

1. Familiarization. Grammar and vocabulary are taught explicitly, usually through reference to a text.
2. Controlled writing. Learners employ fixed patterns.
3. Guided writing. Model texts are imitated by learners.
4. Free writing. Learners develop the patterns they practiced.

The Process Approach It has become a major paradigm in L2 writing instruction. According to Hedgcock (2005) the model requires L2 writers to go through various stages from pre-writing, drafting feedback, revising and editing, reflecting recursive and non-linear processes involved in arriving at the final written product. In contrast to the previous approach it focuses on the learner as he or she goes through the different stages of writing rather than the written text itself. Error correction in L2 writing is very much reduced, and the process oriented approach emphasizes content and text organization at the expense of formal correctness. Careful attention to grammatical accuracy is required only at the final editing stage.

The Post-Process Approach It incorporates and expands the principles of the process approach. The difference, however, is that according to Atkinson (2003) the term encompasses the complex nature of L2 writing as a socio-cognitive, situational and diverse activity. As a result CF can be understood as a complex human activity that takes account of a variety of cultural, institutional and interpersonal contexts. This approach also takes into account the impact of individual leaner differences, such as beliefs and preferences about learning styles and forms of corrective feedback. Hyland and Hyland (2006: 10) characterize the process of error correction in this approach in the following way.

> It is a form of social action designed to accomplish educational and social goals. Like all acts of communication, it occurs in particular cultural, institutional and interpersonal contexts, between people enacting and negotiating particular social identities and relationships, and is mediated by various types of delivery.

While post-process L2 writing researchers have not directly addressed the role of feedback, one clear implication is the need to take into account the cultural and institutional impact of individual learner factors.

3 Written CF in SLA Research

The main interest in corrective feedback concentrated initially on learners' oral performance. There is now a substantial number of studies that have confirmed the positive effect of oral CF on L2 learning (Mackey 2007). In contrast, there are fewer examples of research that have demonstrated the efficacy of written CF, and the extent to which this form of CF can influence acquisition remains a matter of some controversy (cf. Truscott 2007). However, a number of recent studies (e.g. Ferris 2006; Sheen 2011) have shown that both written and oral CF can contribute to language acquisition. As far as written CF is concerned, SLA theories deal with the role of corrective feedback from the perspective of overall writing development, whereas classroom, pedagogically-oriented correction techniques have been primarily used to develop students' ability to revise their written assignment.

According to Reichelt (2001) students' written work does not represent the final product. What matters most, is the process of writing itself, which greatly contributes to L2 acquisition. Corrected learners are more prone to notice the erroneous linguistic form in their writing performances, and their attention to form significantly contributes to second language acquisition. The approach to error correction in writing tasks and oral performances are viewed from the same perspective by SLA researchers.

Another issue refers to the question of focused vs. unfocused correction. Ferris (2004) and Truscott (1996), for example, investigated the effectiveness of corrective feedback from the point of view of the L2 writing process in SLA. Other researchers, e.g. Han (2002) and Lyster (2004) focused on particular grammatical features while investigating the process of correction as a representative of acquisition process. Such an isolation of a single item, according to Doughty and Varela (1998) and Han (2002) proved to be beneficial for interlanguage development. The approach proposed by the above mentioned researchers emphasized the contrast to the previous studies concentrating mainly on unfocused correction techniques.

The positive value of CF, however, was not generally accepted by all SLA and ELT researchers. The error correction phenomenon was perceived as sometimes undesired or even totally harmful in the process of language acquisition. Truscott (1996), for example, emphasized its negative influence and promoted its complete abandonment. Giving an example of his own research, he advised teachers to focus more on their students' writing process itself by drawing their attention to the content of their assignments. By the same token, he promoted reading activities in order to improve learners' writing skills. His critical views on empirical studies of written corrective feedback as proving no inquisitional value resulted in the abundance of theoretical counterarguments and empirical studies supporting great inquisitional value of written correction itself. For example, Ferris (2006), among others, proved correction to greatly contribute to L2 learning and writing accuracy.

4 Key Issues in Written Corrective Feedback

The most important aspects in the analysis of written CF refer to the basic issues connected with the implementation of the procedure of correction, that is *which* errors, *when, by whom, how,* and first of all *whether* should be corrected. The same questions a teacher has to answer before she decides to employ any oral error correction techniques. Let us begin with the review with the fundamental question: Should learner errors be corrected at all?

4.1 Should We Correct Learner Errors?

The value of written corrective feedback has been the object of dispute in the debate among SLA researchers. Ferris (2004), e.g. claims that correction cannot be dismissed and its effects depend on the quality of the corrective procedures. They must be clear and consistent, otherwise CF will not work for improving L2 writing. Truscott (2007), on the other hand, argues that written error correction has little or no effect on the improvement on learners' accuracy in written production. He also warns against a potentially negative effect of error correction, which is supported by Hendrickson (1980), who recognized the dangers of overcorrection resulting from a tendency for teachers to correct linguistic errors at the expense of content and organization. Ferris (2004) admits that a major issue is to balance content feedback and grammar feedback. Hendrickson (1980) distinguished a number of learner factors that teachers need to take into account while providing CF for students, which can be summarized as follows:

(a) They need to know the communicative purpose of writing (e.g. an invitation letter or an application form).

(b) They need to adjust the forms of CF to the students' level of proficiency. Learners' ability to locate their errors and self-correct largely depends on their level of advancement.
(c) They need to take into account error types and their frequencies of occurrence as well as the effects on the intelligibility of the text and individual characteristics of the learner.

We must remember, however, that written corrective feedback is directed at students as "a private practice" (Sheen 2011: 45), thus it is much less stressful and does not usually lead to negative effects in students' future performance.

4.2 Which Errors Should Be Corrected?

SLA researchers and writing experts distinguish several categories of written and spoken errors (c.f. Ellis 2008). They may refer to the particular aspects of learner language development such as (1) identification and description of the sources of L2 errors (e.g. *L1 transfer* vs. *developmental errors*), (2) the relationship between the learner's competence and performance (*pre-systematic, systematic, post-systematic errors*), or (3) a description of the process of acquisition of developmental patterns in L2 (e.g. *overt* vs. *covert errors*, or the surface structure taxonomy of errors, such as errors of *omission, addition, misinformation* and *misordering*). On the other hand, writing experts, ELT methodologists and teachers employ more frequently other categories of error classification, which seem to be more adequate in the L2 classroom error correction, e.g. *global* errors that interfere with comprehension vs. *local* or *surface* errors that do not hinder intelligibility of sentences, *frequent* vs. *infrequent* errors, *treatable* vs. *untreatable* errors or *stigmatizing/ irritating* vs. *non-stigmatizing* errors, that is errors that offend or irritate L2 readers. Ferris (2002) proposes that teachers should first of all correct errors that affect text understanding (*global* errors), occur in a patterned rule–governed way (*treatable* errors) and are *frequent* and *stigmatizing*, although it may not always be easy for a FL teacher to determine whether and to what degree an error is treatable or irritating.

Another issue mentioned previously concerns whether teachers should concentrate on a limited range of errors, or whether corrective feedback should be unfocused, including a wide range of errors. There is no definite answer to this question as either approach has its advantages or disadvantages. If CF covers all sorts of errors learners may not understand the corrections or be discouraged from practicing the skill of writing. If, however, the teacher concentrates on one type of errors many other incorrect forms may go uncorrected.

4.3 Who and When Should Correct Learner Errors?

The question of when to correct written errors is not such an important issue as written CF is usually provided with delay; a student writes his or her text and the teacher then corrects it. In the so called process writing the issue of timing is more important especially when the student produces several forms of the same text, starting from a draft and ending up with the final version. McGarell and Verbeen (2007) suggest that CF should not be provided immediately after the text is written since it may prevent learners from its revising and reorganization that are the necessary components of text editing based on self-correction.

Traditionally, it is the teacher who is responsible for providing corrective feedback on students' written texts, however, as some methodologists claim (e.g. Hendrickson 1980) the teacher's role should not be dominant and learners should also be engaged in the process of correcting their own errors. The problem is that both the student's self-correction or peer correction may be problematic. Learners usually expect the teacher to correct their text and, more importantly, they may lack the necessary linguistic knowledge to self-correct. The same objections apply to peer correction. Although this procedure is often practiced in a foreign language classroom, it is sometimes introduced as a teaching technique rather than a form of error correction. Teachers do not always trust their students' judgements and avoid extensive peer correction as it may lead to the situation of "the blind leading the blind" (Sheen 2011: 48).

4.4 How Can Errors Be Corrected?

The key consideration in the debate of strategies of error correction is the effectiveness of particular types of CF. Our discussion is based on a typology proposed by Ellis (2009). A basic distinction is between direct correction versus indirect correction. The first type of a teacher's intervention requires the provision of a TL form, whereas indirect errors correction calls for indicating an error without giving the L2 form and requires the learner to come up with the correct form. The majority of writing experts advocate the use of indirect CF, as it encourages learners to attend to their errors and self-correct through problem solving activities. Direct feedback provided by the teacher may sometimes be inappropriate because the teacher may misunderstand the students' original content or its meaning. It seems that direct feedback is more appropriate for beginner writers especially when they make syntactic and lexical errors that they are not capable to self correct. The majority of ELT methodologists and teachers seem to believe that learner errors should be corrected both directly and indirectly (cf. Pawlak 2012).

A decisive factor in the use of indirect CF refers to indicating the location of an error. A teacher may opt for clear pointing to an incorrect structure by circling or underlining it or simply signalling the occurrence of an error by writing brief information in the margin of a written text or using a coding system that signals an error type. It seems that the error locating option is more effective since it requires a learner to correct the wrong form and not just to figure out the place where the error is. Corrective feedback can also be analyzed in terms of the meta-linguistic information it contains. Baker and Brickner (2010), for example, describe a direct correction as the one where the corrective act is openly expressed and the learner is instructed to use a particular structure (e.g. 'use present progressive here'). In an indirect correction, the meta-linguistic corrective information is not expressed overtly. The teacher merely suggests the necessity to change the existing incorrect form and replace it with a correct one (e.g. 'Can you change the tense here?'). The study reported by Baker and Brickner (2010) reveals that the majority of university undergraduate students edited their original text most accurately when they were provided with direct correction and the students who received indirect feedback from the teacher produced less correct revisions.

The research by Baker and Bricker, as well as other studies (e.g. Ferris and Roberts 2001) show that ESL learners prefer a direct form of written error correction. Alternatively, teachers try to develop learners' self-editing strategies by encouraging them to locate and correct their own errors. In this procedure teachers first identify the error types and their frequency in the learners' written production and the students' task is to find and correct them. Since they know they have to focus on one error type at a time, the procedure may work quite effectively on condition that learners possess adequate linguistic knowledge to rectify or modify the erroneous forms they have used.

5 A Typology of Written CF Types

Teachers have a number of options for correcting errors in students' written work. Ur (1996: 171), for example, insists that language mistakes should be corrected and learners should rewrite incorporating corrections "not only because it reinforces learning but also rewriting is an integral part of the writing process as a whole". The question is how errors can and should be corrected. A basis for investigating the effects of written CF in the majority of contemporary studies on CF is a distinction between strategies that (1) provide a correct TL form, (2) simply indicate that an error exists. A further distinction relates to the type of meta-linguistic information as to the nature of an error. The following table (see Table 1) presents the typology of written feedback types based on the categories proposed by Ellis (2009: 98–99).

Ellis (2009) mentions another strategy occasionally used by native speakers called *reformulation*. It requires the teacher's rewriting of the whole text written by a learner to make it look as native-like as possible while keeping the original content. As text reformulations are time consuming and require some additional effort on the part of the teacher and the student they are not frequently used in research on written CF.

The Effectiveness of Written Corrective Feedback in the Acquisition of the...   139

Table 1 Types of written corrective feedback (adapted from Ellis 2009: 98–99)

Type of CF	Description
Direct CF	The teacher provides the student with the correct form
Indirect CF	The teacher indicates that an error exists but does not provide the correction
(a) Indicating and locating the error	This takes the form of underlining and use of cursors to show omissions in the student's text
(b) Indication only	This takes the form of an indication in the margin that an error or errors have taken place in a line of text
Meta-linguistic CF	The teacher provides some kind of meta-linguistic clue as to the nature of the error
(a) Use of error codes	The teacher writes codes in the margin (e.g. art = article)
(b) Brief grammatical descriptions	The teacher numbers errors in text and writes a grammatical description for each numbered error at the bottom of the text
The focus of the feedback	This concerns whether the teacher attempts to correct all (or most) of the students' errors or selects one or two specific types of errors to correct. This distinction can be applied to each of the above options. Unfocused CF is extensive, focused CF is intensive
Electronic feedback	The teacher indicates an error and provides a hyperlink to a concordance file that provides examples of correct usage

6 The Research

6.1 Aims and Hypothesis

The research examined the differential effects of the two types of written CF and the extent to which the type of FL instruction mediates the effects of CF on the acquisition of English articles by adult intermediate EFL learners of L1 Polish. The theoretical basis of the study is *The Counterbalance Hypothesis* proposed by Lyster and Mori (2006). The hypothesis predicts a learner's ability to notice the gap between his or her ill-formed utterance and the L2 linguistic form by means of the shift in the learner's attentional focus from meaning to form in a meaning-focused context and from form to meaning in a form-oriented settings. Lyster and Mori (2006: 294) summarize the basic concept of the hypothesis as follows:

> (...) instructional activities and interactional feedback that act as a counterbalance to a classroom's predominant communicative orientation are likely to prove more effective than instructional activities and interactional feedback that are congruent with its predominant communicative orientation.

We may predict that L2 learning will be enhanced if pedagogical intervention in the form of CF runs counter to the preferred classroom orientation. Thus, we may assume that an effective error correction for a form-oriented group needs to encourage communication, whereas the type of CF provided for a communicatively oriented group needs to encourage learners' attention to form. Instructional activities such as corrective feedback should act as a counterbalance to a classroom's predominant orientation and are expected to be more effective than interactional feedback which is congruent with the predominant FL teaching methodology. The study was designed to find out whether the experimental groups (taught and corrected according to the principles of The Counterbalance Hypothesis) would perform better than the control group taught and corrected in the same manner, that is explicitly or implicitly, on the immediate post-tests. It also aimed at confirming or rejecting a hypothesis that written CF targeting a single linguistic feature improved learners' accuracy, especially when meta-linguistic feedback was provided for the learners who received predominately the inductive type of formal instruction.

6.2 Participants and Procedures

The study took place in the spring semester in 2012 and lasted for about 12 weeks. The participants of the study were 59 L1 Polish intermediate learners of L2 English (age 17–18). They were recruited from three local high schools in the area of Lower Silesia, Poland. They attended English class for 45 min four times a week. The Oxford Placement Test (Allan 2004) was used to assess the participants' proficiency in English at the beginning of the research. Four groups of subjects were formed for the purpose of the study: a direct-only correction group taught inductively, a direct-only correction group taught deductively, a direct meta-linguistic correction group taught inductively and a direct meta-linguistic correction group taught deductively. The arrangements of the study groups are presented below (see Table 2).

For the first 3 weeks the participants received 6 h of formal instruction on the use of articles in English. In the following 9 weeks they were asked to write six different assignments as a part of the teaching syllabus. At the end of the treatment they took a post-test that included a free writing task and a test on articles in English (see Appendix 1). The type of instruction was based on the *Counterbalance Hypothesis* principle. In the spring semester both groups used the two dedicated course-books, *Matura Solutions Intermediate* (Falla et al. 2011), and *New Matura Success* (Hastings et al. 2011), which were the basis for the final school leaving exam in English. The form of teaching in the inductive group included group discussion, pair work and individual work. The students were exposed to a large amount of spoken and written input in the form of video and audio recordings, and printed handouts based on authentic materials. They had opportunities to produce spoken and written discourse in different games and exercises.

The students taught explicitly used the same teaching materials, however, both grammatical and lexical issues were presented in the deductive way starting with an explicit language rule illustrated with numerous examples and followed by formal practicing. They did a lot of exercises which checked their knowledge of newly taught language forms and also had opportunities to use English spontaneously in speech and writing. The explicitly taught groups received formal instruction and basic pedagogical explanation on definiteness/indefiniteness in English and the use of articles. The implicitly taught groups practiced the use articles in English,

Table 2 Types of instruction and CF in the research groups

Group Total n = 59	Instruction	Feedback
Group1 (experimental n = 15)	Explicit	Implicit
Group 2 (experimental n = 15)	Implicit	Explicit
Group 3 (control n = 15)	Explicit	Explicit
Group 4 (control n = 14)	Implicit	Implicit

however, they were not given any prescriptive rules and the notions of the definite/indefinite article were not discussed in detail.

The explicitly taught learners were presented with a brief theoretical account of the English article system based on Bickerton (1981). He claims that the meanings of the English articles are universal, but they may be realized differently in different languages, also in article-less languages. He defines [+definite] as "presumed known to the listener", whether by prior knowledge, or general knowledge that a named class exists, uniqueness in the world or a given setting. The feature [−definite] is defined as "presumed unknown to the listener" (Bickerton 1981: 247–248), whether by absence of prior knowledge, or nonexistence of a nameable referent. The semantic universal [±specific] indicates whether a NP refers to a specific entity or whether its referent is non-specific. In other words a learner must be able to perceive the difference of any member, or no member of a class and that of a particular class member. The following examples illustrate the four types of noun phrases with reference to the features of definiteness (known to the hearer [±HK]) and specificity (specific referent [±SR]) (Bickerton 1981).

1. Generics—specific, unknown to the hearer [*the* or *a*], (*A/The* dog is a mammal.)
2. Referential definites—specific, known to the hearer [*the*], (Feed *the* dog!)
3. Non-referential indefinites—non-specific, unknown to the hearer [*a* or Ø], (I want *a* dog.)
4. Referential indefinites [*a* or Ø]—specific, unknown to the hearer, (I have *a* dog.)

Other categories used in the explanation of the English articles were e.g. first mention/second mention (e.g. I saw *a dog. The dog* was black), countable/uncountable nouns (e.g. I like *coffee*. I had *a coffee*), proper names (We visited *the United States* and *Canada*), idioms and fixed phrases (We went there *by bus*).

6.3 Instruments

The students were asked to write the following written assignments: a postcard to a friend, a description of a person they admire, a review of a film they have seen lately, a letter of application to a drama school, an announcement of a charity event and a composition entitled *The future of our civilisation*. They sent their texts in the electronic form via e-mail. All the works were corrected immediately by the teachers and sent back to the authors. The correction methods were based on the corrective feedback types discussed below. The teachers used the available forms of text editing, such as different tools of tracking changes e.g. text insertions, deletions, crossing out and comments added to the text (see Appendix 2).

Four basic types of written CF were used in the study, two direct and two indirect strategies. They differed in the kind of meta-linguistic information provided for the learner. Other available indirect CF types that involve an error treatment without either locating or correcting it were not used in the study because in those types of correction learners would have to locate the errors they had made themselves. A brief description of the four error correction techniques is presented below.

A. Direct Non-meta-linguistic Written Correction This type of correction provides the learner with the written forms, such as crossing out the unnecessary word, phrase or morpheme, inserting a missing word or morpheme, and writing the correct form above or near the erroneous form. For example,

Example 1

a   a   a

A dog stole ~~the~~ bone from butcher. He escaped with ~~having~~ bone.

^   ^   ^

B. Direct Meta-Linguistic Written Correction This refers to the provision of the correct form with an accompanying explanation of some sort. For example,

Example 2

(1)   (2)   (3)

A dog stole bone from butcher. He escaped with a bone.

Teacher: (1), (2)—you need 'a' before the noun when a person or thing is mentioned for the first time. (3)—you need 'the' before the noun when the person or thing has been mentioned previously.

C. Indirect Non-meta-linguistic Written Correction (Located) This correction type differs from the previous one in that it also indicates where the errors are while still not providing the correct form. For example,

Example 3

A dog stole X bone from X butcher. He escaped with having X bone.

D. Indirect Meta-Linguistic Written Correction It involves the provision of meta-linguistic clues about the errors. For example, if the learner has omitted the indefinite article the clue might be as in the example below:

Example 4

A dog stole bone from a butcher. He escaped with having bone.

Teacher: 'What word do you need before a noun when the person/thing is referred to for the first/second time?'

The Effectiveness of Written Corrective Feedback in the Acquisition of the... 143

Table 3 The number and percentage of feedback types used in the free writing task—A film review

Group	DN-M	DM	IN-M	IM	Total (100 %)
1 (E/I)			61 (53 %)	54 (47 %)	115
2 (I/E)	81 (52 %)	74 (48 %)			155
3 (E/E)	78 (54 %)	67 (46 %)			145
4 (I/I)			70 (49 %)	73 (51 %)	143
Both groups	159 (28 %)	141 (25 %)	131 (24 %)	127 (23 %)	558

DN-M direct non-metalinguistic, *DM* direct metalinguistic, *IN-M* indirect non-metalinguistic, *IM* indirect metalinguistic

The key issue is obviously the choice of the most effective correction strategies for providing learners with the necessary feedback information in each study group. The underlying idea behind the study was to diversify the approach to error treatment. The researchers who corrected the students' assignments tried to balance the meta-linguistic and non-meta-linguistic information included in the CF so that the learners received the same number of overt comments about the error they made ('you need 'a' before a noun when it is mentioned for the first time') and indications of the location of the missing or incorrect article (e.g. A dog stole X bone from X butcher). Table 3 below illustrates the frequency and distribution of the types of CF used in the error correction session devoted to writing a film review.

6.4   Results Analysis

After the period of treatment the students were tested on two tasks: (1) free writing task and (2) forced-choice elicitation task. The first task was similar to the written assignments they produced during the whole semester, however, it was longer as the students were requested to write a composition between 220 and 250 words. The size of the writing task complied with the requirements of the written part of the final school-leaving *Maturity Exam*. The study of the learners' use of the English articles was based on the analysis of the first 20 noun phrases (NPs) preceded by the definite [*the*], indefinite [*a/an*] or zero article [*Ø*]. A few students produced shorter texts so that only 15–17 NPs were coded and taken into account in the analysis. The results of the free writing tasks are presented in Table 4.

The results show that the correct use of articles in the free-writing task was problematic for the students who participated in the study. The percentage of correct answers in all groups was about 50, yet, certain differences can be observed between the particular groups. The highest level of accuracy in handling the English articles was noted in the experimental implicit/explicit and explicit/implicit groups (58.2 and 56.6 %, respectively). The results were in accordance with the predictions formulated on the basis of The Counterbalance Hypothesis, which proves the effectiveness of error correction in opposition to the predominant type of teaching. The results in the control groups (implicit/implicit and explicit/explicit) were

Table 4 Percentage of errors in the free writing task (omission and misuse)

Group	Omission (%)	Misuse (%)	Correct (%)
1 (E/I)	17.4	26.0	56.6
2 (I/E)	17.2	24.6	58.2
3 (E/E)	18.7	38.5	42.8
4 (I/I)	22.1	37.9	40.0
All groups	18.8	31.7	49.5

visibly lower, barely exceeding the level of 40 % of the correct answers. An interesting observation may be a relatively low percentage of correct answers in the control groups and a moderate spread between the mean scores in the best group and the weakest group (58.2 and 40.0 %, respectively). This may be due to a relatively smaller influence of corrective feedback on the students' accuracy in free writing tasks in comparison to other writing tasks, such as controlled writing and language tests on English articles, based on meta-linguistic judgement (the elicitation tasks).

As regards the error types in the use of articles, omission was a less serious type of error in comparison to the cases of misuse. The omission of articles among the intermediate learners accounted for less than 20 % of all cases of article use in L2 English. This finding corresponds with other studies of the acquisition of articles in L2 English, which confirmed that omission was a less serious problem for L2 English learners at more advanced levels of proficiency (cf. Tarone and Parrish 1988). The only group in which the learners frequently failed to supply the necessary article was the control inductive/inductive group, which probably suggests that exposure to L2 input in the FL classroom and indirect inductive forms of instruction are not sufficient for L2 learners to acquire such a complex system of determiners as the English articles.

When we analyze the cases of misuse of the articles in English, it is evident that the learners' perception of definiteness/indefiniteness is the key factor responsible for the difference between the experimental and the control groups. The groups that received corrective feedback in opposition to the type of instruction they were provided with made only slightly more than 25 % of errors in the choice of the coded articles. On the other hand, the learners in the control groups made considerably more errors in the correct article choice, almost 40 % of wrong choices. It seems that the contrast between the form of teaching and the type of CF enhances the students' perception of such difficult semantic notions as definiteness/indefiniteness and the contexts in which they are realized.

The results in Table 5 show the correct use of articles in the forced choice elicitation tasks. The percentage of correct answers in all groups is considerably higher in comparison to the results in the free writing task. The highest level of accuracy in handling the English articles was again noted in the implicit/explicit and explicit/implicit groups (70.5 and 62 %, respectively). The level of accuracy in the control groups was evidently lower in comparison to the experimental group results. However, the validity of the Counterbalance Hypothesis is less obvious in this case due to bigger differences between the two experimental groups (70.5 and

The Effectiveness of Written Corrective Feedback in the Acquisition of the... 145

Table 5 Percentage of errors in the elicitation task (omission and misuse)

Group	Omission (%)	Misuse (%)	Correct (%)
1 (E/I)	14.1	15.4	70.5
2 (I/E)	19.0	19.0	62.0
3 (E/E)	17.2	24.1	58.7
4 (I/I)	27.8	25.9	46.3
All groups	19.5	21.1	59.4

62.0 % of correct answers, respectively) and the two control groups (58.7 and 46.3 %). We may assume that the best group (explicit/implicit) benefitted a lot from the indirect type of CF after receiving an extensive pedagogical explanation on the English articles in the deductive form. We may also conclude that the efficacy of the implicit type of error correction in explicitly taught learners was higher and encouraged them to revise their texts and self- correct before producing the final version. This type of CF apparently did not work well for the weakest group in the study (implicit/implicit), possibly because of the lack of any kind of explicit, deductive information directed at the learners as a type of instruction or error correction. We may hypothesize that any kind of teaching in the FL classroom devoid of explicit, deductive instruction/CF may undoubtedly help student develop their communicative skills, but not TL accuracy in the use of such intricate morphological features as articles in L2 English.

When we look at the error types in the use of English articles by the participants in the research, the pattern of article omission in the elicitation test is very similar to the one noted in the free-writing task. The students omitted almost one in five articles in the obligatory contexts and the weakest results again were noted in the implicit/implicit group, with the percentage of omission errors at 22.1 in all contexts. Similarly, the percentage of errors of misuse of the articles was clearly much lower in the experimental groups 26 and 24.6 %, respectively, than in the control group. This confirms the view that the major problem in the correct use of articles in English at the post-elementary level is their misuse rather than omission, irrespective of the task.

Conclusion

Errors in learners' writing appear as frequently as in their oral performance. The occurrence of such incorrect forms can be explained, for example, in terms of L1 transfer, students' previous L2 exposure and the type of formal instruction. One of the main issues in the study of SLA and ELT refers to the significance and forms of written corrective feedback. The research showed that all the treatment groups performed better on the post-tests, but the group taught deductively and corrected implicitly performed slightly better than the other experimental group taught inductively and corrected explicitly and significantly better than the two remaining control groups that were taught

(continued)

and corrected in the same way. The results also showed that written CF targeting a single linguistic feature improved learners' accuracy, especially when the CF completed the predominant type of formal instruction.

The proportion between the types of errors in the use of articles in English (omission- misuse) reflects the general pattern of second language acquisition in which the omission of morphological features is more frequent at the beginning and pre-intermediate level whereas article misuse is a major problem for more advanced learners. In order to reduce the number of errors in the use of articles in L2 English, we suggest that instructional activities such as corrective feedback should act as a counterbalance to the L2 classroom orientation and are predicted to be more effective than interactional feedback which is congruent with the predominant FL teaching methodology.

The techniques used in the study proved very convenient for both the learners and the teachers/researchers. Since the majority of teenage learners and perhaps adults as well prefer electronic forms of communication, they easily and, we may say, quite willingly accept the computer-based forms of writing and error correction. Especially the use of the CF tools such as comments was generally perceived by the students as useful and more interesting than the paper-and-pencil conventional forms of error coding and explanation.

The research also has shown that FL students need diversified types of instruction and error correction. The acquisition of articles in L2 English in the so called *immersion classroom* with minimum grammar explanation and formal practice may take a long time especially when students do not receive any negative evidence, i.e. information on what they do wrong. Similarly, pedagogical grammar presentations based on deductive rules often prove entirely ineffective if not accompanied by learners' access to L2 input and opportunities for authentic language use. Formal instruction based on explicit pedagogical rules and direct error correction in the FL classroom may have limited effects on the students acquisition of less salient, much confusing L2 English structures such as articles, especially when they do not occur in the learner's L1.

A possible reason for the low effectiveness of deductive FI may be the quality of pedagogical rules in formal instruction. They are often too general, vague or ambiguous and usually expressed in complicated meta-language that is conceptually difficult for L2 learners. Even good grammar books written by both native and non-native ELT experts and teachers contain a lot of highly specialized, sophisticated terminology, notions and categories taken from descriptive grammar, such as *anaphora, identifiable* and *uniqueness* (see e.g. Berry 1993). In that situation teachers sometimes simplify the forms and content of formal instruction, whereas learners create their own IL rules, which obviously leads to errors. A good example may be *the first/second*

(continued)

mention rule. Learners often mistakenly assume that every NP mentioned for the first time in a discourse must be preceded by *a* or *an* and every NP mentioned for the second time is anaphoric and must be preceded by *the.* This obviously is not the case, since it is the relationship between the antecedent and the following NP referent and not just their location in the discourse that determines the definiteness of the second mention NP (cf. 'I got *a dog* for my birthday, but I didn't want *a dog.* I wanted a bike').

Finally, another important factor in the analysis of written CF refers to learners' attitude towards error correction and its forms. On the one hand, teachers' correction can be perceived by learners as unnecessary and annoying and remain unnoticed, and on the other hand, it may be desirable and highly expected, aiming at writing improvement. The preference of the different kinds of corrective feedback can also be affected by the learning context and individual learner differences. It seems that the combination of both implicit and explicit language teaching and direct and indirect forms of error correction can be the optimal solution for students who acquire English as a foreign rather than a second language and their opportunities of obtaining comprehensible input containing a particular L2 feature are limited in comparison to learners acquiring a second language in naturalistic conditions.

Appendix 1

The Forced-Choice Elicitation Test on the English Articles (30 Items)

Direction: Underline the missing article a, an, the or zero article (Ø)
    Example: I have (a, an, the, Ø) dog and two hamsters.

1. **Woman:** I bought a blue cup and a green cup. Unfortunately, **(a, an, the, Ø)** blue cup broke before I even got home.
2. **Woman:** Don't go in that yard. **(a, an, the, Ø)** dog will bite you!
3. **Man:** They've just returned from New York. **(a, an, the, Ø)** plane was 5 h late.
4. **Woman:** The pet shop had five puppies and seven kittens. Sue thought for **(a, an, the, Ø)** while and chose **(a, an, the, Ø)** puppy.
5. **Teacher:** Amy, you probably have something on your desk in your room. What is it?
   Schoolgirl: It is **(a, an, the, Ø)** computer.
6. **Boy:** Mum, I haven't got anything to write with.
   Woman: Wait, I have three pens in my bag. I will give you **(a, an, the, Ø)** pen.

7. **Man:** When I was walking down the street (**a, an, the, Ø**) girl came up to me and asked me about the most interesting places in the city. I told her that I couldn't answer (**a, an, the, Ø**) question because I was a stranger there.
8. **Man:** Mark went to see our local football team in training. He even got an autograph from (**a, an, the, Ø**) player. I have no idea which one, but he was very happy.
9. **Man:** (*at the dinner table*) Please pass (**a, an, the, Ø**) butter.
10. **Woman:** We had dinner in that new Italian restaurant. I had (**a, an, the, Ø**) chicken and salad—both were great, but (**a, an, the, Ø**) dessert was far too sweet for my taste.
11. **Boy:** I dropped five coins and found only four of them, (**a, an, the, Ø**) missing coin is probably under (**a, an, the, Ø**) sofa.
12. **Security guard:** If you want to talk to (**a, an, the, Ø**) winner, wait until the end of (**a, an, the, Ø**) race.
13. **Man:** I had to get (**a, an, the, Ø**) taxi from the station. On the way (**a, an, the, Ø**) driver told me there was (**a, an, the, Ø**) bus strike.
14. **Boy:** Paul has many old records. His cousin borrowed (**a, an, the, Ø**) record from him.
15. **Teacher:** A man went to (**a, an, the, Ø**) jungle because he wanted to see a lion or a zebra. He looked all over and looked and looked. Who came running at (**a, an, the, Ø**) man?
    Child: ... (**a, an, the, Ø**) zebra.
16. **Shop owner:** We will offer a huge discount to (**a, an, the, Ø**) next customer.
17. **Woman:** My daughter is studying to be a lawyer. She wants to help (**a, an, the, Ø**) poor.
18. **Man:** We went to a wedding yesterday. I must say (**a, an, the, Ø**) bride was very pretty.
19. **Passenger:** (*At the airport*) Excuse me, I'm looking for (**a, an, the, Ø**) tall, red-haired girl. She's my daughter. She was on (**a, an, the, Ø**) flight 239.
20. **Hotel receptionist:** Are you looking for something, madam?
    Woman: Yes, I'm looking for (**a, an, the, Ø**) brown bag that I left here.

Key: 1 the blue cup, **2** the dog, **3** the plane, **4** a while, a puppy **5** a computer, **6** a pen, **7** a girl, the question, **8** a player, **9** the butter, **10** the chicken, the dessert, **11** the missing coin, the sofa, **12** the winner, the race, **13** a taxi, the driver, a bus strike, **14** a record, **15** the jungle, the man, a zebra, **16** the next customer, **17** the poor, **18** the bride, **19** a tall red-haired girl, flight **20** the brown bag.

Appendix 2

A Sample of a Student's Writing Assignment with Corrections. Noun Phrases Coded for the Analysis of the Article Use Are in Boldface

One week ago I saw **very interesting movie**[1] I would like to write about. **The movie** calls *Noi Albinoi*, was made in Iceland and shows different problems of living in **a small village**. **The main actor** is **18 years old guy**[2] with only one plan for his life. He tries to run away from this little village and look for **better place**[3] to live. **The society** try to convince him to stay because they don't believe he should go away. He doesn't go to **school** and makes new friends that's why **the rest** of the villagers pull him back. He is so frustrated that's why he decides to escape. He jumps to **the boat**[4] to get to **nearest island**[5]. Suddenly **the weather** changes and starts to snowing.

References

Allan, D. 2004. *Oxford placement test 1*. Oxford: Oxford University Press.

Atkinson, D. 2003. L2 writing in the post-process era. *Journal of Second Language Writing* 12: 3–15.

Baker, W., and R. Brickner. 2010. The effects of direct and indirect speech acts on native English and ESL speakers' perception of teacher written feedback. *System* 38: 75–84.

Berry, R. 1993. *Collins Cobuild English guides 3 – Articles*. London: Harper Collins.

Bickerton, D. 1981. *Roots of language*. Ann Abor: Karoma.

Brooks, N. 1960. *Language and language learning*. New York: Harcourt, Brace and World.

Chaudron, C. 1977. A descriptive model of discourse in the corrective treatment of learners' errors. *Language Learning* 25: 153–161.

Chomsky, N. 1975. *Reflections on language*. New York: Pantheon Books.

Doughty, C., and E. Varela. 1998. Communicative focus on form. In *Focus on form in classroom second language acquisition*, ed. C. Doughty and J. Williams, 114–138. Cambridge: Cambridge University Press.

Ellis, R. 2008. *The study of second language acquisition*. Oxford: Oxford University Press.

Ellis, R. 2009. A typology of written corrective feedback types. *ELT Journal* 63: 97–107.

Falla, T., P. Davies, and D. Gryca. 2011. *Matura solutions intermediate*. Oxford: Oxford University Press.

Ferris, D. 2002. *Treatment of error in second language writing classes*. Ann Arbor: University of Michigan Press.

---

[1] You need 'a' before the noun when it is mentioned for the first time.

[2] You need 'a' before the noun when it is mentioned for the first time.

[3] You need 'a' before the noun when it is mentioned for the first time.

[4] You need 'a' before the noun when it is mentioned for the first time.

[5] You need 'the' before the noun in the superlative, 'the nearest'.

Ferris, D. 2004. The grammar correction debate in L2 writing. Where are we, where do we go from here (and what do we do in the meantime. . .?). *Journal of Second Language Writing* 13: 49–62.

Ferris, D. 2006. Does error feedback help student writers? New evidence on the short and long-term effects of written error correction. In *Feedback in second language writing: Context and issues*, ed. K. Hyland and F. Hyland, 81–104. Cambridge: Cambridge University Press.

Ferris, D., and B. Roberts. 2001. Error feedback in L2 writing classes: How explicit does it need to be? *Journal of Second Language Writing* 10: 161–184.

Han, Z.-H. 2002. A study of the impact of recasts on tense consistency in L2 output. *TESOL Quarterly* 41: 387–393.

Hastings, B., R. Raczyńska, and S. McKinley. 2011. *New matura success intermediate*. London: Pearson Longman.

Hedgcock, J. 2005. Taking stock of research and pedagogy in L2 writing. In *Handbook of research in second language teaching and learning*, ed. E. Hinkel, 597–613. Mahwah, NJ: Lawrence Erlbaum.

Hendrickson, J.M. 1980. Error correction in foreign language teaching: Recent research and practice. *The Modern Language Journal* 62: 387–398.

Hyland, F. 2003. Focusing on form: Student engagement with teacher feedback. *System* 31: 217–230.

Hyland, K., and F. Hyland. 2006. Contexts and issues in feedback on L2 writing: An introduction. In *Feedback in second language writing: Contexts and issues*, ed. K. Hyland, 1–19. Cambridge: Cambridge University Press.

Lightbown, P., and N. Spada. 1999. *How languages are learned*. Oxford: Oxford University Press.

Krashen, S.D. 1982. *Principles and practice in second language acquisition*. New York: Pergamon.

Long, M. 1996. The role of linguistic environment in second language acquisition. In *Handbook of second language acquisition*, ed. W.C. Ritchie and B.K. Bahtia, 413–468. New York: Academic.

Lyster, R. 2004. Differential effects of prompts and recasts in form-focused instruction. *Studies in Second Language Acquisition* 26: 399–432.

Lyster, R., and H. Mori. 2006. Interactional feedback and instructional counterbalance. *Studies in Second Language Acquisition* 28: 321–334.

Mackey, A. 2007. The role of conversational intraction in second language acquisition. In *Conversational interaction in second language acquisition*, ed. A. Mackey, 1–26. Oxford: Oxford University Press.

McGarell, H., and J. Verbeen. 2007. Motivating revision of drafts through formative feedback. *ELT Journal* 61: 228–236.

Pawlak, M. 2012. *Error correction in the foreign language classroom: Reconsidering the issue*. Poznan-Kalisz: Wydawnictwo UAM.

Reichelt, M. 2001. A critical review of foreign language writing research on pedagogical approaches. *The Modern Language Journal* 85: 578–598.

Schmidt, R. 2001. Attention. In *Cognition and second language instruction*, ed. P. Robinson, 3–32. Cambridge: Cambridge University Press.

Sheen, Y. 2011. *Corrective feedback, individual differences and second language learning*. Berlin: Springer.

Swain, M. 1995. Three functions of output in second language learning. In *Principle and practice in applied linguistics: Studies in honour of H.G. Widdowson*, ed. G. Cook and B. Seidlhofer, 125–144. Oxford: Oxford University Press.

Tarone, E., and B. Parrish. 1988. Task-related variation in interlanguage: The case of articles. *Language Learning* 38: 21–44.

Truscott, J. 1996. The case against grammar correction in L2 writing classes. *Canadian Modern Language Review* 55: 327–369.

Truscott, J. 2007. The effect of error correction on learners' ability to write accurately. *Journal of Second Language Writing* 16: 255–272.

Ur, P. 1996. *A course in language teaching*. Cambridge: Cambridge University Press.

Formal Instruction in Collocations in English: Mixed Methods Approach

Paweł Szudarski

Abstract Collocations have been shown to be an important aspect of communicative competence in English. Unfortunately, as corpus and psycholinguistic research demonstrates, second language (L2) learners experience difficulties in using collocations and do not seem to notice them in L2 input. In order to remedy the situation, form-focused instruction targeting collocations is suggested as an effective way of improving L2 phraseological competence. Using interview data, this article presents findings from a qualitative inquiry into Polish EFL learners' perceptions of different types of instruction (reading-while-listening vs. reading-only in Study 1 and input enhancement vs. reading-only in Study 2) targeting verb-noun and adjective-noun collocations. A series of interviews with learners and their teacher demonstrates the effectiveness of reading-while-listening and input enhancement as examples of two treatments that can lead to L2 phraseological development. Learners' views on the process of acquiring L2 collocational knowledge are discussed in the broader context of instructed L2 acquisition.

Keywords Mixed-methods • Instructed SLA • Collocations

1 Introduction

The accessibility of computers and New Media has had an enormous impact on applied linguistics in recent years. One of the most illustrative examples is the advent of corpora, databases of linguistic data, which have changed the nature of research on communication and second language acquisition (SLA). Large amounts of authentic data have enabled scholars to discover patterns in language that tended to be ignored by structural and generative approaches (e.g. Chomsky 1965). An area in which this is particularly visible is phraseology. Through the early work of Pawley and Syder (1983), Sinclair (1991) and Nattinger and De Carrico (1992), it became clear that vocabulary should not be seen only as individual words, for much of our lexical knowledge is stored and used as larger phraseological units or chunks.

P. Szudarski (✉)
Kazimierz Wielki University, Bydgoszcz, Poland
e-mail: pawel.szudarski@op.pl

© Springer International Publishing Switzerland 2015
L. Piasecka et al. (eds.), *New Media and Perennial Problems in Foreign Language Learning and Teaching*, Second Language Learning and Teaching,
DOI 10.1007/978-3-319-07686-7_9

In her seminal publication, Wray (2002) introduced the notion of 'formulaic sequences' which is an umbrella term that is used with reference to idioms, collocations, phrasal verbs, binomials, lexical bundles and many more types of phraseological units. However, even though it is convenient to refer to different lexical and lexicogrammatical patterns as formulaic sequences, they are all characterized by distinct features and therefore the work reported in this article will concern only one type of formulaic language—collocations.

Collocations (e.g. 'make a decision', 'terribly interesting') are word partnerships that frequently co-occur in natural discourse (Barfield and Gyllstad 2009) and together with other kinds of formulaic sequences have been emphasized as a vital aspect of proficiency in English (Boers et al. 2006; Ellis 2012). Unfortunately, L2 learners, mainly due to limited exposure to L2 input and L1 interference, experience difficulty with collocations and tend to commit errors, both in speech and writing (Altenberg and Granger 2001; Howarth 1998). Many examples of such collocational errors (e.g. 'take changes') were presented by Nesselhauf (2003) who analyzed a corpus of essays written by German learners of English. Laufer and Waldman (2011) compiled a corpus of L2 writing produced by learners of English in Israel. The authors compared learners' use of collocations with that of native speakers and found that the former used far fewer collocations and committed errors, even at an advanced level of proficiency. In light of these findings, it appears that L2 learners need to be provided with classroom instruction that will address their collocational needs. However, even though some empirical work on teaching collocations is available (e.g. Webb and Kagimoto 2009; Durrant and Schmitt 2010; Sonbul and Schmitt 2013), it offers mainly quantitative findings which do not take learners' perspective into account and reveal little information on how specific pedagogic treatments were perceived by them. Since a quick review of the existing literature on the acquisition of L2 collocations has revealed very few qualitative projects, two studies that are highly relevant to the present work, Ying and O'Neill (2009) and Peters (2009), will be discussed in greater detail.

Ying and O'Neill (2009) studied a group of 20 intermediate Chinese learners of English and explored their perspectives on and reactions to the AWARE approach to learning collocations. AWARE is an awareness-raising, process-oriented learning approach which focuses on different learning strategies that enhance learning collocations and promote learners' active involvement in the process. This approach was implemented for a period of 5 months after which the authors interviewed their participants and analyzed their reflective journals. In general, learners were positive about the approach and welcomed it as a useful addition. It raised their awareness of the importance of collocations and helped them expand their vocabulary repertoire. In learners' opinions, the mastery of collocations could help them use English in a more precise way. Some students also mentioned how gains in their collocational knowledge improved the esthetic value of their language production making it more colorful than before. As far as learning strategies are concerned, learners reported choosing these that best suited their learning styles. Interestingly, some of these strategies were traditionally taught in China (e.g. taking notes of interesting collocation encountered in class). However, there were also new or personalized strategies created by particular learners (e.g. using a special computer program for listing and testing collocations). At the same time, it needs to be stated that there were also some difficulties connected with the implementation of the AWARE approach. Firstly, many students needed a lot of time to understand the concept of collocation and making them appreciate its role in learning English proved to be a challenge. Also, students who were relatively weaker felt that they needed to learn individual words first instead of focusing on more sophisticated patterns and phrases. The major difficulty turned out to be learners' attempts to memorize all the collocations they had noticed. Many students noted down so many examples that they found it unmanageable to try to study all of them in a short period of time. This showed the importance of selecting specific collocations that should be taught and learned. It is clear that there are too many collocations in natural discourse to explicitly address all of them in a time-limited classroom environment. As a result, learners need to be made aware of this fact so that they do not set unrealistic goals and become overburdened with too much work.

Peters (2009) reports some qualitative findings on the acquisition of collocations by advanced L1 Dutch learners of English. Forty-four participants were divided into two groups: both groups were reading a glossed text but one of them was instructed to focus on new vocabulary in general (a general vocabulary task), and the other on new words and collocations (a specific task targeting collocations). In addition to obtaining quantitative data, the author included a qualitative phase in which learners answered seven questions in a questionnaire. Moreover, learners' notes taken during the treatment were analyzed. Since statistical comparisons did not reveal any significant differences between the two treatments, the qualitative findings were particularly revealing because they showed that both groups approached the vocabulary task similarly and focused on the new vocabulary irrespective of the instructions given to them. As far as collocations are concerned, it transpired that their presence on the pre-test and on margins as glosses had been noticed by learners, which was likely to have an effect on their results. In addition, students from both groups found the reading texts to be interesting and they enjoyed completing the vocabulary task (with the exception of one student who did not think it was effective). They also reported that marginal glosses had been helpful and contributed to the improvement of their vocabulary knowledge. The questionnaire also revealed which strategies had been employed by the participants. These were, among others, memorizing target words, writing them down and repeating, underlining and paying more attention to vocabulary. In summary, Peters (2009: 207) advocates the use of qualitative techniques as an addition to quantitative data, "since they can help us to refine our understanding of the learning activity that is taking place".

Following this suggestion, the present study uses a mixed-methods approach (Bergman 2008), that is, it presents findings from a series of interviews that complemented two quantitative studies exploring the effects of formal instruction on the acquisition of collocations by EFL learners. More specifically, reading-while-listening (RWL) was compared with reading-only (RO) in Study 1 (Szudarski 2012), while reading plus input enhancement (IE) was compared with reading-only (RO) in Study 2 Szudarski and Carter (in press). In both studies, participants (36 in

Study 1 and 41 in Study 2) were provided with a 3-week instruction targeting ten verb-noun (e.g. 'keep sanity') and ten adjective-noun (e.g. 'lonely vigil') collocations. The interview data offer qualitative insights into the process of acquiring L2 collocational knowledge and add new information to our quantitative findings.

2 Method

In Study 1, learners read six stories (two stories each week) in which each target collocation appeared six or twelve times (see Appendix 1 for a sample story). In the RO group, learners' only task was to read the stories and answer comprehension questions. With regard to learning collocations, the conditions in this group can be categorized as incidental learning (Schmitt 2010), since no mention of collocations was made throughout the treatment. In contrast, learners in the RWL group read the same stories but simultaneously listened to the recordings of these texts. Such a procedure has been used in previous research and was found to be effective at promoting lexical knowledge (Brown et al. 2008; Webb et al. 2013). There was also a control group that only completed testing measures. In Study 2, the same design was used: two experimental groups and a control group. However, RWL was replaced with IE, that is, learners in the IE group read the six stories where the target collocations were textually enhanced (underlined). Learners in the RO group, similarly to Study 1, were only asked to read the stories and answer comprehension questions.

In both studies, learners' knowledge was assessed by a battery of five tests tapping into both productive and receptive aspects of L2 collocational competence (see Appendix 2 for a sample). Learners' knowledge was tested twice: 1 week before the treatment started (pre-test) and 2 weeks after the treatment ended (post-test). As previous research shows (cf. Nation 2001; Schmitt 2010), vocabulary knowledge is a complex construct that needs to be measured at different levels of mastery. Test 1 was a productive test in which learners had to translate verb-noun collocations from Polish into English. On Test 2, learners' productive knowledge of adjectival collocates was assessed. On the basis of the provided definitions, participants had to write adjectives that formed the target collocations. Test 3 used the same format but targeted verbal collocates. Test 4 was a receptive test of adjective-noun collocations where learners were given English combinations and had to translate them into Polish. Finally, Test 5 was a receptive test of verb-noun collocations in which learners had to choose the correct verb from four response options that had been provided.

Comparisons between learners' pre-test and post-test results revealed interesting findings. In Study 1, RWL was better than RO and led to collocational gains on Test 2 and Test 4. In Study 2, in turn, IE was better than RO resulting in gains on Test 2, Test 3 and Test 5. Since the research concerned classroom instruction, it was decided to complement these findings with a qualitative inquiry into learners' perceptions. As "qualitative interviewing is particularly useful as a research method for accessing individuals' attitudes and values" (Byrne 2004: 182), a series of interviews with students from all the groups as well as their teacher was conducted.

2.1 Research Questions

The research aimed to answer the following questions:

1. How did EFL learners perceive different kinds of formal instruction in L2 collocations?
2. Did learners experience any difficulties with the instruction?
3. To what extent were learners aware of the phenomenon of collocations and its role in acquiring L2 English?

2.2 Interviews: Data Collection and Analysis

The research questions concerned the effectiveness of different kinds of instruction in the acquisition of L2 collocations and consequently it was crucial to explore learners' perceptions of the treatments they had been exposed to. Six students (three from the RWL group and three from the RO group) were interviewed in Study 1 and nine students (three from the IE group, five from the RO group and one from the control group) were interviewed in Study 2. The interviews lasted 10–15 minutes each and ranged from 900 to 1,500 words. The aim of the interviews was to establish how the participants approached both the reading texts and the collocational tests they had been given before and after the treatment. Moreover, it was important to explore the students' views on collocations, potential difficulties they might have encountered and practical ways of dealing with them. All their observations were additionally verified with Sue, a teacher who had implemented all the experimental treatments. Her comments were especially valuable, for she had taught all the groups of learners and was able to compare the teaching process in the different conditions. The interview with her lasted about 35 minutes (over 3,200 words).

The collected data were submitted to content analysis, which, according to Morse (2012), helps one identify different pieces of text that address a specific theme or category. According to the author, themes are well-suited for interpretative descriptions of interviews, for they may be synthesized across different participants of a given research study. Morse (2012: 197) suggests that "once the category contains an adequate number of segments or examples", its characteristic features can be identified, labeled and described. Subsequently, once all categories have been described, one can start looking for possible links between them. Following this as well as methodologies used in previous research (e.g. Amuzie and Winke 2009), the analysis of the interviews involved the iterative process of constant questioning and comparing of the data, which led to the identification of several main themes that emerged from the participants' answers. First the results of the interviews with the students will be presented and this will be followed by the findings from the interview with the teacher.

3 Findings

3.1 Interviews with Learners

All the interviews were conducted individually within a classroom context. Polish, learners' L1, was used so that all informants could express themselves fully. The interviews were guided by an interview protocol that was developed on the basis of the previous research discussed above (Ying and O'Neill 2009; Peters 2009). The findings are presented with reference to three themes that have emerged.

3.1.1 Students' Perceptions of the Instruction

Since the experimental groups in both studies read the same stories, it is possible to compare how they were perceived by the participants. All of the interviewed students found the texts to be easy to read. It is not surprising given the fact that the stories were short and all the words used were among the most frequent ones in English, that is, the first 2,000 word families (Nation 2006). Furthermore, the students seemed to have focused entirely on decoding the meaning of the stories when confronted with them. They did not appear to analyze any linguistic characteristics of the texts. This serves as evidence that the treatment conditions functioned in accordance with our assumption for this study. This is particularly relevant to the RO groups where no mention of collocations was made. Students from this group did not seem to pay much attention to the target collocations, which might explain why no gains in their collocational knowledge were found.

As far as RWL and IE are concerned, most students from the experimental classes did not appear to see them as an intrusion. If anything, they found them to be a pleasant change with some elements of novelty in comparison with their usual classes. This was mentioned by Kinga from the RWL group in Study 1:

Excerpt 1
Kinga (RWL): It [RWL] is good because you can listen to the text and understand something by mere listening.

It needs to be stated that RWL is rarely used in classroom instruction (Brown et al. 2008), for listening and reading are usually perceived as separate skills. However, as the interviews revealed, several students welcomed RWL and treated it as a useful pedagogic practice. Also students in Study 2 confirmed the effectiveness of the treatment that had been used (IE). All of the interviewed students found the stories to be easy to understand and the fact that the target collocations had been underlined did not seem to have led to any problems. In other words, learners from the IE group did not think that the use of IE impeded their reading comprehension process. These questions were asked in light of potential obtrusiveness of such pedagogical techniques. Doughty and Williams (1998: 258) define obtrusiveness as "the degree to which the focus on form interrupts the flow of communication". Since our research was conducted in classroom conditions, Doughty and Williams's flow of communication should be understood as smooth administration of an authentic reading task in which learners answered true/false questions. The interviews with the students suggest that the presence of textual enhancement did not impede the reading process and resulted in the acquisition of collocations.

Furthermore, the comprehension task that was chosen (answering true or false questions) is commonly used in Polish schools and consequently the participants of this research were familiar with such a format of classes. It appears that their approach to the experiment did not differ much from their normal classroom practices. This means that the ecological validity of the study was retained and the students perceived the experiment similarly to their traditional lessons. Interestingly, they treated their participation in this research as an opportunity to check their knowledge. Normally, when their English is assessed, they are usually told which topics or coursebook chapters they need to focus on. In the case of this experiment, the students had not been given any warning before taking the pre-test or post-test. Consequently, the experiment resembled an exam-like situation, which somewhat surprisingly was welcomed by the participants. All high school students in Poland need to take final exams when they are 18. The consequence of this is the fact that many participants of this experiment were highly motivated to study English and treated any language-related activities as exam preparation. This might explain their positive approach to the study. Finally, the element of novelty introduced by the experiment was often mentioned by the participants. It was the first time they had experienced such a research study and therefore they enjoyed participating in its different parts.

Importantly for the purposes of the study, students' answers to the question about the effectiveness of RWL and IE pointed to the recurrence of specific words in all the stories they had read. It needs to be highlighted that such comments were made by students from both groups. For example, Ania from the RO group and Jacek from the IE group noticed that the study was focused on the repetition of the same vocabulary.

Excerpt 2
Jacek (IE): In each text there were the same words.

Somewhat surprisingly, Patryk from the RO group was one of very few students who referred to the recurrence of the same phrases in the stories. The use of the word 'phrases' is worth emphasizing here, since most participants tended to understand vocabulary as individual words (see below). It is especially true for the RO groups where the target collocations had not been enhanced in any way. Arguably, the students tended to devote their attention entirely to the meaning of the stories without noticing that they had been exposed to many examples of collocational patterns.

3.1.2 Receptive and Productive Knowledge

An issue that is relevant to the second research question was the use of five collocational tests. They were often mentioned by the participants as the most difficult aspect of the experiment. Such perceptions are hardly surprising given the difficulty of the tests that measured collocational knowledge. The difficulty of these tests resulted from the fact that the study concerned the acquisition of collocations containing infrequent words unlikely to be known by L2 learners. Naturally, our primary aim was to tap into learners' collocational competence but indirectly the tests also measured their knowledge of individual words. In light of this, it was expected that the participants would find the tests to be challenging. However, it is also important to note that the tests assessed both productive and receptive collocational knowledge, which meant that they had to be administered in a specific order (the productive tests followed by the receptive ones). As previous research demonstrates (Laufer and Girsai 2008; Webb and Kagimoto 2009), collocational knowledge is problematic for L2 learners particularly at a productive level. This was confirmed by the interview data. Test 1, Test 2 and Test 3, which assessed learners' productive ability to recall collocations, were reported as the most difficult ones and this was also borne out by the interview with the teacher.

Another issue that should be pointed out with reference to the tests is how learners' behavior was influenced by the presence of the same items on all the five tests and by the use of the same battery twice (as the pre-test and the post-test). Unsurprisingly, the interviewed students noticed that the tests targeted the same lexical items. However, since the tests were administered in a specific order, starting with the productive Test 1, Test 2 and Test 3 and ending with the receptive Test 4 and Test 5, no correct answers were given away. At the same time, what could have influenced the results to some extent was the possibility of remembering the target items seen at the pre-test. When asked whether they had checked the correct answers after taking the pre-test, some students admitted they had consulted dictionaries and other reference materials. Natalia from the RWL group was one of these students. Arguably, such a behavior has important consequences for the interpretation of the results. First of all, it was easier for such students to complete the same tests during the post-test session and their performance on the test might have reflected not only the effects of the treatment but also learners' autonomous learning. Secondly, this also demonstrates how difficult it is to explore the process of acquiring L2 lexical items in the classroom context over a longer period time. Had the design included a treatment that consisted of only one teaching session, then students' behavior would have been controlled even more and consequently they would not have been able to consult dictionaries or coursebooks. However, in this experiment the treatment consisted of three sessions and therefore there is a possibility that the participants remembered some of the target items and looked them up later on. This could have resulted in some learning that was not accounted for by the design of the study.

3.1.3 Collocations and Their Role in Learning English

The third research question addressed the notion of collocation and its importance in learning English. Many participants tended to view vocabulary only as individual words. This might be partly caused by how collocations are approached by ELT practitioners and materials writers. Even though collocations, idioms and phrasal verbs appear in teaching materials, the way they are selected is often random and the importance of phraseology as an integral element of L2 lexical competence is not sufficiently emphasized (Koprowski 2005). This results in a lack of phraseological awareness on the part of L2 learners who focus mainly on individual words. It is also seen in learners' beliefs revealed in their answers to the question concerning their ambitions and aims for studying English. Even though they acknowledged that vocabulary was an important aspect of linguistic competence and they wanted to develop it during lessons, in practical terms they perceived this process as learning large numbers of new words rather than studying how they combine in collocational and colligational patterns.

Interestingly, in response to the question about the classification of collocations, students' views were divided. Some of them treated them as grammatical features (e.g. Radek from the control group; Maciej from the RO group), others categorized them as lexical knowledge (e.g. Dominika from the RO group) and yet others as a separate linguistic skill (Jacek from the IE group). The fact that collocations were seen as tokens of grammatical knowledge by some learners leads to further consequences. In many students' opinions, grammatical accuracy is considered less important when one's aim is to function communicatively in an L2 and consequently collocations should be studied only at higher levels of proficiency. Such comments are indicative of how L2 learners approach fluency and accuracy as aims for L2 development (Brumfit 1984).

Furthermore, the participants were also asked about the most effective ways of promoting collocations in the classroom. Some students mentioned learning through associations, a common technique that is used by many L2 learners as far as learning new vocabulary is concerned. Its potential for learning collocations, however, remains to be explored. Additionally, some individuals (e.g., Natalia from the RWL group) listed underlining collocations as a useful technique that could help them acquire collocations more effectively. In Peters's (2009) study that had a similar design, L1 Dutch learners of English also referred to underlining as a helpful learning strategy. Moreover, when asked about specific strategies they could recommend as useful and practical ways of learning English, some students mentioned vocabulary lists where English words are presented with their Polish equivalents. This resembles what Chinese learners reported in Ying and O'Neill's (2009) study where they admitted they had relied on this strategy quite heavily. Finally, many students listed free time activities that involve using English such as browsing websites, listening to songs and watching films. The fact that different examples of collocations could be found in such sources had been treated by the interviewed participants as evidence that word combinations were an important element of everyday speech and writing. However, irrespective of how students seemed to classify collocations, they stressed the importance of such combinations.

Excerpt 3

Radek (control): This is how people speak, how we use it in practice so it is important.

Łukasz (IE): They are not necessary for communication but they make utterances sound better.

Maciej (RO): Collocations are needed so that one's use of L2 is smooth and automatic without thinking too much.

Given these views on collocations and their role in learning a foreign language, it appears that future research should determine how to influence L2 learners' perceptions. As the complexity of English phraseology cannot be denied (e.g. O'Keeffe et al. 2007), learners' awareness of the inseparability of lexis and grammar needs to be raised and it can only be done in the language classroom, since for many learners it is the only source of L2 input. Hopefully, more studies like the one reported by Ying and O'Neill (2009) showing how an effective use of collocations can contribute to L2 fluency will appear soon. Such research should help L2 learners and their teachers realize that it is worth putting effort in developing L2 phraseological competence.

3.2 Interview with the Teacher

The effectiveness of any pedagogical practice depends to a large extent on the teacher who is administering it in the classroom. Therefore, it was necessary to explore the perceptions of the teacher (Sue) who participated in this study. Since the whole study was based on Sue's active participation, her remarks and comments were an important addition to the interpretation of the results. The main focus of the interview was to evaluate the teaching process in terms of how she implemented it in the experimental groups, what her impressions were and how she viewed the acquisition of collocations in this context.

3.2.1 Perceptions of the Experiment

In Sue's opinion, a good rapport with her students contributed to the fact that she found the teaching process to have run smoothly without experiencing any major difficulties during the experimental treatments. She also noted that in their regular classes students were often given different kinds of reading tasks and consequently the texts presented to them during the experiment were perceived as both pleasant and accessible. Sue commented that all the lessons comprising this research resembled the format of classes that she normally conducted, which reflects the ecological validity of the study.

With regard to differences between the experimental groups, Sue pointed out that students from the IE group in Study 2 quickly recognized that the research was focused on collocations. In contrast, the RO group did not seem to have noticed which linguistic form the study had targeted despite the fact that the students from this group took the same tests as the IE group. This echoes the findings from the interviews described above. Importantly, Sue's comments on the reading comprehension process corroborate what has been found in the interviews with the students: the stories were easy to understand and answering the comprehension questions did not pose too much difficulty.

Furthermore, Sue also discussed how the teaching process differed in the experimental groups. She noted that even though all participants represented a similar level of proficiency in English (i.e. intermediate), there were some qualitative differences between the groups that might have influenced her approach to teaching. This shows the benefits of conducting a mixed-methods study. Despite the fact that the experimental groups were carefully selected and their knowledge did not differ quantitatively before the treatments started, there were still qualitative differences that would not have been found without the interview data (e.g. how much attention particular participants needed during the treatment). Consequently, it should be remembered that whenever research is conducted in the classroom, many different factors specific to a local context play a role and they must be taken into account before definite conclusions are formulated.

Another point that Sue underlined were students' reactions to the collocational tests. In both studies, students quickly signaled to her that the tests had contained the same items. Being tested on the same items is a rare practice in Polish schools. Therefore, the confrontation with the five tests targeting the same vocabulary was an element of novelty. Moreover, the teacher noted that Polish students were usually trained to try to figure out what the correct answer was even if it resulted in pure guessing. During this experiment, this is exactly what the participants had been asked to avoid doing. Such a procedure was likely to have caused difficulties for the participants, especially on Test 5 when they had been given several response options to choose from.

3.2.2 Teaching Collocations

Since the research questions concerned the acquisition of L2 collocations, Sue was asked about their role in the learning/teaching process. In her view, collocations should not be taught in isolation and therefore highlighting them in pre- or post-reading/listening activities appealed to her. She approved of the integration of language skills, for this approach offers many opportunities for highlighting collocations. She admitted to drawing her students' attention to specific phrases that are misused by them. Except for difficult collocations with delexical verbs (e.g. 'take a

162 P. Szudarski

photo'), she also referred to colligations (e.g. 'interested in', 'listen to'). In Sue's opinion, raising phraseological awareness via different methods early in the process of SLA brings many benefits that learners will appreciate as their proficiency develops. For example, according to Laufer and Girsai (2008), contrasting the use of collocations in L1 and L2 is an effective way of enhancing learners' collocational competence. For Sue, this suggestion did not seem to be convincing and she favored focusing on collocations exclusively in English.

Excerpt 4
Sue: I advocate introducing thinking in English right away; thinking in English structures.

However, Sue also stated that using translation could be an effective practice, especially when less time is available for giving explanations in English. She usually relied on L1 translation when she wanted her students to notice different collocational patterns in English and Polish. Sue believed that using examples from both languages could help learners realize that direct L1–L2 translation was not always possible due to cross-linguistic phraseological differences.

When asked about what learners tended to focus on in learning an L2, Sue stated that this was usually determined by their overall goals, that is, their level of proficiency in English. As collocational knowledge can be regarded as an element of L2 grammatical competence by some learners, they might pay attention to it only if they want to improve accuracy. However, if communicative competence is their primary goal, they will tend to ignore such higher-level aspects of L2 mastery, not realizing what benefits phraseological competence can bring. This is an interesting finding that might explain why L2 learners struggle with collocations and use them much less frequently than native speakers (Laufer and Waldman 2011). Finally, with regard to the question on which collocations should be prioritized in teaching, Sue stated that frequency seemed to be the most important criterion. In her view, learners should first acquire these phrases that are frequently used for different communicative purposes.

Conclusion
The study is an example of a corpus-informed pedagogic intervention aimed at improving EFL learners' collocational competence. It demonstrates benefits of mixed methods research in which the qualitative data on learners' perceptions provided a better understanding of the process of acquiring L2 collocations in the classroom context. Contrasting different types of formal instruction revealed that both RWL (in Study 1) and IE (in Study 2) were more effective than RO. The above analysis of the interviews showed that learners in the RO group focused mainly on the decoding of the meaning of the stories and consequently did not pay attention to the target collocations. On the other hand, as the results from the RWL and IE groups indicate, raising learners' awareness of collocations through subtle implicit treatments

(continued)

can lead to positive changes in L2 phraseological knowledge. These findings were confirmed by the teacher who treated these approaches to teaching collocations as effective practices.

Hopefully, this study shows how L2 phraseology, an area of research that has been brought to the fore of SLA research by the recent surge of corpus-based work, can be developed through form-focused instruction. More empirical work exploring the acquisition of other aspects of communicative competence identified by corpus linguistics (e.g. semantic prosody, lexical creativity or valency patterns) is warranted. Moreover, it would be useful to replicate this study with learners representing other L1 backgrounds and English proficiency levels, for these factors are known to play an important role in developing L2 competence. It is anticipated that, as more research becomes available, our understanding of how learners acquire L2 lexical knowledge and later put it into practice in real life communication will be broadened.

Appendix 1

Story1

Mary was a psychologist and she worked for a social welfare agency. Her responsibilities involved deciding who should have custody of children and protecting them. Since her job gave her a rare insight into families where children were not loved and moral precepts were not followed, Mary had a deep aversion to all those who abused children. For her, it was a matter of human decency to provide such children with help. But this often meant making hard decisions and Mary sometimes had a grumble about all the stress her job involved. So, in order to keep her sanity, whenever she had time, Mary played the guitar in a band. Sometimes the band was invited to perform at banquets that were held in different companies. Their performances were great so they were often given an ovation.

Through her work, Mary had met many different people. She once met Tom, a 17-year old student who had been referred to her by his school. He had always been a good student willing to make forays into different school activities. He had often held raffles for students and organized parties on different occasions. But lately he had changed. One of his friends accidentally gave him a nudge. Tom got angry and when his friend apologized Tom's quick retort was "Get lost". On the following day, Tom took a swipe at another friend and hit him in the face for not borrowing him a book. After this incident, Tom was immediately sent to Mary and she tried to identify reasons behind his behaviour. Everything became clear to her when she saw Tom's house. Untidy heaps of clothes and empty bottles were everywhere. When she entered the kitchen, she saw Tom's father lying drunk on the floor behind a wooden pillar. It turned out that Tom's father had been fired and he had started drinking which often led to <u>drunken brawls</u> at home. In such conditions, Tom found it hard to <u>keep his sanity</u> and his behaviour at school was his way of coping with all the stress.

Mary had a <u>deep aversion</u> to alcohol and naturally she felt sorry for Tom. Since helping others was <u>a moral precept</u> she had always followed, she didn't leave Tom on his own. First, she wanted him to calm down and spend some time on his own so she isolated him from everybody else. Then, after this <u>lonely vigil,</u> when Tom thought everything through, Mary asked him to help her in her office. He had never <u>made forays</u> into this kind of work before so it gave him a <u>rare insight</u> into what administrative work involved. People's complaints, <u>quick retorts</u>, rude comments were common. So now Tom fully understood why office workers sometimes <u>had a grumble</u> about their job.

Also, Mary knew that Tom played the trumpet so she encouraged him to perform with her band. The city hall was <u>holding a banquet</u> and Mary's band was invited. Tom was very nervous but he played really well so after the performance he was <u>given an ovation</u> by all the guests in the room. Tom thanked everyone and decided to walk home. As he was <u>taking a shortcut</u> in a nearby park, he saw his father. It turned that Mary had invited him and he came to see Tom's performance. He told Tom that his performance was an <u>amazing feat</u> and he apologized for his recent behaviour. These words meant so much for Tom. As soon as he got home, he called Mary to thank her. None of this would have happened without her special support. But she didn't feel special. For her, helping others was just a matter of <u>human decency</u>.

True or False

Mary's job involved making decisions about people's lives.
Mary played in the band because she needed money.
Mary found a reason why Tom had changed so much.
Mary asked Tom to help her at work.
Tom's father refused to come to his son's concert.

Appendix 2

Test 1

Translate the following phrases into English. You must provide <u>both a verb and a noun. Don't provide adjectives or prepositions.</u>

Formal Instruction in Collocations in English: Mixed Methods Approach 165

Robić kurs
Mieć przerwę
Wydać bankiet
Przeprowadzić loterię
Zrobić błąd

Test 2

Complete these 25 phrases with <u>one word</u> so that they express the meaning provided in the brackets. The missing words are adjectives. If you think more than one answer is possible, give all alternatives. The number of dashes indicates the number of missing letters.

d _ _ _ aversion (a strong dislike associated with something unpleasant)

i_ _ _ _ _ _ _ _ _ task (a piece of work that cannot be done because of its difficulty)

e_ _ _ _ _ _ _ _ trip (a journey from one place to another that costs a lot of money)

o_ _ _ _ _ _ _ proposal (a plan of action that has not been suggested before and offers a new and fresh idea)

a_ _ _ _ _ _ _ _ letter (an unnamed and/or unidentified piece of writing sent to somebody)

Test 3

Complete the phrases with <u>one verb</u> so that they express the meaning provided in the brackets. Don't use the verbs from the brackets. If you think more than one answer is possible, give all alternatives.

to _____ homework (to complete exercises resulting from one's school duties)

to _____ a breath (to draw air into the lungs)

to _____ sanity (to be able to think in a normal way)

to _____ a mistake (to perform a wrong action as a result of lack of knowledge)

to _____ custody (to be legally responsible for somebody or something)

Test 4

Translate these 25 phrases into Polish. Remember to translate <u>both the adjective and the noun.</u>

difficult decision
deep aversion
impossible task
original proposal
anonymous letter

Test 5

Choose the verb that best completes the following phrases in such a way that the meaning provided in the brackets is expressed. If you don't know the answer, <u>don't guess</u> and choose response (e) I don't know.

1. to _____ homework (to complete exercises resulting from one's school duties)

(a) give   (b) make   (c) do   (d) take   (e) I don't know

2. to _____ a breath (to draw air into the lungs)

(a) do   (b) make   (c) hold   (d) take   (e) I don't know

3. to _____ a mistake (to perform a wrong action as a result of lack of knowledge)

(a) give   (b) make   (c) take   (d) do   (e) I don't know

4. to _____ a swipe (to try to hit somebody with one's hand)

(a) have   (b) give   (c) take   (d) hold   (e) I don't know

5. to _____ an answer (to provide a spoken or written reply)

(a) give   (b) take   (c) hold   (d) do   (e) I don't know

References

Altenberg, B., and S. Granger. 2001. The grammatical and lexical patterning of make in native and non-native student writing. *Applied Linguistics* 22: 173–195.

Amuzie, G.L., and P. Winke. 2009. Changes in language learning beliefs as a result of study abroad. *System* 37: 366–370.

Barfield, A., and H. Gyllstad (eds.). 2009. *Researching collocations in another language.* Houndmills: Palgrave Macmillan.

Bergman, M.M. 2008. The straw men of the qualitative-quantitative divide and their influence on mixed methods research. In *Advances in mixed methods research*, ed. M.M. Bergman, 11–21. Los Angeles, CA: Sage.

Boers, F., J. Eyckmans, J. Kappej, H. Stengers, and M. Demecheleer. 2006. Formulaic sequences and perceived oral proficiency: Putting a lexical approach to the test. *Language Teaching Research* 10: 245–261.

Brown, R., R. Waring, and S. Donkaewbua. 2008. Incidental vocabulary acquisition from reading, reading-while-listening, and listening to stories. *Reading in a Foreign Language* 20: 136–163.

Brumfit, C.J. 1984. *Communicative methodology in language teaching: The roles of fluency and accuracy.* Cambridge: Cambridge University Press.

Byrne, B. 2004. Qualitative interviewing. In *Researching society and culture*, 2nd ed, ed. C. Seale, 179–192. London: Sage.

Chomsky, N. 1965. *Aspects of the theory of syntax*. Cambridge, MA: MIT Press.

Doughty, C.J., and J. Williams. 1998. Pedagogical choices in focus on form. In *Focus on form in classroom second language acquisition*, ed. C.J. Doughty and J. Williams, 197–262. New York: Cambridge University Press.

Durrant, P., and N. Schmitt. 2010. Adult learners' retention of collocations from exposure. *Second Language Research* 26: 163–188.

Ellis, N. 2012. Formulaic language and second language acquisition: Zipf and the phrasal teddy bear. *Annual Review of Applied Linguistics* 32: 17–44.

Howarth, P. 1998. Phraseology and second language proficiency. *Applied Linguistics* 19: 24–44.

Koprowski, M. 2005. Investigating the usefulness of lexical phrases in contemporary coursebooks. *ELT Journal* 59: 322–332.

Laufer, B., and N. Girsai. 2008. Form-focused instruction in second language vocabulary learning: A case for contrastive analysis and translation. *Applied Linguistics* 29: 694–716.

Laufer, B., and T. Waldman. 2011. Verb-noun collocations in second language writing: A corpus analysis of learners' English. *Language Learning* 61: 647–672.

Morse, J.M. 2012. The implications of interview type and structure in mixed-methods designs. In *The SAGE handbook of interview research. The Complexity of the craft*, ed. J.F. Gubrium, J.A. Holstein, A.B. Marvasti, and K.D. McKinney, 193–204. Los Angeles, CA: Sage.

Nation, I.S.P. 2001. *Learning vocabulary in another language*. Cambridge: Cambridge University Press.

Nation, I.S.P. 2006. How large a vocabulary is needed for reading and listening? *The Canadian Modern Language Review* 63: 59–81.

Nattinger, J., and J. De Carrico. 1992. *Lexical phrases and language teaching*. Oxford: Oxford University Press.

Nesselhauf, N. 2003. The use of collocations by advanced learners of English and some implications for teaching. *Applied Linguistics* 24: 223–242.

O'Keeffe, A., M. McCarthy, and R. Carter. 2007. *From corpus to classroom: Language use and language teaching*. Cambridge: Cambridge University Press.

Pawley, A., and F. Syder. 1983. Two puzzles for linguistic theory: Native-like selection and native-like fluency. In *Language and communication*, ed. J. Richards and R. Schmidt, 191–226. London: Longman.

Peters, E. 2009. Learning collocations through attention-drawing techniques: A qualitative and quantitative analysis. In *Researching collocations in another language*, ed. A. Barfield and H. Gyllstad, 194–207. Houndmills: Palgrave Macmillan.

Schmitt, N. 2010. *Researching vocabulary: A vocabulary research manual*. Basingstoke: Palgrave.

Sinclair, J. 1991. *Corpus, concordance, collocation*. Oxford: Oxford University Press.

Sonbul, S., and N. Schmitt. 2013. Explicit and implicit lexical knowledge: Acquisition of collocations under different input conditions. *Language Learning* 63: 121–159.

Szudarski, P. 2012. EFL learners' perceptions of formal instruction in collocations. Paper presented at the Topics in Applied Linguistics Conference, University of Opole, Poland, November 12–14, 2012.

Szudarski, P. Reading-while-listening and teaching collocations in L2 English (in preparation).

Szudarski, P., and R. Carter. The role of input flood input enhancement in EFL learners' acquisition of collocations (under review).

Webb, S., and E. Kagimoto. 2009. The effects of vocabulary learning on collocation and meaning. *TESOL Quarterly* 43: 55–77.

Webb, S., J. Newton, and A. Chang. 2013. Incidental learning of collocations. *Language Learning* 63: 91–120.

Wray, A. 2002. *Formulaic language and the lexicon*. Cambridge: Cambridge University Press.

Ying, Y., and M. O'Neill. 2009. Collocation learning through an AWARE approach: Learner perspectives and learning process. In *Researching collocations in another language*, ed. A. Barfield and H. Gyllstad, 181–193. Houndmills: Palgrave Macmillan.

Some Implications for Developing Learners' Figurative Language Competence Across Modalities: Metaphor, Metonymy and Blending in the Picture Modality

Przemysław Wilk

Abstract The paper argues for developing learners' figurative language competence across modalities. Specifically, focusing on the picture modality, the article attempts to show the importance of figurative thinking in the new media age multimodal communication. The sample analysis of pictures and images representing the recent issue of the EU crisis addresses the significance of three conceptual phenomena, namely, metaphor, metonymy, and blending, in the conceptualization of such a highly abstract phenomenon. In general, it is argued that language users almost invariably turn to figurative language resources to conceptualize abstract phenomena that cannot be conceptualized by means of literal language. Hence, developing learners' figurative language competence seems to be of critical importance in foreign language instruction. The article also argues that picture modality is a reasonable starting point for the development of learners' figurative language competence as it is our sense of vision that plays the most fundamental role in conceptualizing the reality.

Keywords Figurative language competence • Metaphor • Metonymy • Blending

1 Introduction

The advent of the Internet has undoubtedly been a turning point in terms of the nature of communication as it has dawned an era of virtually unlimited worldwide communication. The beginning of the twenty-first century has brought about yet a greater and easier possibility to communicate with others by introducing such social networking services as *Facebook* or *Tweeter*, which have gained almost immediate appreciation and tremendous popularity worldwide. One could probably risk a statement that to communicate in the twenty-first century means by and large to 'post' and to 'click', and arguably to 'like'. Posting simple comments and images,

P. Wilk (✉)
Opole University, Opole, Poland
e-mail: pwilk@uni.opole.pl

© Springer International Publishing Switzerland 2015
L. Piasecka et al. (eds.), *New Media and Perennial Problems in Foreign Language Learning and Teaching*, Second Language Learning and Teaching,
DOI 10.1007/978-3-319-07686-7_10

usually accompanied by a number of emoticons, has become an easy way to share one's opinions and feelings. It is not uncommon that instead of some actual language one comes across a sequence of commonly used acronyms, such as *lol*, which, maybe not surprisingly, have almost attained the status of lexical units and easily undergo syntactic and morphological processes, for example, the past form *lolled*. It seems then that communicating in a more traditional way, that is, in the written language mode, has been substantially supplemented by other modes of communication, notably the image.

What needs to be acknowledged at this point is the fact that one of the basic human cognitive abilities is to use our language figuratively. Langacker (2009: 46–47), emphasizing the significance of figurative thinking, claims that conceptualization does depend on various imaginative capacities, such as metaphor, metonymy, or blending. I believe that one of the primary functions of figurative language is to help conceptualize highly abstract phenomena. This claim corresponds with Croft and Cruise's (2004: 193) observation that "a speaker uses an expression figuratively when he/she feels that no literal use will produce the same effect". They also emphasize the fact that using language figuratively "may simply be more attention-grabbing, or it might conjure up a complex image not attainable any other way, or it may permit the conveyance of new concepts."

In light of the above observations, the present article concentrates on one particular aspect of communication, namely, communicating via images, or in more technical terms, via the picture modality (cf. Forceville 1996). In my analysis, I focus upon a recent issue of the EU crisis, which has drawn a wide response among the Internet users and has given rise to a number of images representing its various conceptualizations. As the EU crisis is a highly abstract phenomenon which exists only in our socially constructed reality, it should not be surprising that it is conceptualized in a figurative manner. Hence, to be able to communicate successfully, which undeniably entails understanding figurative language, people need to have some knowledge and skill pertaining to non-literal language use. Since a massive part of our language is figurative in nature, there seems to be a growing need to implement some elements of figurative language education into the curricula to foster figurative language competence among learners. In this paper, I argue for developing figurative language competence among learners by focusing on three cognitive mechanisms, namely, conceptual metaphor, metonymy, and blending, and illustrating how they interact to help the abstract phenomenon of the EU crisis achieve 'human scale cognition' (cf. Fauconnier and Turner 2002).

2 Figurative Language and Figurative Language Competence

It has been over 30 years since the publication of Lakoff and Johnson's (1980) *Metaphors we live by*, which claimed that metaphor is one of the most fundamental human cognitive mechanisms. It was also in *Metaphors we live by* that the importance of another conceptual mechanism central to language and thought and closely related to conceptual metaphor, namely conceptual metonymy, was addressed. Although, throughout the last three decades, Lakoff and Johnson's (1980) original ideas have undergone significant changes, which in a more or less direct way gave rise to Conceptual Blending Theory (Fauconnier and Turner 2002), it is indisputable that the year 1980 triggered a considerable interest in figurative language, which has since been studied, among others, within the cognitive linguistics paradigm. There have been innumerable studies on figurative language from both theoretical as well as more analytical perspectives which have brought about some disagreement as to the status of figurative language and the cognitive mechanisms of conceptual metaphor, metonymy, and blending (see e.g. Evans 2010, for discussion). Goossens (1990) has even argued for a close interaction of metaphor and metonymy and introduced into the literature the concept of metaphtonymy, which is either of the two combinations: metaphor from metonymy or metonymy within metaphor. Irrespective of the current state of affairs, there can be no doubt that human language and thought is to a great extent figurative. Moreover, cognitive linguists agree, though to different degrees, that the three cognitive mechanisms, namely metaphor, metonymy, and blending, are conceptual phenomena central to human thought.

Acknowledging the centrality of the figurative processes in human thought, and hence language, it may be surprising that relatively little attention has been given to this phenomenon in foreign language teaching and learning. Kellerman (2001) notices that it has taken a long time for applied linguists to introduce metaphor into the curricula and pedagogical practice in general. Nevertheless, it is still rather uncommon to come across courses addressing the importance of figurative language in any area of foreign language instruction, be it writing, reading, listening or speaking. Traditionally, it is very often the case that in foreign language teaching process teachers put a great emphasis on the students' grammatical competence, which is developed through studying grammar and vocabulary. The shortcoming of this traditional approach is, however, the fact that it ignores some fundamental aspects of our cognitive abilities relating to language use, namely, our ability to perceive and make analogy between two or more things, which gives rise to figurative language and lies at the heart of metaphoric process of meaning extension.

The importance of figurative language in the context of foreign language instruction concerning different language skills has been recognized by many scholars (e.g. Danesi 1992; Epstein and Gamlin 1994; Johnson and Rosano 1993; Kathpalia 2011; Littlemore and Low 2006a, b; Pickens and Pollio 1979). Majority of these studies deploy the term *metaphoric/metaphorical competence* with reference to the knowledge of and ability to use metaphor. I would argue that the above term is not quite adequate, as it seems to limit figurative language processes to metaphor, or at least seems to give it primacy over other figurative language processes. I advocate to use the term *figurative language competence* (cf. Littlemore and Low 2006a) to include other figurative language mechanism, such as metonymy and blending, within our scope of attention. Littlemore and Low

(2006a) have used the term *figurative language competence* and explained the significance of figurative thinking in the four components of Bachman's (1990) model of language competence, namely, grammatical, textual, illocutionary, and sociolinguistic competence. In my paper, I would like to argue for a need to develop learners' *figurative language competence*, which I understand as the knowledge of and the ability to identify, understand and use figurative language, in the context of foreign language teaching and learning. My attempt in this paper, however, is not to focus on any of the four language skills in particular but to argue for fostering learners' figurative language competence in general. In light of the fact that it is our visual perception that plays the most fundamental role in our conceptualization of the reality, which translates into the fact that we engage our visual system to understand language—a central tenet of simulation semantics (cf. Bergen 2012)—I suggest that a reasonable starting point for the development of learners' figurative language competence is the picture modality. It seems that it is much easier for learners to perceive certain figurative processes in the picture modality than in the written language mode, for example. Hence, in my paper, I present a sample analysis of some figurative language processes in the picture modality which might be the first step to foster learners' figurative language competence across different modalities. It is not my aim here, however, to suggest how this kind of analysis could be implemented into the foreign language instruction.

3 Metaphor, Metonymy and Blending

In this section, I introduce and explain the concepts of metaphor, metonymy and blending. I supplement the discussion of metaphor with a relatively new concept of multimodal metaphor. It should be noticed, however, that the discussion provided here is definitely not exhaustive in that it ignores some technical and theoretical intricacies these cognitive processes involve as focus on such details is far beyond the scope of this paper.

A conceptual metaphor is a cognitive mechanism which involves perception of one conceptual domain in terms of another conceptual domain, where a conceptual domain is understood as any piece of organized human experience. Hence, metaphors are analyzed as stable and systematic relationships between two conceptual domains. Lakoff and Johnson (1980) refer to metaphor as a cross-domain mapping in the conceptual system. The relationship between conceptual domains can be represented in the following way: CONCEPTUAL DOMAIN X IS (or AS) CONCEPTUAL DOMAIN Y, where X and Y represent the source and target domains respectively. Cross-domain mapping implies that some most salient elements of a conceptually concrete domain correspond to elements in a more abstract conceptual domain, as represented in Fig. 1. An important characteristic of conceptual metaphors is that they account for only one-way symmetrical mappings from source to target domains. According to Lakoff (1993: 245), such cross-domain mappings "are not arbitrary, but grounded in the body and in everyday experience and

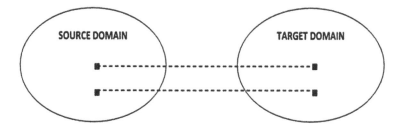

Fig. 1 Conceptual metaphor: a basic diagram

knowledge." Hence, conceptual metaphors capture systematic and conventionalized conceptualizations of everyday human experience.

The concept of multimodal metaphor (Forceville 2006; Forceville and Urios-Aparisi 2009) is founded on Lakoff and Johnson's (1980) Conceptual Metaphor Theory, yet it takes the phenomenon of metaphor into a new dimension, namely, different modalities (or modes). Forceville (2006: 384) defines a multimodal metaphor as a metaphor whose "target and source are each represented exclusively or predominantly in different modes." It is precisely the fact that the source and target domains are realized in different modalities that distinguishes multimodal metaphors from monomodal ones, that is, the ones which are realized exclusively in one modality. Libura (2012: 122) notices, however, that Forceville's (2006) use of the word *predominantly* is to some extent ambiguous as it leads to arbitrary choices concerning the degree to which a particular domain is realized in different modalities. Therefore, she advocates El Refaie's (2009: 191) suggestion to extend the category of multimodal metaphor so that it includes "all instances of metaphor where the target and source are represented exclusively, predominantly or *partially* [my emphasis] in different modes." This extension of the category of multimodal metaphor definitely allows one to categorize a much greater number of metaphors as instances of a multimodal metaphor.

Lakoff and Johnson (1980) see metonymy as a conceptual mechanism which links two conceptual entities, the vehicle and the target (cf. Kövecses and Radden 1998), within the same cognitive domain in a way that the former provides mental access to the latter. Hence, metonymy is ascribed a purely referential function, which can be explicated in the following notation: X for Y. Radden and Kövecses (1999: 18–19) point out, however, that metonymy should not be understood simply as a process of substitution because it interrelates the two concepts to create a new meaning. Although there exists a number of different approaches to metonymy, each using its own nomenclature, the common denominator of all approaches is the fact that metonymy is a conceptual process occurring within one cognitive domain. Langacker (2008: 69), for example, refers to metonymy as a shift in the profile which takes place when "an expression that ordinarily profiles one entity is used instead to profile another entity associated with it in some domain." In a similar vein, Croft (1993: 348) explains that "metonymy makes primary a domain that is

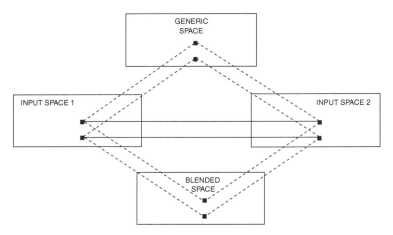

Fig. 2 Conceptual blending: a basic diagram (Fauconnier and Turner 2002: 46)

secondary in the literal meaning" and suggests to perceive metonymy as a process of domain highlighting.

Conceptual Blending Theory (cf. e.g. Coulson 2000; Fauconnier and Turner 2002, 2008; Grady 2005; Libura 2010) makes use of the construct of mental space, which Fauconnier and Turner (1996: 113) define as "conceptual packets constructed as we think and talk, for purposes of local understanding and action." Mental spaces contain elements of and are structured by cognitive models (cf. Lakoff 1987). Accordingly, as Grady et al. (1999) notice, mental spaces are not equivalent to domains. Spaces depend on domains in a sense that they are informed by more general structures connected with a given domain. A conceptual bled arises in networks of mental spaces. A basic network of mental spaces is diagrammatically represented in Fig. 2. A conceptual blend consists of four mental spaces, namely, input space 1, input space 2, generic space, and blended space. Two input spaces can loosely be associated with the source and target domains in Lakoff and Johnson's (1980) Cognitive Metaphor Theory. It is input spaces that a blend inherits its major conceptual structure from. A generic space contains conceptual structure common to both input spaces. Arrived at in the process of conceptual blending operations (cf. Fauconnier and Turner 2002), a blended space has its own unique emergent content received from two input spaces and a generic space. Grady et al. (1999) emphasize that such a four-space model allows for simultaneous projections from both input spaces directly into a blended space. Hence, blends are not characterized by systematic unidirectional mappings between the target and source domains but, as Hart (2010: 118) puts it, they involve "a dynamic construal operation involving four mental spaces". It is precisely this dynamic nature of blends that allows for novel conceptualizations.

4 Data Collection and Classification

The data for my analysis comprise images and cartoons and hence fall within the category of picture modality (cf. Forceville 2006). The common denominator of the cartoons and images is the fact that they represent various conceptualizations of the EU crisis and the EU itself. To retrieve the data, I used the Google search engine, which offers the option of searching the Web for images. I based the search on a keyword phrase, namely *EU crisis*. As the search results included an abundance of images and cartoons on the EU crisis, my next step was to establish some general categories to classify my data into. As I aimed to discuss metaphor, metonymy, and blending as conceptual phenomena, it was of crucial importance to me that the categories capture some recursive patterns in conceptualizing the EU and the EU crisis. Eventually, I was able to establish five categories, namely, (1) the one euro coin construal, (2) the EU currency symbol construal, (3) the EU flag construal, (4) the domino construal, and (5) the ship/boat construal. It is important to make a caveat here that the names of the categories are my own choice and are based on how a particular group of images and/or cartoons conceptualizes the EU. It is also crucial to mention that there were some rare cases of images and cartoons which conceptualized the EU crisis or the EU itself in a very peculiar and unique way, for example, as a pack of mountain bikers riding down a steep and dangerous cliff, some of them falling into the precipice. Consequently, it was not possible to assign each such a unique image to one of the five categories; neither was it reasonable to establish new categories for such images as they were simply isolated occurrences. Therefore, my data comprise only these instances which reflect a particular recursive pattern in conceptualizing the EU and the EU crisis. According to my observation that, in the age of the new media, communication has become multimodal, I also discuss one instance of a multimodal metaphor (cf. El Refaie 2009; Forceville 2006; Forceville and Urios-Aparisi 2009), where I show that the interplay of two modalities enhances and leads to the reinforcement of a particular conceptualization of the EU crisis.

5 Analysis of Examples

In this section I present my analysis and discuss the findings. The section is divided into six subsections: the first five are concerned with one of the five categories enumerated in the previous section while the last subsection features a discussion of a multimodal metaphor. Importantly, to illustrate and support my discussion, I provide only a representative example of a given category which, via picture modality exclusively (necessarily except for the multimodal metaphor), reflects the general pattern of conceptualizing the EU. The rationale for this decision was first and foremost to conform to space constraints. Nonetheless, in my presentation of a particular category, I discuss a variety of different construals of the EU crisis which I was able to identify during my analysis, even though they are not illustrated with relevant images or cartoons. I start my discussion with the relatively simple construals of the EU and the EU crisis to consequently move towards the more complex ones which employ a number of metonymic, metaphoric and blending mechanisms in order to conceptualize the EU and the EU crisis.

5.1 The One Euro Coin Construal

One of the least complex but most frequent construals of the EU is a metonymic representation of the EU as the one euro coin (see Fig. 3). What we deal here with is the conventionalized conceptual PART FOR WHOLE metonymy, which is instantiated here as THE ONE EURO COIN FOR THE EU. Arguably, it can also be claimed that due to the lack of any contextual information this metonymy can be explicated as THE ONE EURO COIN FOR THE EUROZONE. Irrespective of the decision whether the coin stands for the EU as a whole, which is the view I advocate in this paper, or just the Eurozone, the basic metonymic construal of the target is the same. As far as the crisis is concerned, there are several construals to be found in my data. In Fig. 3, we can see that the crisis is represented as a crack in the coin. It can be argued that the crack symbolizes the disintegration of the EU, which leads to the isolation of the single member states represented by the pieces of the coin.

The other common construals of the crisis in this category are the one of fire and the one of water. In the case of the former, the one euro coin is on fire and as a consequence of being exposed to high temperature, it starts to melt. In the case of the latter, the coin is approximately half immersed in a body of water, which unequivocally suggests that the coin is going under. As will be evidenced in the following sections of my paper, the water construal of the EU crisis is very commonly employed.

I was also able to identify one particularly interesting instance of the EU crisis construal in my data, namely, a knife stabbed right in the middle of the one euro coin with a visible bleeding wound. This construal differs from the others in that it

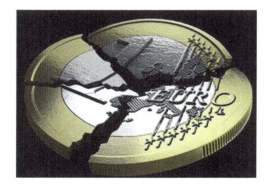

Fig. 3 The one euro coin construal (available at http://frontpagemag.com/2012/bruce-thornton/the-e-u-is-speeding-for-the-iceberg/)

clearly attributes blame for the crisis to some human factor, as it seems reasonable to conclude that only humans are capable of stabbing somebody or something with a knife. Additionally, the fact that the coin bleeds can be ascribed to a metaphorical construal of the EU as a living organism, which is based upon the ORGANIZATIONS ARE ORGANISMS metaphor (cf. e.g. Lakoff and Johnson 1980), but can also be explained in terms of the Great Chain of Being (cf. e.g. Krzeszowski 1997).

5.2 The EU Currency Symbol Construal

The EU currency symbol construal is very similar, in conceptual terms, to the one euro coin construal discussed in the previous section. As can be seen in Fig. 4, the EU is construed once again through the cognitive mechanism of metonymy as the EU currency symbol. It is based on the same conceptual pattern, namely, the PART FOR WHOLE metonymy. The crisis is construed here as the process of melting, arguably, as was the case with the one euro coin, because of exposure to high temperature, though this aspect is left implicit. Among a number of other construals of the crisis I was able to identify, there are the already mentioned crack and water, which I will not discuss here to simply avoid repetition.

There are, however, also some creative construals, such as an image where the EU is construed as a battered harp in the shape of the EU currency symbol some of whose strings are broken, which makes it difficult for the musician to play the instrument. The crisis manifests itself here as the poor condition of the instrument, including the broken strings. It is clear that in this case it is not only the metonymy alone that is operative here but also the ORGANIZATIONS ARE INSTRUMENTS metaphor which maps some elements of the harp onto the target domain of the EU.

Another interesting cartoon construes the EU crisis in terms of a murder committed on the EU metonymically construed as the EU currency symbol. The EU lies on the sidewalk secured by the police with the yellow police tape with a labeling saying 'crime scene'. In the background we can see a suitcase with a label 'financial

Fig. 4 The EU currency symbol construal (available at http://www.thecorner.eu/euro/page/24/)

forensics'. This construal, founded on the cognitive domain of murder, necessarily activates the portion of our extralinguistic knowledge (or a cognitive model profile in Evans's (2009) terms) which tells us that only human beings can commit murder, which in the case of the cartoon boils down to the fact that it is a human that is to blame for the EU crisis.

5.3 The EU Flag Construal

As visible in Fig. 5, the underlying construal of the EU in this category is the PART FOR WHOLE metonymy where the vehicle is the constellation of stars identical with the one on the EU flag. Hence, the metonymy can be explicated as THE EU FLAG FOR THE EU. The EU crisis in Fig. 5 is construed as a jigsaw puzzle undergoing the process of decomposition, or alternatively, undergoing the process of fitting jigsaw puzzle elements together. Irrespective of the two possible ways of perceiving it, the understanding goes that unless all the elements of the jigsaw do fall to their place, the whole picture cannot be seen. Translating this into the EU crisis construal, it seems logical that the EU will not hold together if any of the member countries is out of its place in the structure of the EU family.

Another noteworthy construal of the EU crisis is an image where we can see a heavy blue sky with a circular constellation of stars resembling the one on the EU flag. Inside the circle there is the EU currency symbol, whose aim is to disambiguate the context, that is, this metonymic construal of the EU clearly establishes the one and only interpretation of the image: it is definitely the EU that is of concern here. The crisis is conceptualized as a process of single stars coming off the whole constellation, leaving holes in the structure. The stars which have come off and lie on the ground no longer shine brightly but have faded away.

I find one more construal of the EU crisis particularly worthy of discussion, namely, an image where the EU is construed as a dandelion clock, whose flower is represented as the EU flag star constellation. The crisis is metaphorically construed as death, which itself is personified and metaphorically represented as a human skeleton wearing a scarf with a word 'crisis.' The process of the EU disintegration manifests itself in the death's attempt to blow the flower off its stem.

Fig. 5 The EU flag construal (available at http://studentthinktank.eu/blogs/the-centripetal-theory-of-governance-a-borderless-union/)

5.4 The Domino Construal

The fundamental figurative representation of the EU common to all images in the domino category is a primary structural metaphor (ABSTRACT) ORGANIZATION IS PHYSICAL STRUCTURE (cf. Kövecses 2002). As can be seen in Fig. 6, the metaphor is instantiated here as THE EU IS A DOMINO, which is diagrammatically represented in Fig. 7. It is clear from the diagram that some salient constituents of the source domain are mapped onto the target domain: (1) domino tiles correspond to the EU member states, which is reinforced by the A NATIONAL FLAG FOR A NATIONAL STATE metonymy discussed in the previous section; (2) the set-up of domino tiles corresponds to the EU structure; and (3) domino toppling corresponds to the disintegration of the EU. With these correspondences established, it is clear that the crisis is construed here as the process of domino toppling. Knowing the mechanism of domino toppling, which consists in toppling the first tile in the whole set-up to instigate a chain reaction in which the first tile knocks the second over, which consequently falls onto the next one and continues until all tiles have fallen, the mechanism can be easily applied to the process of the EU disintegration, which in this case boils down to a situation in which problems,

Fig. 6 The domino construal 1 (available at http://next-europe.info/2011/12/26/debt-crisis-2011/)

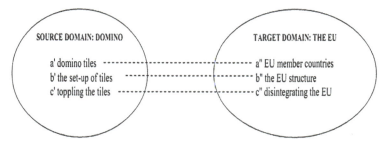

Fig. 7 The domino metaphor

Fig. 8 The domino construal 2 (available at http://injapan.gaijinpot.com/live/banking-investments/2012/02/16/euro-crisis/)

be it economic or any other, of one EU member state exert a more or less direct impact on the other EU member states. Crucially, the fact that the first domino tile in the whole set-up stands metonymically for Greece, where the crisis broke out, does not seem accidental. In fact, in all the images and cartoons employing the domino construal that I was able to collect, the first domino tile always stands for Greece, which reflects the situation at the dawn of the EU crisis and clearly establishes who is to blame for such a state of affairs.

The interpretation of the domino construal in terms of Lakoff and Johnson's (1980) Conceptual Metaphor Theory suffices in all but one example in my data. As visible in Fig. 8, the mechanism of domino tiles toppling cannot be applied here to explain the construal of the crisis, as, though the first tile indeed falls down, in no way can it trigger a chain reaction of domino tiles toppling. Still, there can be no doubt that the image makes use of the domino construal, as we can clearly see domino tiles. Moreover, it is also clear that what the image tries to depict is the EU crisis, which is reinforced by the already mentioned instantiation of the PART FOR WHOLE metonymy, namely A NATIONAL FLAG FOR A NATIONAL STATE.

To explain how it is possible to arrive at such an interpretation and what conceptual operations are at play here is beyond the explanatory power of Conceptual Metaphor Theory. These issues can be tackled, however, by Fauconnier and Turner's (2002) Conceptual Blending Theory. Indeed, as I argued elsewhere (Wilk 2012), compared to Conceptual Metaphor Theory, Conceptual Blending Theory offers more insight into how a conceptualization is arrived upon and in general offers a greater potential for the study of figurative language. In the case of the image in Fig. 8, I argue that the blend inherits its structure from three input spaces which together allow for a coherent and plausible interpretation of the EU crisis. I represent the bled diagrammatically in Fig. 9. It can be easily seen that the blended space inherits its unique structure from the three input spaces, namely (1) the domino input space 1, (2) the EU input space 2, and (3) the communicating tubes system input space 3. There are also clear correspondences between the three input spaces, namely, (1) domino tiles correspond to the EU member states and to the

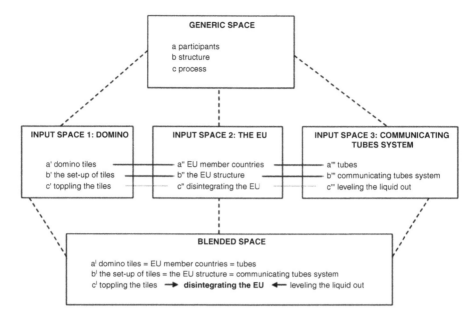

Fig. 9 The domino blend

tubes in the communicating tubes system, (2) the set-up of domino tiles corresponds to the EU structure and to the system of communicating tubes; and (3) domino toppling corresponds to disintegration of the EU and to leveling the liquid out in the communicating tubes system.

Having established these correspondences, it is possible now to account for the conceptual operations responsible for the interpretation of the construal of the crisis presented in Fig. 8. It should be noticed that the interpretation is facilitated especially by the fact that the blended space inherits the 'c' component from the input space 3, that is, it needs to be assumed that the EU structure, apart from being similar to a set-up of domino tiles, also resembles a communicating tubes system, which consequently entails that any increase or decrease of liquid in any of the tubes affects the amount of liquid in all other tubes, which translates directly into the fact that a problem a given EU member state is affected by has some more or less direct bearing on the other EU members as well as the EU as a whole.

5.5 The Ship/Boat Construal

Before I move on to specific examples and discussion of the ship/boat metaphor, I would like to make one remark on the nature of meaning which is relevant to my discussion of this particular construal. In light of cognitive access semantics (cf. - e.g. Evans 2010), no two lexical items are the same, which implies that the two lexical items underlying the construal of the EU, namely, ship and boat, due to their different conceptual content, may give rise to different mappings between the source and target domain of conceptual metaphor. Zinken (2007) points to some basic differences between the two lexical items in question. Although they are similar in their conventional meanings as both refer to basic types of vehicles used to travel on water, they differ in some aspects. First, a boat is usually a small vehicle, whereas a ship tends to be much bigger. Second, a boat is relatively simple in terms of technological advancement as it prototypically requires rows or a sail for locomotion. A ship, on the other hand, is technologically much more advanced. Third, when compared to a boat, a ship requires more expert knowledge on the part of the captain to steer it. With these differences in mind, Zinken (2007) demonstrates how the two lexical items differ in their behavior as metaphor vehicles and hence give rise to different figurative meanings. In my analysis, however, I ignore the differences between the two concepts as they are not relevant to my discussion and, more importantly, cannot be verified as my data are deprived of any further context.

Figures 10 and 11 represent the ship and the boat construals of the EU respectively. As mentioned in the previous paragraph, the basic cognitive mechanism operative here is metaphor. As can be seen in the ship/boat diagram in Fig. 12, the metaphorical construal of the EU is founded upon the following correspondences between the source and target domains: (1) the ship/boat corresponds to the EU, (2) passengers correspond to the EU member states, and (3) the process of sinking corresponds to the process of disintegrating the EU.

Additionally, in the case of the boat construal (see Fig. 11), the EU is metonymically construed as the EU currency symbol. In fact, all images employing the boat construal of the EU make use of the same metonymic pattern. Similarly, there are also two metonymies operative in the ship construal of the EU. As is visible in Fig. 10, at the stern of the ship there is the EU flag flying in the air, which instantiates the THE EU FLAG FOR THE EU metonymy. There is also the EU currency symbol on the funnel of the ship, which activates the already familiar THE EU CURRENCY SYMBOL FOR THE EU metonymy. In my data, quite frequent was also a metonymic representation of Germany and France as Chancellor Merkel and President Sarkozy respectively, which is founded upon the A HEAD OF STATE FOR THE STATE metonymy. As far as the EU crisis is concerned, in all

Fig. 10 The ship construal (available at http://www.economist.com/node/16536898) Courtesy: Peter Schrank

Some Implications for Developing Learners' Figurative Language... 183

Fig. 11 The boat construal (available at http://www.allvoices.com/cartoons/c/88802999-eurocrisis)

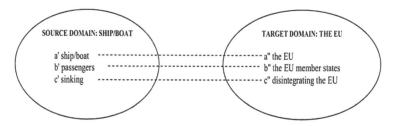

Fig. 12 The ship/boat metaphor

instances of the images and cartoon falling within the ship/boat category, it is in general construed in terms of dangerous waters posing a potential threat to the vessel. In Fig. 10, the crisis is construed as a kind of whirlpool capable of sucking the vessel underwater. In Fig. 11, the crisis is quite straightforwardly conceptualized as a high waterfall the boat is unavoidably approaching.

5.6 A Multimodal Metaphor

As defined earlier, a multimodal metaphor is the one which draws *exclusively* or *predominantly* on different modalities to represent the source and target domains

Fig. 13 A multimodal metaphor (available at http://blogs.hindustantimes.com/dabs-and-jabs/tag/euro-crisis/) Courtesy: Shreyas Navare, Hindustan Times, India

(Forceville 2006). According to this definition, it is not really certain if the metaphorical construal of the EU crisis as represented in Fig. 13 can be categorized as an instance of multimodal metaphor. It can be clearly seen that the source domain, that is, a football game, is represented *exclusively* in the picture modality, yet it begs the question whether the target domain, that is, the EU crisis, is represented *predominantly* in the written language mode (on a typology of modalities/modes see e.g. Forceville 2006). Even though it can be claimed with a high dose of certainty that in this particular case the target domain is indeed represented *predominantly* in the written language modality, accepting El Refaie's (2009) extended definition of a multimodal metaphor definitely solves the problem of classification as the target domain is surely represented at least *partially* in the written language mode.

Having categorized it as a multimodal metaphor, it can be said now that the metaphorical construal of the EU crisis in Fig. 13 can be explicated as THE EU CRISIS IS A FOOTBALL GAME. Apart from this underlying metaphorical construal of the EU crisis, there are some other cognitive mechanism which enhance the interpretation of the cartoon. It can be claimed that the crisis is also metaphorically construed as fissures in the rock supporting the football pitch and the players on the pitch, by means of the general PART FOR WHOLE metonymy, stand for the EU member states.

Crucially, though not discernible at first glance, there is one more primary metaphor (cf. Lakoff and Johnson 1980) which is central to the construal of the EU crisis in this cartoon, namely, QUANTITY IS VERTICAL ELEVATION (also known as the MORE IS UP metaphor). Kövecses (2002: 70) explains that there are two concepts central to this metaphor, namely, quantity and verticality. While quantity is based on a MORE and LESS scale, verticality consists of an UP and DOWN scale. The metaphor manifests itself in the analyzed cartoon both in the picture and the written language modalities. Quantity as the source domain is exclusively represented in the written language mode as two noun phrases, namely, the 'haves' and the 'have-nots', which pertain to the amount of money possessed. Consequently, as no communication exists outside context, it is highly plausible that the 'haves' are represented here by the two biggest players in the EU, that is, Germany and France. Following this line of reasoning, it can also be claimed that France and Germany are metonymically conceptualized as Chancellor Merkel and President Sarkozy. As far as the target domain of the QUANTITY IS VERTICAL ELEVEATION metaphor is concerned, it is represented here in both modes. In terms of the picture modality, the target domain manifests itself in a deviant structure of the pitch: there are clearly two different levels of the pitch visible. In the written language modality, the target domain is instantiated by two linguistic exponents, that is, the spatial prepositions 'up' and 'down'. Overall, the QUANTITY IS VERTICAL ELEVEATION metaphor seems to suggest that no compromise in terms of the EU crisis is attainable as there is no middle ground (as suggested by the caption below the cartoon), which, arguably, is the result of the 'haves' not being willing to cooperate.

Conclusions

Following an observation that communication in the present day, especially via the Internet, has been greatly simplified and on a regular basis makes use of various modalities, such as picture modality, for instance, I have demonstrated that conceptualizing such a highly abstract concept as the EU crisis in terms of picture modality takes place via figurative thinking. Focusing on three cognitive mechanisms, namely, conceptual metaphor, metonymy, and blending, I have shown how they interact to create conceptualizations of the EU and the EU crisis, which even though at times quite complex, serve the purpose of making the abstract concept of the EU crisis more accessible in respect of our human experience. However, it seems reasonable to claim that without some training and practice in figurative language interpretation, some of the conceptualizations might turn out to be too complex to be comprehended by learners, for example. Hence, I hope that my sample analysis hints at the significance of developing figurative language competence among learners. I also believe that the process of fostering figurative language competence should start with image, that is, the picture modality, as the visual perception is the primary sense responsible for our conceptualization of the reality. With some initial training on figurative language in the picture modality, learners might continue to develop their figurative language competence in other, arguably, cognitively more demanding, modalities, notably the written and spoken language modality, which seem to occupy the central position in foreign language instruction.

References

Bachman, L. 1990. *Fundamental considerations in language testing.* New York: Oxford University Press.

Bergen, B. 2012. *Louder than words: The new science of how the mind makes meaning.* New York: Basic Books.

Coulson, S. 2000. *Semantic leaps.* Cambridge: Cambridge University Press.

Croft, W. 1993. The role of domains in the interpretation of metaphors and metonymies. *Cognitive Linguistics* 4: 335–370.

Croft, W., and D.A. Cruise. 2004. *Cognitive linguistics.* Cambridge: Cambridge University Press.

Danesi, M. 1992. Metaphorical competence in second language acquisition and second language teaching: The neglected dimension. In *Georgetown university round table on languages and linguistics*, ed. J.E. Alatis, 489–500. Washington, DC: Georgetown University Press.

El Refaie, E. 2009. Metaphor in political cartoons: Exploring audience responses. In *Multimodal metaphor*, ed. Ch. Forceville and E. Urios-Aparisi, 173–196. Berlin: Mouton de Gruyter.

Epstein, R., and R. Gamlin. 1994. Young children's comprehension of simple and complex metaphors presented in pictures and words. *Metaphor and Symbolic Activity* 9: 179–191.

Evans, V. 2009. *How words mean: Lexical concepts, cognitive models, and meaning construction.* Oxford: Oxford University Press.

Evans, V. 2010. Figurative language understanding in LCCM theory. *Cognitive Linguistics* 21: 601–662.

Fauconnier, G., and M. Turner. 1996. Blending as a central process of grammar. In *Conceptual structure, discourse and language*, ed. A.E. Goldberg, 113–130. Stanford: CSLI Publications.

Fauconnier, G., and M. Turner. 2002. *The way we think: Conceptual blending and the mind's hidden complexities.* New York: Basic Books.

Fauconnier, G., and M. Turner. 2008. Rethinking metaphor. In *The Cambridge handbook of metaphor and thought*, ed. R. Gibbs, 53–66. Cambridge: Cambridge University Press.

Forceville, Ch. 1996. *Pictorial metaphors in advertising.* London: Routledge.

Forceville, Ch. 2006. Non-verbal and multimodal metaphor in a cognitivist framework: Agendas for research. In *Cognitive linguistics: Current applications and future perspectives*, ed. G. Kristiansen, M. Achard, R. Dirven, and F. Ruiz de Mendoza Ibàñez, 379–402. Berlin: Mouton de Gruyter.

Forceville, Ch., and E. Urios-Aparisi. 2009. Introduction. In *Multimodal metaphor*, ed. Ch. Forceville and E. Urios-Aparisi, 3–17. Berlin: Mouton de Gruyter.

Goossens, L. 1990. Metaphtonymy: The interaction of metaphor and metonymy in expressions for linguistic actions. *Cognitive Linguistics* 1: 323–340.

Grady, J.E. 2005. Primary metaphors as inputs to conceptual integration. *Journal of Pragmatics* 37: 1595–1614.

Grady, J.E., T. Oakley, and S. Coulson. 1999. Blending and metaphor. In *Metaphor in cognitive linguistics*, ed. G. Steen and R. Gibbs, 101–124. Philadelphia: Benjamins.

Hart, Ch. 2010. *Critical discourse analysis and cognitive science: New perspectives on immigration discourse.* Houndmills: Palgrave Macmillan.

Johnson, J., and T. Rosano. 1993. Relation of cognitive style to metaphor interpretation and second language proficiency. *Applied Psycholinguistics* 14: 159–175.

Kathpalia, S.S. 2011. Metaphorical competence in ESL student writing. *RELC Journal* 42: 273–290.

Kellerman, E. 2001. New uses for old language: Cross-linguistic and cross-gestural influence in the narratives of native speakers. In *Cross-linguistic influence in third language acquisition*, ed. J. Ceñoz, B. Hufeisen, and U. Jessner, 170–191. Clevedon: Multilingual Matters.

Kövecses, Z. 2002. *Metaphor: A practical introduction.* Oxford: Oxford University Press.

Kövecses, Z., and G. Radden. 1998. Metonymy: Developing a cognitive linguistic view. *Cognitive Linguistics* 9: 37–77.

Krzeszowski, T.P. 1997. *Angels and devils in hell: Elements of axiology in semantics*. Warszawa: Energeia.

Lakoff, G. 1987. *Women, fire and dangerous things: What categories reveal about the mind*. Chicago: The University of Chicago Press.

Lakoff, G. 1993. The contemporary theory of metaphor. In *Metaphor and thought*, 2nd ed, ed. A. Ortony, 202–251. Cambridge: Cambridge University Press.

Lakoff, G., and M. Johnson. 1980. *Metaphors we live by*. Chicago: The University of Chicago Press.

Langacker, R.W. 2008. *Cognitive grammar: An introduction*. Oxford: Oxford University Press.

Langacker, R.W. 2009. Metonymic grammar. In *Metonymy and metaphor in grammar*, ed. K.U. Panther, L.L. Thornburg, and A. Barcelona, 45–71. Amsterdam: Benjamins.

Libura, A. 2010. *Teoria przestrzeni mentalnych i integracji pojęciowej: Struktura modelu i jego funkcjonalność*. Wrocław: Wydawnictwo Uniwersytetu Wrocławskiego.

Libura, A. 2012. Teoria metafory pojęciowej wobec badań nad komunikacją multimodalną. In *Nowe zjawiska w języku, tekście i komunikacji IV: Metafory i amalgamaty pojęciowe*, ed. M. Cichmińska and I. Matusiak-Kempa, 117–129. Olsztyn: Instytut Filologii Polskiej UMW w Olsztynie.

Littlemore, J., and G. Low. 2006a. *Figurative thinking and foreign language learning*. Houndmills: Palgrave Macmillan.

Littlemore, J., and G. Low. 2006b. Metaphoric competence and communicative language ability. *Applied Linguistics* 27: 268–294.

Pickens, J.D., and H.R. Pollio. 1979. Patterns of figurative language competence in adult speakers. *Psychological Research* 40: 299–313.

Radden, G., and Z. Kövecses. 1999. Towards a theory of metonymy. In *Metonymy in language and thought*, ed. K.U. Panther and G. Radden, 17–59. Berlin: Mouton de Gruyter.

Wilk, P. 2012. Immigration metaphors in press discourse. In *Nowe zjawiska w języku, tekście i komunikacji IV: Metafory i amalgamaty pojęciowe*, ed. M. Cichmińska and I. Matusiak-Kempa, 291–307. Olsztyn: Instytut Filologii Polskiej UMW w Olsztynie.

Zinken, J. 2007. Discourse metaphors: The link between figurative language and habitual analogies. *Cognitive Linguistics* 18: 445–466.

Design and Style of Cultural and Media Studies Textbooks for College Students

Katarzyna Molek-Kozakowska

Abstract This paper uses the conceptual framework of multimodal discourse analysis in order to investigate the dominant styles and designs in selected Cultural and Media Studies (CMS) university textbooks. For many EFL students who major in philology, CMS courses are obligatory and thus constitute a type of content and language integrated learning (CLIL). The data from a description and evaluation of four popular textbooks indicate that there is a discernible move away from traditional literacy towards visuality and orality in textbook design and style. This tendency is evident in the use of segmentation and listing in composition, dialogic layouts and informal registers in exposition and visual aids for the purposes of explanation, illustration and memorization. The study aims at elucidating the gains and losses inherent in this transition, particularly with respect to fostering students' critical literacy.

Keywords Design • Style • Multimodal discourse analysis • College textbooks • Critical literacy

1 Introduction

The fact that university textbooks by leading commercial publishers are more and more multimodal, universalized, informal, even entertaining, testifies to the broader trend of how this domain of academic discourse is being colonized by pop-cultural forms. Presumably, textbook authors aim to engage a generation of students raised in a media-saturated world of access and choice, while publishers can advertise such textbooks as user-friendly and practice-oriented, which is what, indeed, many textbooks are like. However, the crossover between popular media culture and academia may have indirect negative consequences for students' critical literacy—a set of skills for deconstructing meanings and demystifying hegemonic ideologies inscribed in texts via various semiotic resources. It can be observed that some characteristics of communication in the new media are reflected in the newest

K. Molek-Kozakowska (✉)
Opole University, Opole, Poland
e-mail: molekk@uni.opole.pl

© Springer International Publishing Switzerland 2015
L. Piasecka et al. (eds.), *New Media and Perennial Problems in Foreign Language Learning and Teaching*, Second Language Learning and Teaching,
DOI 10.1007/978-3-319-07686-7_11

textbook designs. For example, textbook pages tend to be "navigable" with combinations of visually and verbally presented information. Dialogic formats of exposition, cross-references and window-like inserts in textbooks all but imitate the hypertextuality and interactivity of web-based materials. In addition, paragraph structure and section titling often resemble the style of user manuals, while visual aids, such as pictures, lists, graphs and even cartoons are seamlessly integrated into academic presentations.

This project has been motivated by a belief that "design can be a means for controlling the actions of others" (Kress and van Leeuwen 2001: 7). It uses the categories of multimodal discourse analysis in order to investigate the stylistic preferences and dominant patterns of design on the basis of selected leading Cultural and Media Studies (henceforth CMS) textbooks. The aim is firstly to identify the prevalent modes of representation and conventions of interaction as regards the contents of introductory courses in CMS. The analysis is to show whether we can indeed observe a move from pure literacy in the direction of more visuality and orality in the textbook design and style. In the course of both quantitative and qualitative analysis it is demonstrated how 'model' students, as well as 'model' educators, are constructed via textual organization and rhetorical style and how they are being positioned to accept the authorial stance. Thus, the article addresses the implications of certain preferences for print, oral and visual affordances as specific pedagogical tools for minimizing negotiated readings. The question that is kept in the background of these explorations is to what extent, if any, such textbooks encourage students to be self-reflective about their cultural practices and to be critical of their ingrained ideologies. It is worth stressing here, however, that this project does not aim to advise students and educators which textbooks to use, since this choice largely depends on local circumstances. Evaluative insights offered here concern some general trends in textbook style and design, which are likely to impinge on university-level learning and teaching practices.

2   The Medium Is the Message? The Context and Rationale for the Project

Although no study of design or style of texts can aspire to specific insights or generalizations about their actual influence on readers, among various theories of media effects, one tradition has substantial bearing on the present project. This tradition is sometimes called *technological determinism* and, as a whole, deserves a dose of skepticism. Its main champion, Marshall McLuhan, proves that the media used at any given point in time influence human cognitive and communicative dispositions in that they extend the human horizon of experience. In his most important work, *Understanding Media: The Extensions of Man* (1964), McLuhan elaborates on how first the print and later the electronic media technologies have transformed our ways of acquiring, remembering, communicating and recording information. Importantly, he understands media effects not as resulting from mere exposure to media content, but rather as deriving from the essential "form of a medium," which "shapes and controls the scale and form of human associations and action" (1964: 9), especially when it is routinely consumed. In this study, the growing availability of new media technologies is seen as the key factor instigating a transition from page-like to screen-like formats in many domains of communication, including education.

Another publication that impinges on the question of how media technologies influence human communication and cultural formation is Walter Ong's 1982 *Orality and Literacy: The Technologizing of the Word.* This (still debated) study has shed light on the ways in which human thinking and interacting tends to be disparately shaped in cultures dominated by either oral or written traditions. Away from the controversies surrounding the debate whether either orality or literacy are culturally superior, it is worth revisiting some of Ong's characteristics of spoken and written modes, vis-à-vis the visual mode, as these modes will play a major role in the subsequent discussion.

The spoken mode, and the oral cultures in which it is the dominant form of expression and thought, according to Ong (1982: 29–43), can be characterized as sequential (narrative-driven), aggregative (rather than analytic) and specific (context-bound) rather than objectively distanced. Oral expression is situationally delimited by (self)references to participants and to shared immediate surroundings (i.e. through deixis), as well as to performed actions (e.g. through the active voice). Due to human memory limitations, the spoken mode tends to be repetitive—copious or redundant—and arranged in co-ordinative (rather than subordinative) patterns. There is a tendency for oral cultures to express more concrete and evaluative propositions, as opposed to more abstract and objective expressions facilitated by writing and most likely by print, and the accompanying process of editing. As a result, oral cultures are also likely to be more homeostatic, participatory and conservative.

The long-term effects of literacy and print culture, according to Ong (1982: 72–108), include the displacement of situated interaction, the interiorization of thinking processes, the decontextualization and abstraction of thought, and the increase in attention to detail and arrangement. For example, the narrative in most types of educational discourse has been replaced with such forms of arrangement as enumerating, classifying, comparing and contrasting, demonstrating causes and results. Such forms of reasoning (sometimes also graphically presented in the forms of tables, diagrams, flow-charts or graphs) are nowadays routinely used even with the youngest readers/writers. As a result, it can be observed that complex arrangements that involve various semiotic resources are used in mature literate cultures to indicate conceptual relations and hierarchies of knowledge. This may be correlated with the fact that literate cultures tend to be more progressive.

Despite obvious differences in medium and form, and disparate implications thereof, there is nevertheless some overlap between some characteristics of speech and writing, on the one hand, and writing and image, on the other. Needless to say, both speech and writing are instantiations of the lexical resources and grammatical principles of a specific language, while visual images are usually drawn from universal or cultural semiotic reservoirs. In terms of arrangement, both speech and writing are made of discreet elements arranged in a linear fashion and thus pre-ordered by the sender to be interpreted by the receiver; by contrast visual images are compositional blocks—holistic units—whose processing is not that rigidly enforced by any code (Kress and van Leeuwen 1996: 23). As a result, visual images allow for a fair degree of subjectivity in ordering and construing meaning.

While speech is driven by the logic of sequencing of the sounds in time, writing and image are both predicated on spatial arrangements. If speech is instantiated by voice and its cadences (as well as body language), then writing relies heavily on syntactic patterns, with punctuation only marginally being capable of reconstituting the intonation, pitch and voice quality of talk. Unlike speech, writing is unit-organized, and as such, it is both horizontally and vertically arranged, which it shares with images. In images, both "the point of entry" and "the reading path" (Kress 2003: 156–160) are mostly up to the reader, while the verbal modes do not offer such freedom. On the other hand, visuals require specific and concrete "epistemological commitments" (Kress 2003: 2), such as colour, size, shape, direction, where language allows for more indeterminacy, abstractness and conceptual intricacy. As a result, it can be claimed that reading a description requires more effort put into imagining than viewing an image.

It needs to be observed, however, that in the contemporary mediatized world, rigid distinctions between modes of expression and their diverse implications for cultural practices no longer matter that much. This is because most mediated texts we encounter tend to be "multimodal ensembles" (Kress 2003: 20; Machin and Mayr 2012: 12) that take strategic advantage of spoken, written and visual representations. In the classroom, for example, it has been demonstrated that various modes facilitate various kinds of learning and, when effectively combined, enhance memorization (Gardner 1993). Also, with the rise of humanistic teaching that takes into account students' individual differences and preferences (such as learning styles, multiple intelligences, affective needs and diverse motivations, cf. Moskovitz 1981), insisting on identifying *the best* way of transmitting knowledge seems anachronistic. Assuming that each mode has different advantages and disadvantages, it follows that integrating various modes should optimize learning for larger groups of students. Contemporary textbook authors, aware of the exposure of learners to new media, seem to take multimodality particularly seriously. And yet, it should be remembered that when students' cognitive resources are 'scattered' to process information and construe meanings out of various modalities, there is a risk of diminishing their opportunities for creative and critical engagement with that meaning (Janks 2010: 155–158).

To summarize, one can detect a reflection of designs characteristic of new media, in which information is coded and transmitted in multiple modalities, back on the formats of print materials. The starting point in this study is that that the formerly print-dominated medium of the textbook has been 'enriched' or 'corrupted' (depending on one's normative stance) by properties appropriated from the visual and the oral modes. This has been a steady process that seems to

Design and Style of Cultural and Media Studies Textbooks for College Students 193

have finally touched some of the academic genres (cf. Martin and Veel 1998; Trumbo 1999). For example, Kress (2003), who aims to re-define literacy in the new media age, notes that contemporary print materials, including school textbooks, are becoming increasingly 'display-oriented':

> Contemporary pages are beginning to resemble, more and more, both the look and the deeper sense of contemporary screens. Writing on the page is not immune in any way from this move, even though the writing of the elite using the older media will be more resistant to the move than writing elsewhere. It is possible to see writing once again moving back in the direction of visuality, whether as letter, or as "graphic block" of writing, as an element of what are and will be fundamentally visual entities, organized and structured through the logics of the visual. (Kress 2003: 6–7)

As a consequence of the import of the visual as well as the oral onto the printed in textbook design, a question may be raised as to the results and merits of such a change. The larger questions that arise are: How exactly is this transition bound to change the ways information is presented, interaction conducted and knowledge shaped within this re-designed and re-styled medium? What can be gained and what can be lost as a result of such a transition? And particularly, how are the new designs likely to influence students' critical literacy—the mainstay of humanistic education? By critical literacy we mean here a set of skills used by students to confront the social, ideological, even economic, aspects of institutional discourse, particularly those that are naturalized as 'common sense' (Holme 2004: 69). Critical literacy allows them to identify how, for example, academic texts can be used to either re-affirm or resist dominant cultural meanings. Being critical does not mean being sceptical with respect to textbook information. Rather, it means being able to interrogate the designs and styles which tend to be applied conventionally in the academia, in order to show how they may reinforce particular social ideologies, political doctrines and educational philosophies (cf. Molek-Kozakowska 2013).

3 The Conceptual Framework: Texts, Modes, Affordances, Designs, Reading Paths

Before proceeding to the analysis, it is worth presenting the conceptual framework of multimodal discourse analysis (Kress 2003; Kress and van Leeuwen 1996, 2001; Machin 2008; Machin and Mayr 2012) in view of applying its main categories for textbook evaluation. First, in discourse studies a *text* is to be understood broadly to mean a communicatively purposeful, relatively formally and thematically delimited and generically recognizable product of a discursive practice (de Beaugrande and Dressler 1981). Texts may be produced in one *mode* (e.g. conversations over the telephone almost exclusively rely on the spoken mode, classified ads on the written mode, and family photos on the visual); however, as mentioned above, with the advent of new media technologies, most texts we now encounter may well be produced drawing on the resources of various modalities. For multimodal discourse analysts, each mode has its distinct *affordances*, i.e. meaning potentials delimited by the material and semiotic properties of the medium in which the mode is constituted. In addition, there are some long-lasting socio-cultural conventions (constraints, preferences) in the use of a particular mode. For example, the range of possible gestural expression in face-to-face encounters is fairly broad, but the cultural conventions of a given speech community may significantly restrict it.

Since modes are materially, semiotically and culturally delimited resources for representing and communicating meaning, the text's *design* (Kress and van Leeuwen 1996: 4) is the representation that is fashioned from available modalities, according to their affordances, and with the aim to most effectively achieve the communicative purpose. In addition, representations are hardly neutral; they are relative to the social, institutional and ideological contexts of designing. The notion of design highlights "a deliberateness about choosing the modes for representation, and the framing for that representation" (Kress and van Leeuwen 2001: 45) in order to provide for "the organization of what is to be articulated into a blueprint for production" (Kress and van Leeuwen 2001: 50). While *design* is about the choice of the modes of representation, *style* is how the resources of the particular mode are appropriated. For example, photos may be published in color or in black-and-white; readers may be addressed directly and informally or indirectly and formally.

A key element of textual design is the *composition* (on the production side) or the *reading path* (on the reception side), the latter being an important category in the present study. The reading path is an idealization of how a text is bound to be read 'properly' or 'conventionally' (Kress 2003; Kress and van Leeuwen 1996). At the same time, it is supposed that following a different reading path is likely to produce a differing reading. Basing on the concept of the reading path, Kress (2003: 54–56) proposes an opposition between reading the text as it is told—*reading as interpretation*—and reading the world as it is shown, or reading as imposing salience and order—*reading as design*. While interpretation is defined as basically following a prescribed reading path of the traditional written text, reading as design is navigating and constructing meaning, often by selecting and picking on various modalities to arrive at a satisfactorily coherent construal. It is possible to take issue with the idea of such a simple dichotomy as the one drawn above, since interpretation does not have to involve a mechanical decoding of sequentially ordered signs, but an intellectual and emotional engagement with them. At the same time, reading as design may be so deeply reliant on one's media-derived habits that it ceases to be creative. Many would like to see reading as interpretation (especially in the academic context) as a situated, purposeful and reflective literacy practice, regardless of whether the text is arranged according to a linear or non-linear design.

Another problem is that since *reading as design* is fundamentally constructive— i.e. cognitive resources are engaged in construing meaning—it seems that fewer resources are delegated to the task of deconstructing the hegemonic meaning and problematizing the apparent neutrality of the representation. It can be hypothesized that the more contrived the design and the more challenging the construal, the more obscure the texts' strategic projection that results in making us accept its claims. The claim that reading as interpretation is contemplative and retroactive, while reading designs is creative and proactive (Kress 2003: 56), is also problematic.

Reading a text in a predominantly written mode requires the constant productive effort of imagining: the filling of signifiers with significations at various levels of textual organization and the checking of initial hypotheses against in-coming information. Meanwhile, reading of many multimodal designs equals accepting the imaginations of designers, especially if we are likely to follow some conventionalized reading paths inherent in the designs (from centre to periphery, from large to small, or from left to right). It seems fair to posit that some designs, as well as some texts, are not created to problematize or defamiliarize the routines of their reception or open the text to critical re-interpretations. Epistemologically speaking, the problem of how knowledge is delimited does not depend on the modes themselves, but rather on the conventions of representation (e.g. realism, fantasy) that transcend modality distinctions. What matters nowadays is how to be able to read increasingly multimodal designs critically and to recognize the interests behind the designs drawing on given modes, resources and conventions.

4 Design and Style of Selected College Textbooks

This study is devoted to an analysis and evaluation (in the sense of elucidating the gains and losses) of the recent changes in the ways university textbooks tend to be designed: with visual and oral modes backgrounding the affordances of writing and print. It is not to claim that the transition from print linearity to the more visual logic and oral rhetoric of the textbook is necessarily a change for worse. Academic writing has long been criticized for its stylistic distancing from the familiar patterns of the spoken mode (Fairclough 1992; Janks 2010). The inaccessibility and eliteness of academic texts has been perpetuated with added formal complexity. It is claimed (Kress and van Leeuwen 1996; Kress 2003) that any mode is partial in its representation, due to its distinct affordances. Insisting on print-only materials at college level would amount to restricting, rather than developing, students' critical literacy. However, the problem is that any transition in pedagogical practices is located in a specific socio-cultural context. In a media-saturated, consumer-oriented neoliberal market, it is legitimate to consider how such a transition reflects producers' (commercial publishers') interests rather than consumers' (faculty's and students') needs. The question that is still open is whether what consumers are offered in place of the print-dominated publications is of comparable merit. Since each mode has its advantages and limitations, there are possible improvements in the teaching/learning process, but there are also possible losses, which need to be spotlighted before the new designs are naturalized and we no longer have any choice.

The study is based on a survey of currently available coursebooks for Cultural and Media Studies. For many EFL students majoring in philology, CMS courses are obligatory and thus constitute a type of content and language integrated learning (CLIL). The following part of the paper is an analysis of four selected textbooks introducing CMS. Although sales or circulation figures for these books could not be found, their availability in catalogues of CMS-related libraries and through the bookseller Amazon.com, as well as the fact that two of them have already been republished, was treated as an indication of their popularity with CMS students/instructors. Each textbook is analysed in terms of its (1) model audience, (2) contents and chapter composition, (3) page layout and peculiar supra-textual features. Attention is devoted to specific features of the design, including the number and type of dominant visual elements (analysed quantitatively when possible), as well as the general stylistic properties of verbal expositions (analysed qualitatively on representative examples). This kind of multimodal analysis focuses on the conspicuous patterns of design and style that distinguish a given textbook from the other publications. It is impossible to conduct a comparative analysis of the four designs as they are radically different. In the closing comments, attention is directed to the realizations of visuality and orality vis-à-vis traditional literacy of the print mode. The analysis is completed with the evaluation of the main implications of given designs for critical dispositions.

4.1 How to Do Media and Cultural Studies *by Jane Stokes*

First published in 2003 by Sage, this book has been repeatedly reprinted (most recently in 2013) with minor changes or updates. *How to Do Media and Cultural Studies* is aimed at instructors and students at the undergraduate level and its blurb stresses the role of student independence in doing research. The author focuses on practical advice on anything from framing the research objectives to choosing the right methodology, to finding sources (e.g. the address, phone number and website of the British Library is given, pp. 172–173), to selecting the right referencing style.

The book is 198 pages long and includes an introduction, six chapters, two appendices, a reference list and an index. Each chapter starts with an overview, contains a short introduction, several sections with several dozen subsections, and finishes with a discussion. Chapters are organized to roughly mirror the undertaking of a research project: (1) Getting started, (2) Sources and resources, (3) Analyzing media and cultural texts, (4) Researching media institutions and culture industries, (5) Methods of analysing audiences, (6) Presenting your work. Table 1 shows quantitative information about the book's organization and design:

The visual design of the textbook is consistent and not too elaborate: there are only two levels of section headings (marked in bold and italics), chapter overviews are shaded grey, figures include only graphs, not photos, and case studies are printed in different font type and size. What is striking, however, is how the text is divided into numerous short sections and sub-sections. All have very clear headings, mostly in the form of imperatives or phrases with participles, e.g. "Define you object of analysis" (p. 14), "Getting started" (p. 7), "Choosing the right method" (p. 18). This division and arrangement of information, together with the textual composition and page layout, resemble the style of user manuals, with clearly laid out instructions and warnings. Some pieces of advice and

Design and Style of Cultural and Media Studies Textbooks for College Students 197

Table 1 Features of design in *How to Do Media and Cultural Studies* by Jane Stokes

Type	Sections	Sub-sections	Tables	Case studies	Figures
Number	59	172	19	13	3

Own source

instruction are indeed basic and it is questionable if students undertaking their independent research projects really need to be instructed about brainstorming techniques (p. 13), or the arrangement of the table of contents (p. 158).

The pervasive use of direct address and imperative, dialogic patterning, catchy phrases, as well as inclusive *we* facilitates following the author's points and advice. For example:

> You may wonder, 'What is an appropriate subject for academic research in a field where all areas of culture seem open to study?' Remember that our fields of study were largely originated by people who were prepared to study what others considered to be unworthy of academic investigation. (p. 8)

In addition, there is much repetition and emphasis of information (within paragraphs, sections, chapters, and across written and visual modes), as well as cross-reference and exemplification.

Case studies are another important pedagogical tool: they are summary reports of previous (classical) studies in which particular methods discussed in the textbook were applied. Case studies are deemed important for students to get acquainted with for two reasons: firstly, to see how a given method has been applied in a particular context of an insightful study; secondly, to show how to replicate a similar undertaking. As a result, there is a risk of students giving up on their alternative, critical or creative ideas for research projects for the sake of choosing something offered by the author on the list of exemplary topics. A prime example of this kind of advice is the following:

Some ideas for semiotic analysis are listed below:

- the image of the boy band—themes of masculinity and youth
- the semiotics of music videos by a particular artist or within a particular genre
- signs of 'hip' and 'youth' in fashion advertising today and in the 1960s
- semiotics of the bad boy: Eminem's star persona (p. 73)

To conclude, this textbook, despite being practical and enriching, is likely to foster complacency and reproductiveness of certain research conventions. In a larger perspective, it "canonizes" Cultural and Media Studies projects, instead of encouraging students to critically interrogate some of their results and conclusions.

4.2 **Introducing Cultural Studies** *by Brian Longhurst et al.*

Introducing Cultural Studies (2008) is the second (revised) edition of a popular introductory textbook published by Longman and co-authored by an interdisciplinary team of researchers and lecturers mainly from the University of Salford, UK—Brian Longhurst, Greg Smith, Gaynor Bagnall, Garry Crawford and Miles Ogborn (with Elaine Baldwin and Scott McCracken who collaborated at the first edition). The intended audience is under- and postgraduate students in the humanities and social sciences who need a comprehensive and authoritative introduction to the field.

The book is 347 pages long with 303 pages of text (after excluding 17-page-long index and 26-page-long bibliography). The text is laid out in two columns per page throughout the body, and in three columns in boxes. The book consists of 2 parts, 10 chapters, 71 subchapters, 110 numbered sections and 17 additional unnumbered subsections (not listed in contents). The levelling and length of sections differs slightly among chapters (presumably authored by different individuals in the team). All sections are titled (193 headings); all boxes are labelled (100 headings); each chapter is finished with a *further reading* section (10 standard headings). Statistically, then, there is more than one heading per page. In practice, there are no pages that contain continuous unbroken print only. The body of the text is supplemented with various additional designs that stand out visually (see Table 2):

Chapter and section structure is fairly uniform. Each chapter (numbered, titled and visually distinguished) begins with a 3-4-paragraph-long introduction that contains a list of 3–5 learning objectives in a box. The text of the chapter is divided into subchapters and sections, whose flow is frequently broken with explanatory or contextualizing information in shaded boxes, as well as visuals, figures, tables, graphs or lists (see Table 2 for details). The contents of the boxes (definitions of key concepts, bio-notes of key scholars, contextual information) are related to the themes taken up in the current section; however, sometimes referring back and

Table 2 Features of design in *Introducing Cultural Studies* by Brian Longhurst et al.

Boxes (separated, shaded blue or gray) 100				
Key influence 20	Defining concept 21	Recap/learning objectives 20	Tables, in-text inserts 39	
Visual images (aka figures) 49				
Photos 32	Chapter openers 10	Cartoons 3	Drawings 3	Maps 1
Visual/verbal combinations 37				
Boxed recap lists 10	Boxed learning objectives lists 10	Graphs 9	Opposites in columns 8	
Listings 66				
In text/box text/tables 46		In recap/learning objectives boxes 20		

Own source

forth to previous or subsequent chapters is necessary. Each section begins with an outlining paragraph and finishes with a summarizing paragraph, which also relates the section's last theme to the main themes of the following section. As a result, each chapter involves a fair degree of repetitiveness, which is a pedagogical tool that seems to have displaced the old-fashioned college requirement of note-taking to enhance memorization. The textual practice of including transitions between individual sections indicates that much effort had been put by authors into organizing a large body of disparate CMS information into a coherent and progressive exposition. Each chapter finishes with a 3-4-paragraph-long, relatively general, section of *Conclusions* (devoted to a review of the main ideas and a summary of its argument) followed by a boxed list labelled *recap* and a *further reading* section in a considerably smaller font size.

Some section titles are formulated as clauses or even as questions (mainly in Chapter 1), rather than phrases, which suggests a dialogic format for information exchange (possibly with students bringing their own experience to answer a question). This is not the case, however, as no questions remain unanswered and open for students' discussion or exploration. Also each chapter sets out a uniform pattern for what should be learned and remembered (with its learning objectives/recap lists). This restricts not only students but also teachers in their choice of materials to cover and the order of learning priorities. It seems that in the attempt at making their life easier with such a design, some important aspects of studying CMS as discovery, and above all—self-discovery, are lost.

As regards the style of exposition, the text is replete with exemplifications. The origins of many examples can be traced back to common knowledge and everyday experience (cf. BMW as a "symbol," p. 2; tradition exemplified as "what it means to be a mother or a father," p. 7). On the one hand, such a stylistic convention facilitates the process of relating some theoretical models to tangible cultural practices or known forms, but on the other, it discourages thinking in terms of abstract categories and establishing or discovering larger principles or mechanisms. Another problem with such exemplification is that it treats Western mainstream cultural forms and practices as "the norm." At the same time some boxes elaborate on "exotic" cultures (Azande p. 8, Trobriand Islanders p. 9, Creole English p. 47, counter-school culture p. 103, cyberpunk p. 188, body-building p. 230, youth subcultures p. 245).

Unlike in some other popular discourses, addressing the reader directly is not yet a common stylistic convention of most academic textbooks. However, there are cases in this textbook when the readers are invoked collectively and inclusively with the authors as *we*. This implies a common educational context and shared objectives and values. The authors also project a "care-taker" persona in their going to great lengths to limit the amount of jargon, to indicate what is the most important in the exposition (bold print), and to exemplify profusely. Last but not least, they try to alert students to the difficulties they may encounter when getting acquainted with some "difficult theories" (p. 36) or problems they may face when confronted with "abstract language" (p. 64). That is also why nominalizations tend to be avoided in the textbook, and terminological nuances are clarified and exemplified with the use of clauses rather than phrases.

The consequences of such a design and style of the textbook are difficult to establish with complete certainty; however, it is beyond any doubt that readers are provided with a predictable and easy-to-follow structure replicated in each chapter. This means that they do not have to attend to the text to discover its structure; they can focus on the content. Since headings are elaborate, frequent and precise, and transition phrases and transition paragraphs ensure the continuity of the text, students are not pushed to develop expectations or hypotheses and do not have to discover the relations between ideas discussed in neighbouring sections. These links are to be taken for granted. Also, as many new technical terms or key concepts are defined in boxes right beside, students are not encouraged to consult outside sources (glossaries, lexicons, encyclopaedias) for alternative or competing definitions.

4.3 **Introducing Cultural Studies** *by David Walton*

Introducing Cultural Studies: Learning through Practice (2008) by David Walton is the first edition of another of Sage's introductory textbooks advertised in the Introduction as "a publication useful for tutors looking for a book as a source for straightforward exercises to get students motivated to practice cultural studies for themselves" (p. 1). It is 309 pages long (plus another 14 pages of an index), and divided into 5 parts and 14 chapters. Chapter titles are intriguing with some emotion-laden words and exaggerations (e.g. Chapter 2: The Leavises and T.S. Eliot combat mass urban culture) or puns (e.g. Chapter 12: Crying Woolf! Thinking with feminism; Chapter 14: Consolidating practice, heuristic thinking, creative cri-tickle acts and further research). Presumably, these witty constructions are to draw students' attention to the idea that textbooks can be fun to read and the academia is not to be thought of as humourless. The conflation of the double—entertaining and informative—functions of the textbook is evident at various levels of its design: in its dialogic formats of exposition, inserts and listings, practice exercises and notes, the style of headings and body text, and, most visibly, cartoon drawings.

It must be admitted that the textbook's innovative project is predicated on a radical re-design of the traditional, fairly well-structured and predictable composition of academic texts made coherent by virtue of hierarchies of paragraphs, sections and chapters. Here the length and structure of each chapter varies considerably. although each chapter begins with a 1-2-paragraph-long introduction outlining the main learning goals in bullet points, which is followed by the main body of the exposition peppered with inserts and exercises, and closed with a summary, a reference list and an annotated *further reading* section. The research tradition, methodology, fields of interests and main theses of Cultural Studies are introduced in the such stylized forms as dialogues, polemics, a personal letter or a list. For example, Chapter 1 features the author's polemic with Matthew Arnold (pp. 15–21), Chapter 2—a (handwritten) letter about the lecture by the Leavises (pp. 31–33), Chapter 3—a dialogue between Sherlock Holmes and Dr Watson about the Frankfurt School (pp. 49–60), Chapter 4—a dialogue between Humphrey and Bogart about the writings by Richard Hoggart (pp. 74–85), Chapter 5—a dialogue between E.P. (a student) and Thompson (a teacher) about the ideas of E.P. Thompson on the British working class (pp. 90–107), Chapter 6—a conversation between siblings/students Vidal and Ladvi Tandow (anagrams of the author's name) about Raymond Williams's contribution to Cultural Studies (pp. 112–133), Chapter 8—a dialogue between the philosopher Antonio Gramsci (sick and confined to prison) and his doctor about the notion of hegemony (pp. 193–195). Remaining chapters also include dialogues featuring fictional characters (e.g. Jekyll and Hyde, Gollum, Shrek, The Voice of Chastity, Ms Representation), or voices of classical authors in polemics about various concepts and ideas (e.g. George Eliot and contemporary feminist critics).

Appropriating a dialogue for a textbook exposition may be an effective pedagogical tool, since such conversations are usually designed as if proceeding between someone knowledgeable (the original author of the idea) and someone aspiring to learn more (a student). This is likely to simulate the actual context of experience of actual readers. Alternatively, the conversation might involve proponents of various traditions in a (well-managed) argument for their respective stances. However, presenting a selection and interpretation of original authors' ideas in direct speech may mislead readers into accepting this construction as their authentic expression. This format might also blur the historical conditions in which particular conceptions were framed. Another problem is how seriously one is to treat some of the arguments if they are presented in highly stylized, humorous and fictionalized forms. Presumably, the author's purpose has been to engage students in a critical-creative discursive practice of re-imagining the historical and institutional contexts of the key ideas in Cultural Studies in order to encourage them to appropriate some of these categories for the analysis of their own lived cultural experience. To what extent the simulation of conversational or polemical formats has actually helped them to do so remains to be seen.

It must also be highlighted here that the dialogues are frequently broken and interspaced with other visual designs (cartoons, diagrams, flow charts) and textual bylines (oversimplification warnings, help-files and practice tasks), as specified in Table 3.

1-2-paragraph-long *oversimplification warnings* include extensions and additional points to consider with respect to a given claim taken up in the dialogue. *Help files* are short inserts that offer definitions of technical terms (e.g. diaspora, bricolage), elaborations on concepts, categories or ideas (e.g. utilitarianism, luddism), historical contexts (e.g. the Enlightenment), glossaries (e.g. of dated working class vocabulary). *The voice of contemporary criticism* is usually a short remark about the controversial nature of the claims, while *a dialogue with social sciences* is a confrontation with alternative conceptions stemming from other disciplines. Listing is a very common device for both an introduction and

Table 3 Features of design in *Introducing Cultural Studies* by David Walton

Visual elements 37				
Drawn cartoons 25	Diagrams 6	Flow-charts 2	Tables 4	
Inserts 41				
Oversimplification warnings 14	Help files 17	The voice of con-temporary criticism 3	A dialogue with social sciences 3	Mock exam: question–answer 4
Specific textual lay-outs 80				
Listings (bullet points/numbers) 63		Block quotations 17		
Practice 54				
Practice exercises 23		Notes on practice 31		

Own source

consolidation of contents. The listings specified in Table 3. do not include extended lists of sources (bibliography and further reading, films, journals or websites), which feature within and particularly at the end of each chapter.

Another striking characteristic of the textbook is that *practice exercises* are located not only at the end but also within the body of each chapter. For example, after an important concept has been defined and elaborated upon, there is bound to be at least a short practice exercise devoted to considering or reflecting how that concept might be applicable in a different context. The idea of a *heuristic* is introduced to stimulate students' own analytic endeavours. Heuristics are provided in the form of fill-in diagrams in which the general categories/elements are to be replaced by students with specific information. For example, they are to read a rap song and list the ideological, economic, social or aesthetic aspects of this cultural product. Such exercises are only partly creative, since students are not to select the aspects they want to explore, but to fill in what is required. For more extended practice tasks, there are additional *notes on practice*. These are in fact suggested answers or possible explanations to the problems or questions posited in the exercises.

The textbook's design, as described above, may impress as offering diverse reading paths with optional or additional material in various inserts, and profuse repetition and cross-referencing; however, it is rather unlikely for either students or tutors to opt for an alternative route than that designed by the author and publisher in their ordering of information and activity. Despite the apparent poli-vocality of dialogic formats, informal ways of addressing readers, and the frequency of question-answer interaction patterns, there is a strong sense of authorial authority.

Linguistically, this is strengthened with a conspicuous first-person author's voice. He is, after all, the inventor of the textbook's innovative design, the scriptwriter and director of the dialogues and polemics, the narrator of the presentations, a task-dispenser and a guideline-provider.

4.4 Introducing Cultural Studies *by Ziauddin Sardar (Text) and Borin van Loon (Illustrations)*

This fourth textbook is discussed here to problematize the notion of criticality vis-à-vis modality. *Introducing Cultural Studies* by Ziauddin Sardar and Borin van Loon is a 173-page-long black-and-white comic book published in 1999 by Icon Books in the UK and distributed by Penguin Books Ltd. As a result, the graphic affordances are its main mode of design. It may not have been designed strictly as a college textbook, but it targets young people who might consider CMS as a subject of study in the future or readers interested in finding out more about some culture-related buzzwords. The book includes only two pages of *further reading* referring to a selection of authors mentioned in the text and little annotation and referencing throughout the body. Notwithstanding its cursory introduction to the field, the authors manage to adopt a critical (ironic or even acerbic) perspective on the ideas and practices championed by Cultural Studies practitioners.

The book contains from one to six frames per page, which often function as elements of a larger composition. The frames contain print exposition in the form of biographical notes on important authors, outlines of theoretical tenets, results of studies, points in polemics, critical reviews of traditions of research, as well as extended exemplifications (cf. Indian restaurant, pp. 14–22). The textual format includes expositions, listings, question-answer sequences, as well as captions and quotes. All this is variously laid out to be aligned with visual images: realistic or abstract imagery, caricatures, re-drawn classical artwork, and, above all, visual symbolism and metaphor. Much of the information is introduced in accordance with the comic-book convention of spoken words placed in balloons, either by a leading character (a cartoon humanoid figure that looks female, exotic, not fully clad and with a balloon-like belly), or by various other fictional or actual characters (incl. philosophers, theorists, scholars, authors, readers). There is much overlap between information presented verbally and visually, e.g. the word "hot" (p. 5) is accompanied by fire and smoke in the background. There is also much repetition of concepts, ideas as well as visual frames, which mostly enhances the coherence of the introduction and aids in remembering information. The variety of font styles and sizes is striking, with key terms often bolded and main arguments underlined.

The oral mode that is constitutive of the comic-book format transpires in the exposition with many colloquial phrases, conjunctions, elisions, embeddings and unfinished clauses (e.g. "Culture seems to be (almost) everything and cultural studies the study of (almost) everything!" p. 5). However, what is really striking is the degree of verbal and visual alignment, which could be interpreted as an effective pedagogical tool for enriching the exposition, contextualizing the information, and facilitating memorization. In addition, cognitive and affective rewards derived from reading an academic comic-book lie in the process of discovery of visual/verbal metaphoricity. The visual requirement for constant epistemological commitments enables one to re-think some of the frozen verbal metaphors in academic discourse (e.g. "a mode of inquiry that does not subscribe to the *straitjacket* of institutionalized disciplines" p. 8; "to put Cultural Studies on the *map*" p. 24; "cultural *casualties* and victims as well as *winners*" p. 33; "Marx was *hauled* back" p. 39; "I've *wrestled* with Althusser" p. 47, italics mine). Such phrases are graphically illustrated as if they were meant literally. In addition, verbal play and visual symbolism often accompany the presentation.

The combination of orality and visuality typical of the comic-book format does not preclude criticality, at least in the case of this introductory textbook. The book adopts a critical slant in many ways, for example by (1) pinpointing the contradictions and limitations of Cultural Studies, (2) infusing with irony the idea of treating some of the theorists as the discipline's 'founding fathers,' (3) recognizing the 'fashions' that sometimes drive research in the humanities and social sciences, (4) re-evaluating the implications of some long-standing critical concepts in the field (cyberculture, Orientalism), (5) diversifying and internationalizing the scope of presented examples (from Anglo-American to French, Australian, Asian culture), (6) introducing on-going polemics in the field without trying to resolve them, (7) informing about theoretical advances and studies emanating from non-Western centres of scholarship. The overall conclusion that can be drawn from this analysis is that the dominant mode(s) of presentation should not be straightforwardly correlated with the degree of criticality fostered by a textbook a priori, rather, the critical merits of any publication should be evaluated on the one-by-one basis.

Conclusions

The following are some generalized observations regarding various levels of textbook design and style, together with some of the implications of particular linguistic, compositional and semiotic resources.

First, contemporary textbooks are marked for typographic variations. The use of bold or italicized print, larger or smaller fonts, as well as coloured print/shading is meant to attract attention to specific information and thus to provide guidance in readers' choice of the reading path. The printed text as a visual unit is also designed to look good, not only to inform well. The value of the book is increasingly dependent on the complexity of its design: plain books do not sell well any more.

Secondly, chapter and section titles, captions and headings function primarily to anchor attention. They are instrumental in delimiting identifiable themes to facilitate scanning and searching for desired information. But

(continued)

headings also hierarchize themes. Heading structure is used to bring vertical, not only horizontal order in the material (most notably in the table of contents). Question-answer formats are to facilitate smooth progression and minimize resistance. Captions limit the variety of interpretations of visuals.

Page layout and page flow influence the level of acceptance of meanings. Information in graphs, bullet points or tables differs from information inscribed in sentences and paragraphs. For example, presenting information in points, lists or bullets is likely to impress as higher in importance, more official, and worthy of attention: "bullet points are (...) 'fired' at us, abrupt and challenging, not meant to be continuous and coherent, not inviting reflection and consideration, not insinuating themselves into our thinking. They are hard and direct, and not to be argued with" (Kress 2003: 16–17). Positioning within a page draws on conventional cultural expectations. For example, information on the left hand-side is likely to be treated as 'accepted, given,' while information presented on the right is likely to be interpreted as 'new.' The items at the top of the list will be regarded as more important than the items placed towards the bottom.

Chapter/section layout determines not only textual structures but also conceptual arrangements, and yields hierarchies of knowledge. In the 'traditional' print paradigm, a sentence inheres a proposition, a paragraph develops an argument, a section coheres thematically, a chapter constitutes a comprehensive and exhaustive exposition, and a report draws on data and examples to build an argumentation to substantiate a given thesis. Hardly any diagrams, photo-stories or hyperlinked texts could do that.

Register (formality/informality markers) and linguistic style (an aggregate of preferred linguistic forms) are common indicators of social distance or social status within a community of practice. Low-profile authorial stance—built with such stylistic choices as 'solidarity' terms of address, colloquialisms, and references to common knowledge—may project a relation of partnership rather than of authority. This, in turn, may lower the chance of readers' resistance to presented claims and critical evaluation of argumentation. In a relation of collegiality there is usually more tolerance and acceptance.

The written mode and the spoken mode are not necessarily to be thought of as two sides of the same coin (language) to be flipped—applied interchangeably. Writing has different material affordances (spatial and visual) than speech (temporal, aural). Writing should not be thought of as a transcription of speech—it is a different mode of thinking and communicating, a different literacy practice than oral communication (Kress 2003). An attempt at returning writing to patterns characteristic of speech may be misguided. So is interpellating the student as an interlocutor rather than a reader. Since reading allows for individual speed and the possibility of rereading and

(continued)

engaging with various interpretations of the text, textbooks should take the advantage of this affordance. For example, using a written (fictional) dialogue for the exposition of an academic argument seems to be an artificial, if innovative, device, whose merits are yet to be seen.

It seems that the style and design of contemporary textbooks, as outlined above, is aimed at producing students with functional literacy rather than critical literacy. At the college level, most textbooks have not yet been reduced to piles of worksheets; however, this analysis shows that some changes in CMS textbook formats that imitate popular media culture may be seen as a hindrance to students' critical dispositions.

Textbooks are now designed to be user-friendly, approachable, entertaining, with clearly laid out information that is to be accepted and learnt, not negotiated or problematized (e.g. selection is limited, reading paths are imposed, outside reference made unnecessary). Although practical application of presented ideas is welcome, a critical reflection on the hierarchies of knowledge is not encouraged. Indeed, it seems harder to challenge claims presented in graphs, visuals, bullet points, informal conversations, than in paragraphs and chapters. However, in an era of a growing uncertainty about what is true or authoritative, it is increasingly important to provide students with principled means for interrogating claims around truth and authority. This study has been devoted to raising awareness of the affordances and encouraging the assessment of the rhetoric of various modes, designs and styles, which are central to fostering critical literacy. This paper is not to argue for the return to the traditional print-only, formal-style textbooks. These, as we well know, were also used as ideological tools to constrain rather than enhance criticality and intellection. The case has been made to evaluate the advantages as well as disadvantages of new textbook designs before appropriation.

References

Primary Sources

Longhurst, B., G. Smith, G. Bagnall, G. Crawford, and M. Ogborn. 2008. *Introducing cultural studies*. Harlow: Longman.
Sardar, Z., and B. van Loon. 1999. *Introducing cultural studies*. Cambridge: Icon Books.
Stokes, J. 2003. *How to do media and cultural studies*. London: Sage.
Walton, D. 2008. *Introducing cultural studies: Learning through practice*. London: Sage.

Secondary Sources

De Beaugrande, R., and W.U. Dressler. 1981. *Introduction to text linguistics*. London; New York: Longman.

Fairclough, N. (ed.). 1992. *Critical language awareness*. London: Longman.

Gardner, H. 1993. *Creating minds*. New York: HarperCollins.

Holme, R. 2004. *Literacy: An introduction*. Edinburgh: Edinburgh University Press.

Janks, H. 2010. *Literacy and power*. London: Routledge.

Kress, G. 2003. *Literacy in the new media age*. London; New York: Routledge.

Kress, G., and T. van Leeuwen. 1996. *Reading images: The grammar of visual design*. London: Routledge.

Kress, G., and T. van Leeuwen. 2001. *Multimodal discourse: The modes and media of contemporary communication*. London: Hodder Arnold.

Machin, D. 2008. *Introduction to multimodal analysis*. London: Hodder Arnold.

Machin, D., and A. Mayr. 2012. *How to do critical discourse analysis: A multimodal introduction*. London: Sage.

Martin, J., and R. Veel (eds.). 1998. *Reading science*. London; New York: Routledge.

McLuhan, M. 1964. *Understanding media: The extensions of man*. Toronto: McGraw-Hill.

Molek-Kozakowska, K. 2013. How to foster critical literacy in academic contexts: Some insights from action research on writing research papers. In *Language in cognition and affect*, ed. E. Piechurska-Kuciel and E. Szymańska-Czaplak, 95–110. Heidelberg: Springer.

Moskovitz, G. 1981. *Caring and sharing in the foreign language classroom*. New York: Newbury House.

Ong, W. 1982. *Orality and literacy: The technologizing of the word*. New York: Metheuen.

Trumbo, J. 1999. Visual literacy and science communication. *Science Communication* 20: 409–425.

Towards Teaching English for Pharmaceutical Purposes: An Attempt at a Description of Key Vocabulary and Phraseology in Clinical Trial Protocols and European Public Assessment Reports

Łukasz Grabowski

Abstract With the exception of medical schools or medical universities, English for Pharmaceutical Purposes is rarely taught as a specialist language course or ESP module at the university-level (e.g. designed specifically for training translators of specialist texts). This may be caused by, among other factors, the lack of comprehensive description of vocabulary and phraseology used across different pharmaceutical text types and genres, e.g. patient-pharmacist interactions, patient information leaflets, clinical trial protocols etc. This preliminary study is designed as an initial step to develop a description of vocabulary and phraseology, namely keywords, n-grams consisting of 4 words and phrase frames based on n-grams consisting of 4 words all used in clinical trial protocols and European public assessment reports written originally in English. The analyses are aimed to provide an initial description of the use of distinctive lexis and phraseology found in the said text varieties. The results offer new, yet still preliminary, data for further descriptions of English used for pharmaceutical purposes to be conducted in the future.

Keywords English for specific purposes • Pharmaceutical texts • Register variation • Keywords • Lexical bundles • Phrase frames

1 Introduction

One of the perennial problems pertaining to didactics of English for Specific Purposes (ESP), notably at courses targeted at non-native speakers of English, refers to teaching and instilling in students confidence in terms of the proper use of domain-specific vocabulary and phraseology. More specifically, the problem refers to the use of collocations and co-occurrence patterns that occur hand-in-hand

---

Ł. Grabowski (✉)
Opole University, Opole, Poland
e-mail: lukasz@uni.opole.pl

© Springer International Publishing Switzerland 2015
L. Piasecka et al. (eds.), *New Media and Perennial Problems in Foreign Language Learning and Teaching*, Second Language Learning and Teaching,
DOI 10.1007/978-3-319-07686-7_12

with specialist terminology, in some studies referred to as phraseological competence (Biel 2011, 2013). The idea at the heart of this paper is that a description of the most frequent linguistic patterns may constitute a good starting point to help teachers or instructors achieve the aforementioned aim. This has profound implications for language learning, traditionally considered to involve item-learning as well as system-learning (Ellis 1997, cited in Liu 2012: 28), the former referring to acquisition of formulaic sequences and phraseologies stored and retrieved from memory as single items and semantic wholes (setting aside various definitions and operationalizations of different types of multi-word units and of the criteria adopted for their identification).

Hence, the aim of this very preliminary study is to undertake an attempt at a corpus linguistic description of key vocabulary and phraseology in English for Specific Purposes, in particular in terms of exploration of keywords, lexical bundles and phrase frames used across different text types found in the pharmaceutical sector of the economy. Although medical language has been explored from a multitude of perspectives, including applied linguistics, SLA and FLA (e.g. Brooks 2001; Glendinning and Holmstroem 2005; Hoekje and Tipton 2011), also targeted specifically at Polish students of English used for various pharmaceutical purposes (Ciecierska et al. 1983; Donesch-Jeżo 2000, 2002, 2007; Kierczak 2009), one may notice a dearth of studies explicitly addressing the problem of register variation in English used within the pharmaceutical industry, in particular in terms of describing recurrent patterns of vocabulary and phraseology. Such studies conducted so far are either scarce or dispersed as fragments of larger studies on medical discourse in written contexts. Also, some linguistically-oriented studies have either considered such text varieties to be parts of medical discourse (Biber and Finegan 1994; Gotti and Salager-Meyer 2006) or focused on a single text variety and a limited selection of linguistic features (e.g. Gledhill 1995a, b; Paiva 2000). Up to date, according to the author's knowledge, there has been only one study (Gledhill 1995a)—integrating phraseology, corpus linguistics and genre analysis—aimed to explicitly address the problem of phraseology (more specifically, of collocational patterns) used in pharmaceutical texts.

It appears, however, that it is difficult, if not impossible, to find any studies aimed to show that language used in various pharmaceutical contexts varies depending on a text variety or discourse community. From that it follows that English used for various pharmaceutical purposes is dissolved or watered down within a more general English for Medical Purposes (EMP), English for Specific Purposes (ESP) or English for Occupational Purposes (EOP), to name but a few. Consequently, the English language used in different pharmaceutical contexts is rarely referred to as pharmaceutical discourse or English for pharmaceutical purposes. This observation is corroborated by the frequency data extracted from Google (as of 10 February 2014) showing that the former expression, namely 'pharmaceutical discourse' occurs 783 times, while the latter, namely 'English for Pharmaceutical Purposes' occurs only 16 times, and it is used only twice in the context of applied linguistics—as a name of a specialist language course at the university-level offered at the University of Calabria, Italy (del Vecchio 2012) and at the Medical University of Warsaw, Poland (WUM 2014).

Consequently, there are no readily available descriptions of linguistic variation in a particular pharmaceutical text variety relative to other text varieties from the same specialist domain of language use (an attempt, similar in terms of methodology to the one presented in this paper, at comparing patient information leaflets and summaries of product characteristics is undertaken in Grabowski (2013), yet it is also of preliminary character). The lack of comprehensive descriptions of the most frequent and distinctive vocabulary and phraseology used across a wide range of pharmaceutical text varieties may therefore be one of the reasons why English for Pharmaceutical Purposes is rarely taught as a specialist language course at the university-level, notably in translation-oriented classes; also, the lack of such descriptions may adversely impact students' competence in terms of properly and adequately using specialist terms in texts (notably the collocations and co-occurrence patterns that go hand in hand with terminology).

Thus, the rationale behind this preliminary study is the idea of linguistic variation defined as variability in the choice of linguistic forms in different situational contexts of language use (Biber 2006; Biber and Conrad 2009). More specifically, it is hypothesized that two pharmaceutical text varieties—clinical trial protocols (henceforth CTPs) and European public assessment reports (henceforth EPARs)—found in different contexts of the use of medicines will prioritize different lexical and phraseological patterns and thus reveal a high degree of variation in terms of the use, distribution and function of the most frequent and distinctive vocabulary and phraseology. Furthermore, it is hypothesized that the reasons for this variation are different communicative purposes, functions, situational contexts of use as well as production circumstances and typical users of the pharmaceutical text varieties under study. Thus, a specific aim of the analyses is the identification—using corpus linguistics methodology—of the most distinctive linguistic patterns (keywords, lexical bundles and phrase frames), typical of the CTPs and EPARs.

There are two main characteristics of the preliminary study presented in this paper. Firstly, it is conducted from a register-perspective whereby a linguistic characterization of text varieties is tantamount to identification of frequent and pervasive linguistic features (Biber and Conrad 2009: 6). Secondly, following Biber and Conrad (2009: 51), the research is based on three components, or methodological keystones, of register analysis, namely a comparative approach (which in this study means a comparison of electronic corpora of two pharmaceutical registers), quantitative analysis (i.e. identification of register features on the basis of information on frequency and distribution of lexical and phraseological items found across two pharmaceutical text varieties) and a representative sample of texts (i.e. a range of texts with a high number of linguistic characteristics typical of a particular pharmaceutical register). This allows one to determine—in a more objective way as compared with the intuition-based approach prioritizing unusual and rare linguistic patterns—whether a given linguistic feature is more frequent and pervasive in one register than in another. All in all, following the methodology proposed by Biber and Conrad (2009: 51–81), in this paper the preliminary description of register variation across two pharmaceutical text varieties, namely the CTPs and EPARs, focusses on their situational, linguistic and functional characteristics, which make up three stages of the study.

As regards the first stage of register analysis, namely situational characteristics of a register, it is based on the assumption that "linguistic differences can be derived from situational differences, because linguistic features are functional" (Biber and Conrad 2009: 9). Further, Biber and Conrad (2009: 47) propose a framework for analysis of situational characteristics of registers, including a description of a number of situational factors, such as participants and the relations between them, channel of communication, production circumstances, setting, communicative purpose and topic. This analytical framework is used in the description and further comparison of the situational characteristics of the CTPs and EPARs

The second stage, namely description of linguistic features and their functions, is the most important from the perspective of this descriptive study. Although registers can be described in situational terms, they can also be compared in terms of their linguistic characteristics. Such an approach is known as the study of register variation (Biber 2008: 823). According to Teich and Fankhauser (2010: 4), "register variation is inherent in human language: a single speaker will make systematic choices in pronunciation, morphology, word choice, and grammar reflecting a range of situational factors." As regards this study, it focusses on systematic choices of lexis and phraseology (i.e. keywords as well as lexical bundles and phrase frames) in the CTPs and EPARs.

Finally, the third stage refers to functional interpretation of the results from situational and linguistic analyses of registers (Biber and Conrad 2009: 64). In other words, at this stage the aim is to pinpoint the links between distinctive situational characteristics of a given register and its distinctive linguistic characteristics in order to explain why particular linguistic patterns occur therein (Biber and Conrad 2009). As this stage of the study is a qualitative one, it is paramount to illustrate particular interpretations with examples of use of lexis and phraseology in their textual (e.g. by using concordances or text fragments) and situational context (e.g. by explaining the situational rationale behind the choice of particular linguistic features). However, due to the limitations as to the size of this paper, the results of the preliminary analyses are only summarized in tables and briefly commented upon rather than presented in the form of individual concordances illustrating the actual uses of keywords, lexical bundles and phrase frames in their textual environment. Also, due to the large number of linguistic data, more detailed presentation of linguistic and/or phraseological profile of individual pharmaceutical text varieties as well as of larger patterns of register variation across multiple pharmaceutical text types shall be developed in the future.

2 Method

This preliminary study focuses on the analysis of register variation manifested in the use of vocabulary and phraseology. To that end, it adopts a similar approach to the one employed by Biber (2006), Roemer (2009) and Goźdź-Roszkowski (2011), who used key vocabulary and lexical bundles, among other grammatical and syntactic characteristics, as register features. However, in this study, apart from keywords (Scott 1997, 2008b) and lexical bundles (Biber et al. 1999), phrase frames (Fletcher 2007) are also tested as additional linguistic exponents of register variation, or register features, across pharmaceutical text types. This allows for inclusion in the analyses of both contiguous and non-contiguous multi-word units, the decision intended to facilitate preparation of a more comprehensive description of vocabulary and phraseology in the CTPs and EPARs.

The first register feature explored in this study are single-word units, namely keywords, which—according to Scott (2008b: 176)—are those words "whose frequency is unusually high in comparison with some norm". More specifically, these are words which occur more frequently in a text or corpus (or a particular text type) than in another text or collection of texts (or text types) contained in a reference corpus. Goźdź-Roszkowski (2011: 35) argues that keywords can "reveal not only a great deal about the subject matter, the 'aboutness' of a particular genre, but they can also specify the salient features which are functionally related to the genre". Furthermore, Goźdź-Roszkowski (2011: 35–38, 64–66) demonstrates that keywords are typically investigated through their typical co-occurrence patterns in texts or corpora, the approach that allows one to classify the keywords into semantic or functional categories reflecting their various aspects (e.g. a type of information they convey, role in the organization and structure of particular discourse, evaluative charge, semantic prosody etc.).

The second register feature subject to the analysis are multi-word units called lexical bundles, described as sequences of three or more words that occur frequently in natural discourse and constitute lexical building blocks used frequently by language users in different situational and communicative contexts (Biber et al. 1999: 990–991). More often than not, lexical bundles are not idiomatic in meaning and not perceptually salient. Quite to the contrary, meanings of lexical bundles are typically transparent from the individual words contained in them (Biber et al. 2003: 134). The rationale behind using lexical bundles as register features and—at the same time—as one of the exponents of function-related register variation is the claim made by Biber (2006: 174) who argues that "the functions and meanings expressed by these lexical bundles differ dramatically across registers and academic disciplines, depending on the typical purposes of each".

Finally, the third register feature are non-contiguous multi-word units called phrase frames, originally introduced by Fletcher (2007) and defined as sets of variants of an n-gram identical except for one word. As it was demonstrated by Roemer (2009), in her comparison of native and non-native students' academic writing, phrase frames may be used as a means of comparing pattern variability across different text types or registers (Roemer 2009: 91) and hence they may provide further insight into how fixed multi-language units are in a given register and what degree of variation they exhibit. For example, a high number of variants of a phrase frame is tantamount to high productivity of that phrase frame and to a higher degree of phraseological variation within a given text variety. So far, phrase frames have been used as exponents of register variation in the study conducted by Roemer (2009), namely the exploration of the phraseological profile of native and non-native students' academic writing (two specialist registers)—the preliminary study that provided motivation to use a somewhat similar approach to examine and compare the degree of phraseological variation across different types of pharmaceutical texts.

The research presented in this paper uses a radical corpus-driven approach whereby the linguistic data found in the corpus of texts are not adjusted to fit any predefined categories or linguistic theories. On the contrary, the results of an empirical corpus-driven analysis of frequencies of recurrent patterns of language use, exemplified by keywords, lexical bundles and phrase frames, provide the basis for a preliminary description.

As far as the linguistic and functional characterization of the CTPs and EPARs are concerned, the analyses are modelled on the selected studies conducted by Biber (2006, 2009), Goźdź-Roszkowski (2011) and Roemer (2009). First, the keywords are generated against a custom-designed pharmaceutical reference corpus including, apart from the CTPs and EPARs, samples of patient information leaflets, research articles on pharmacology, as well as samples of chapters/sections from academic textbooks on pharmacology (c. 2.8 million word tokens). Second, functional profiles of keywords in the CTPs and EPARs are compared. Next, 50 - top-frequency lexical bundles in the CTPs and EPARs are generated and compared in terms of their functions, using the functional typology proposed by Biber et al. (2003) and Biber (2006), later used and slightly modified by, among others, Goźdź-Roszkowski (2011). The study ends with a comparison of phrase-frame variation, based on the most frequent n-grams consisting of 4 words.

Although this preliminary study focuses on, and is limited to, exploration of the CTPs and EPARs, the research material is a purpose-designed corpus of English pharmaceutical texts with 2,773,630 words in total, split into five sub-corpora ranging from 248,841 words (in the case of research articles on pharmacology) to 956,545 words (in the case of the EPARs), representing five pharmaceutical text varieties (Table 1).

As for the text varieties explored in this preliminary study, clinical trial protocols (240 complete texts) were downloaded from the Clinical Trials Register (CTR) database of the European Union, hosted by the European Medicines Agency (EMA 2012) and available at https://www.clinicaltrialsregister.eu/index.html. The European public assessment reports (40 complete texts), on the other hand, were downloaded from the Open Source Parallel Corpus (OPUS) Project website (Tiedemann 2009).

As for the remaining text varieties, patient information leaflets (463 complete texts) were extracted from the Patient Information Leaflet (PIL) corpus 2.0 hosted

Table 1 Make-up of a purpose-designed corpus with English pharmaceutical texts

Text type	Number of text samples	Size (word tokens used for a wordlist)
Clinical trial protocols (CTP)	240	468,957
European public assessment reports (EPARs)	40	965,545
Patient information leaflets (PILs)	463	474,458
Research articles (RAs)	22	248,831
Chapters from academic textbooks (ATs)	86	615,839
Total size:	851	2,773,630

by the Open University (Bouayad-Agha 2006), available at: http://mcs.open.ac.uk/nlg/old_projects/pills/corpus/PIL; Research articles on pharmacology (22 text samples) were extracted from selected volumes of two international academic journals in the field of pharmaceutical sciences (*International Journal of Pharmaceutical Sciences and Research* (available at: http://www.ijpsr.com/), *The International Journal of Pharmacy and Biological Sciences* (available at: http://www.ijpbs.com/) and from one monograph entitled *Drug Interactions in Infectious Diseases* (Piscitelli and Rodvold 2005). Finally, selected samples of chapters/sections from academic textbooks (86 text samples) were extracted from titles such as *Modern Pharmacology with Clinical Applications* (Craig and Stitzel 2004) and *Introduction to Pharmacology* (Hollinger 2003). The study corpus was compiled for personal non-commercial research and therefore it is not publicly available. Finally, the following computer programs purpose-designed for text analysis were used in order to obtain and process data for the different types of linguistic analyses, namely WordSmith 5.0 (Scott 2008a) and kfNgram (Fletcher 2007).

In accordance with the hypothesis adopted in this study, different pharmaceutical text varieties prioritize different vocabulary and phraseology because of varying discipline-specific practices associated with the situational contexts of use of the CTPs and EPARs. In order to test this hypothesis, the study has the following specific aims:

(a) To identify 'register features', such as keywords, lexical bundles and phrase frames, typical of either the CTPs or EPARs
(b) To determine whether any similarities or differences in the use of vocabulary (keywords) and phraseology (lexical bundles and phrase frames) are contingent on situational contexts of use of the CTPs and EPARs

3 Results

3.1 Situational Characteristics of CTPs and EPARs

In general terms, clinical trial protocols (CTPs), also referred to in the United Kingdom as 'clinical studies protocols', present results of experiments on human or animal subjects conducted in order to explore pharmacological and pharmaco-dynamic effects related to the use of medicines, including any adverse reactions or any other matters impacting their safe and efficient use (Montalt Resurrecio and Gonzalez Davies 2007: 80–81). As a rule, a CTP is submitted to a competent regulatory authority (e.g. Medicines and Healthcare Products Regulatory Agency (MHRA) in the United Kingdom to request authorization for conduct of a clinical trial of any medicinal product designed for human use. In the European Union, the CTPs are prepared in accordance with the Clinical Trials Directive (2001/20/EC), issued by the European Parliament and the Council of the European Union as well as with a number of derivative documents related to the said Directive (Montalt Resurrecio and Gonzalez Davies 2007: 81).

As regards their communicative purpose, the CTPs provide information on objectives, purpose and design of a clinical trial, selection and treatment of subjects as well as methodology and organization of the trial (Montalt Resurrecio and Gonzalez Davies 2007: 81). According to Mallick et al. (2006: 23–24), "a well-designed protocol reflects the scientific and methodological integrity of a trial", and therefore it is important for conducting clinical trials in a safe and cost-effective manner. According to Montalt Resurrecio and Gonzalez Davies (2007: 81), the CTPs can be written by either a chief researcher (in the case of trials conducted in more than one centre or institution) or a principal researcher (in the case of trials conducted in a single centre or institution).

Furthermore, the CTPs are used as reference documents by various professionals involved in the trial, such as investigators, study site coordinators, pharmacists, research nurses, dispensing staff, laboratory staff as well as study monitors, data managers, pharmacovigilance specialists, statisticians, regulatory inspectors, report writers, or members of ethics committees (Fitzpatrick 2005: 2; Wang and Bakhai 2006: xii). Thus, the CTPs have either a singular, individual addressor (i.e. a researcher or lead investigator) or are written collaboratively by a team of researchers, including a lead investigator (an expert clinician) and his or her co-investigators (e.g. a clinical scientist, statistician and other researchers). Also, a group of renowned experts is chosen to peer review the document and provide their consultations and opinions (Mallick et al. 2006: 24). The CTPs have an institutional addressee (e.g. a competent authority, such as MHRA in the United Kingdom) and a high number of intermediate users referring to the CTPs in the course of clinical trials. Consequently, both the addressor and the addressee have similar level of expert background in the field and so a relatively equal status.

As regards contents and generic macro-structure of the CTPs, they are highly conventionalized in that they follow a standard form and provide the same types of information in a fixed order, as specified in the Directive 2001/20/EC and related documents. This information (presented in sections A-P) includes the following: summary of the trial, protocol information, sponsor information, applicant identification, information on investigational medicinal products (IMPs), information on placebo, general information on a clinical trial, description of population of trial subjects, specification of investigator networks involved in a trial.

The second text variety explored in this paper are the European public assessment reports (EPARs) compiled by the European Medicines Agency (EMA); they include reports on scientific evaluation, discussion and conclusion for every medicine granted a Marketing Authorization by the European Commission (EMA 2012). The main purpose of this text variety is to provide a summary of the grounds for an opinion of the Committee for Medicinal Products for Human Use (CHMP)—based on the review of documentation submitted by an applicant, i.e. a pharmaceutical company—concerning granting or refusal of a marketing authorization for a specific medicinal product (EMA 2012). This document is targeted primarily at specialist readers or public authorities. However, in order to make their contents understandable to the public, the EPARs contain a summary (i.e. a short description of the main attributes of a medicinal product) written in a plain style understandable for non-specialists in the field. The legal basis for creation and availability of the EPARs is contained in Articles 12(3) and 13(3) of Regulation (EC) No 726/2004 (EMA 2012).

As regards typical generic macro-structure of the EPARs, it is highly conventionalized and consists of the following elements: a summary for the public, authorization details, product information (including summary of product characteristics, specification of a manufacturing-authorization holder responsible for batch release, specification of conditions of marketing authorization, description of labeling and package leaflet) and assessment history of a medicinal product (EMA 2012).

These documents typically have a specific institutional addressor (European Medicines Agency) and institutional (e.g. pharmaceutical companies, national regulatory authorities) or singular addressee (e.g. a pharmacist). Thus, there also seems to be little asymmetry in terms of the level of specialist knowledge between an addressor and addressee of the EPARs.

3.2 Keywords

Due to the emphasis on selectivity as the priority for generation of keywords, the log likelihood test with a p value set at 0.000001 and the minimum frequency set at 25 are used to obtain fewer but more representative number of keywords. Furthermore, the keywords are revealed through a comparison of a wordlist generated for an individual sub-corpus (e.g. the CTPs or EPARs) with a wordlist generated for the entire study corpus (minus the sub-corpus for which keywords are generated, i.e. either the CTPs or EPARs). According to Goźdź-Roszkowski (2011: 36), such an approach to identification of keywords unique to particular genres and text types is more effective than a comparison against a larger general reference corpus.

All in all, the keyword generation procedure, conducted with the help of the Keyword facility of WordSmith Tools 5.0 (Scott 2008a), revealed 716 of positive keywords in the CTPs and 1873 in the EPARs. As such a number of keywords is not amenable to interpretation, only 50 keywords with the highest keyness value are subjected to more detailed analyses.

In order to identify the functional relationship between keywords and situational factors, such as production circumstances of the CTPs and EPARs and their typical communicative purposes and target audiences, the next step is to propose a functional classification of the 50 keywords. In what follows, a domain-specific and text-type specific functional classification of keywords found in the CTPs and EPARs has been developed (Table 2)—based on the one proposed by Goźdź-Roszkowski (2011)—through examination of context and co-text of occurrence of these keywords.

Table 2 shows salient functional categories of keywords identified in the CTPs and EPARs. Predictably, given their situational characteristics, the CTPs are marked by the occurrence of keywords marking participation (*sponsor, committee, sponsor's, subject, subjects, (competent) authority, (member) state, country, organization*), including institutional keywords (*EudraCT, EEA, MHRA*), as well as procedural keywords (*trial, investigation, classification, designated, therapy, identification, description, protocol*) referring to various stages of a clinical trial. The keyword status of these items dovetails with the main communicative purpose of the CTPs, which is to convey specific information concerning objectives, purpose and design of a clinical trial, selection and treatment of subjects, methodology and organization of the trial as well as on its sponsors and organizations involved in the trial. Also, in the CTPs one may find a high number of general language keywords which, together with their immediate collocates, express a range of specialist meanings (*advanced therapy, medical condition, trade name, orphan drug etc.*). For example, the latter collocation, namely an *orphan drug*, constitutes a specialist term defined as "a drug for which the target population is limited or for which the disease it treats occurs only rarely" (Hollinger 2003: 387). Since the CTPs are highly conventionalized in terms of their generic macro-structure, the majority of keywords are used in the titles of sections or subsections (from A to P), e.g. "B.1.1 *Name* of *Sponsor*: (...)" contains two keywords (in italics) which occur in every CTP found in the corpus. Finally, it should be noted that the CTPs are written in a highly formal, concise and precise style, with a large number of specialist terms and formulaic expressions.

The EPARs, on the other hand, have more keywords referring to brand names of medicines or names of chemical substances (e.g. *haemoglobin, insulin, aransep, alfa darbepoetin, apriprazole, rosiglitazone, epoetin*), names of medical conditions and side-effects (e.g. *observed disorders, anaemia, hypoglycaemia*), use and/or administration of medicinal products (e.g. *subcutaneous, injection, pre-filled syringe, pen, dose, weekly*), measurement units corresponding to chemical substances or medicines [e.g. *dl, mmol, g, IU*—defined as a unit of potency required to

Table 2 Functional classification of keywords

No	Functional category	CTPs	EPARs
1	Citation keywords		*See*
2	Keywords referring to participants	*Sponsor, committee, sponsor's, subject, subjects, (competent) authority, (member) state, country, organisation*	*Patients*
3	Keywords referring to names of substances		*Haemoglobin, insulin, alfa, apriprazole, rosiglitazone, actraphane, darbepoetin, epoetin, erythropoietin, agenerase*
4	Keywords referring to names of medicines		*abilify, aranesp*
5	Keywords referring to use of medicines	*EudraCT, EEA, MHRA,*	*Subcutaneous, injection, syringe, dose, weekly, pen, pre-filled,*
6	Keywords referring to pharmaceutical form of medicines		*Excipient*
7	Keywords referring to medical conditions and side-effects		*Disorders, anaemia, hypoglycaemia, observed, risk*
8	Modality keywords		*Should*
9	Procedural keywords	*Trial, investigation, classification, designated, therapy, identification, description, protocol*	*Studies, treated*
10	Institutional keywords	*EudraCT, EEA, MHRA,*	*EU*
11	General language keywords	*Yes, no, present, concerned, advanced, outside, not, end, name, condition, origin, involves, information, orphan, criteria, ethics*	*With, special, uncommon, common, once, were, was, tel*
12	Recommendation "advisory" keywords		*Recommended*
13	Aboutness keywords	*Product, medicinal, medical*	*Products, batch, package*
14	Specialist and legal terms as key words	*IMP, INN, opinion, decision, status*	
15	Keywords referring to symbols and classifications	*Number, code, type*	
16	Keywords marking internal text organization		*Section, particulars*
17	Measure keywords		*dl, mmol, g, IU*

produce a desired biological effect and agreed upon as international standard (Pickar 2004: 67)] as well as keywords marking internal text organization (e.g. *section, particulars*). Overall, the EPARs have higher number of keywords referring to chemical substances found in medicines and to the use of medicines, the finding that may be due to their communicative purpose (scientific evaluation or discussion of properties of medicinal products). The CTPs, on the other hand, have more keywords referring to participants or parties involved in clinical trials as well as to procedures corresponding to different stages of the trials, the reflection of the CTPs' communicative purpose, namely of providing information on objectives, purpose and design of the clinical trials.

3.3 Lexical Bundles

This part of the study consists of a comparison of lists of the most frequent 4-word lexical bundles in the CTPs and EPARs, which are generated with the help of kfNgram (Fletcher 2007). The hashes ('#') stand for various numbers used in pharmaceutical texts under scrutiny. The 20 most common 4-word lexical bundles in both sub-corpora are displayed in Table 3.

The data reveal that there is no overlap among the top-frequency lexical bundles in the CTPs and EPARs. Quite to the contrary, 8 out of 10 top-frequency bundles in the EPARs contain numbers which refer to the quantity or concentration of chemical substances found in medicinal products (e.g. *than # g dl, dl # mmol l*) or to sections of a document (e.g. *# name of the* [*medicinal product*]).

In order to identify the functional relationship between lexical bundles and situational factors related to the use of the two text varieties, such as production circumstances of the CTPs and EPARs and their typical communicative purposes and target audiences, the next step of the study consists in a concordance-based qualitative functional analysis of lexical bundles. In what follows, a domain-specific and text-type specific functional classification of lexical bundles found in the CTPs and EPARs has been developed—based on the one proposed by Biber (2006) and Goźdź-Roszkowski (2011)—through examination of context and co-text of occurrence of the 50 top-frequency 4-word lexical bundles. The results are summarized in Tables 4 and 5 below.

Table 5 shows certain differences in terms of the function of the most frequent lexical bundles used in the CTPs and EPARs. It was revealed that the CTPs are dominated by discourse-organizing (28) and referential bundles (22), with no single stance bundle among the 50 most frequent ones. This accords with the communicative purpose of this text variety, which is to objectively—in a scientifically rigorous way—convey detailed information on, among others, purpose, design and methodology of clinical trials. Hence, the expectation concerning non-occurrence of lexical bundles expressing personal feelings, opinions, attitudes or assessments in the CTPs has been confirmed at this stage of the study. On the contrary, one may find in the CTPs a large number of referential bundles conveying

Table 3 20 top-frequency 4-word lexical bundles

	CTPs	EPARs
1	*information not present in*	**# # # #**
2	*not present in EUdract*	*eu # # #*
3	*in the member state*	*# g dl #*
4	*the member state concerned*	*dl # mmol l*
5	*be used in the*	*g dl # mmol*
6	*to be used in*	*of the medicinal product*
7	*IMP to be used*	*# name of the*
8	*scope of the trial*	*name of the medicinal*
9	*information on the trial*	*than # g dl*
10	*objective of the trial*	*and sight of children*
11	*the trial involves multiple*	*of the reach and*
12	*in the trial has*	*reach and sight of*
13	*cell therapy medicinal product*	*the reach and sight*
14	*sometic cell therepy medicinal*	*out of the reach*
15	*a classification for this*	*your doctor or pharmacist*
16	*active substance of biological*	*# special precautions for*
17	*active substance of chemical*	*of the marketing authorisation*
18	*administration for this IMP*	*# eu # #*
19	*an orphan drug in*	*the marketing authorisation holder*
20	*another type of medicinal*	*particulars to appear on*

Table 4 General functional classification of lexical bundles

	CTPs	EPARs
Referential bundles	22	41
Discourse organizers	28	6
Stance bundles	0	3

factual information on clinical trials, e.g. location of a trial, procedures and stages of a trial, institutions engaged in the conduct of clinical trials, attributes of investigational medicinal products subjected to clinical trials etc. (e.g. *information on the trial, scope of the trial, objective of the trial, cell therapy medicinal product, gene therapy medical product, description of the IMP, classification for this product*).

Among the 50 top-frequency lexical bundles in the EPARs, there are 41 referential bundles while stance bundles and discourse organizers are marginal (3 and 6, respectively). These differences are content- and purpose-related. Since the EPARs' primary function is to present results of scientific evaluation of medicinal products, they are dominated by referential bundles, such as measurement/quantity bundles (e.g. *# mmol l in, # mg # mg, greater than # g, than # g dl*, etc.), attributive bundles (e.g. *and address of the, name and address of, and route s of, reach and sight of*), identification/focus bundles (e.g. *special precautions for disposal, with*

Table 5 Detailed functional classification of lexical bundles

	CTPs	EPARs
Referential bundles		
Identification/focus bundlesIdentification/focus	*information on the trial, scope of the trial, objective of the trial, cell therapy medicinal product, gene therapy medical product, description of the IMP, classification for this product*	*special precautions for disposal, and sight of children, the reach and sight, with other medicinal products, drive and use machines, to drive and use*
Location bundles	*in the member state, member state concerned*	*out of the reach*
Attributive bundles	*somatic cell therapy medicinal, active substance of biological, active substance of chemical, another type of medicinal, indication as an orphan, medicinal product containing genetically*	*and address of the, name and address of, and route s of, reach and sight of, # name of the, name of the medicinal*
Participative bundles		*your doctor or pharmacist, the marketing authorisation holder*
Institutional bundles	*Committee on Advanced therapies*	*eu # # #, # eu # #, # # # eu, # # eu #, number s eu #, s eu # #*
Terminological bundles		*authorisation number s eu, # marketing authorisation number, marketing authorisation number s, expiry date exp #, # expiry date exp, # list of excipients*
Procedure-related bundles	*IMP has been designated, administration for this IMP, IMP to be used, designated in this indication, has a marketing authorization, has issued a classification*	*route s of administration*
Measurement bundles/Quantity		*# mmol l in, # mg # mg, greater than # g, than # g dl, # g dl #, dl # mmol l, g dl # mmol, # # # #, # # to #, # to # #, # years of age*
Discourse organizers		
Condition bundles		
Topic introduction/focus	*the trial involves multiple, information not present in, CAT has issued a, combination product that includes, immunological medicinal product such, medicinal product such as, a classification for this, issued a classification for, in this indication as, has been designated in, been designated in this, be used in the, to be used in, an orphan drug in*	*solution for injection in, for injection in a, particulars to appear on, # special precautions for*

(continued)

Towards Teaching English for Pharmaceutical Purposes: An Attempt at a... 223

Table 5 (continued)

	CTPs	EPARs
Clarification/topic elaboration bundles	*not present in EUdract, of the IMP to, of administration for this, containing genetically modified organisms, in the clinical trial, drug in the community, in the trial has, involve an advanced therapy, involving a medical device, as an orphan drug, but does not involve, does not involve an, one involving a medical, not involve an advanced*	*of the reach and*
Structuring bundles		*see section # #*
Stance bundles		
Desire bundles		*the dose should be*
Obligation/directive bundles		*keep out of the*
Ability bundles		*ability to drive and*

other medicinal products) or terminological bundles (e.g. *marketing authorisation number s, authorisation number s eu*).

3.4 Phrase Frames

For the purposes of this study, phrase frames (i.e. identical variants of n-grams except for one word, marked with the symbol *) are identified with the use of a program kfNgram (Fletcher 2007) and 20 top-frequency 4-word phrase frames (short 4-p-frames) found in the CTPs and EPARs are compared in terms of pattern variability (Table 6). Those 4-word phrase frames which either go over sentence boundaries (i.e. are divided by full-stops or semi-colons) are not analyzed. The 'hits' column presents the total token frequency of all variants of a given phrase frame while the 'variants' column presents the number of variants (i.e. different types) of a given phrase frame. As a rule, the higher the number, the higher the productivity of a given phrase frame (Roemer 2009: 96).

Table 6 reveals that only one 4-p-frame (*the * of the*) out of the 20 most frequent ones overlaps in the CTPs and EPARs. It shows that their writers prioritize different phrase frames, which further confirms topic- and function-related differences between the two text types. In particular, the EPARs have a high number of top-frequency 4-p-frames with numbers (marked with #), which refer to either measurement units (e.g. '# * # mg' or '* # and #') or document structure (e.g. '# * of the'). Also, the only overlapping 4-p-frame is more productive in EPARs than CTPs, i.e. the p-frame *the * of the* occurs in EPARs 646 times and has 47 variants

Table 6 Top-20 4-p-frames in CTPs and EPARs

	CTPs	Hits (tokens)	Variants (types)	EPARs	Hits (tokens)	Variants (types)
1	*of the trial	2704	8	* # and #	942	25
2	* member state concerned	1310	2	# and # *	867	46
3	be * in the	1134	3	* the medicinal product	825	5
4	to be * in	1125	3	the medicinal product *	757	29
5	used in the *	871	3	if you are *	756	29
6	* in the trial	870	5	in the * of	736	34
7	* of the IMP	866	2	# * # mg	717	18
8	active substance of *	866	2	* solution for injection	672	16
9	**the * of the**	794	14	* marketing authorisation holder	663	6
10	of the trial *	737	7	**the * of the**	646	47
11	the trial involves *	720	2	the * should be	646	11
12	* the clinical trial	690	2	# * of the	646	6
13	status of the *	688	2	marketing authorisation holder *	645	29
14	trial has a *	673	2	on the * of	630	21
15	used in * trial	576	2	solution for injection *	628	20
16	of * for this	573	2	* if you are	624	36
17	* the marketing authorization	504	2	should not be *	616	13
18	* information on the	495	2	# * eu #	613	10
19	objective of * trial	493	2	of * medicinal product	602	2
20	of the * of	490	3	of the medicinal *	599	2

while in the CTPs it occurs 794 times and has only 14 variants. Overall, the higher number of variants of the most frequent 4-p-frames in the EPARs (405 vs. 70 in the CTPs) means that the said patterns are largely responsible for the scope of a phraseological profile of the former text variety and attest to its high degree of formulaicity. Although both text varieties are highly conventionalized, this result shows that the CTPs are more clichéd and fixed in terms of their phraseological patterns while the EPARs are less schematic and more varied in terms of the scope of formulaic language used.

Discussion and Conclusions

The results of this preliminary research revealed that the patterns of use of the most frequent and distinctive vocabulary and multi-word units vary across the CTPs and EPARs. More specifically, it was revealed that the CTPs have more keywords marking participants and institutions involved in clinical trials as well as those referring to procedures and various stages of the clinical trials. Also, in the CTPs there is a high number of general language keywords, which together with their immediate collocates express a range of specialist meanings (*advanced therapy, medical condition, trade name, orphan drug etc.*). On the other hand, the EPARs were found to have more keywords referring to names of chemical substances found in medicinal products and measurement units, names of medical conditions and side-effects as well as to the use and/or administration of medicinal products. Likewise, the functional analysis of the 50 most frequent lexical bundles revealed further differences. It was demonstrated that the CTPs are dominated by discourse-organizing and referential bundles, with no single stance bundle among the 50 most frequent ones whereas in the EPARs one may find more referential bundles (identification/focus, participative, institutional, terminological and quantity bundles). As regards the degree of pattern variability among phrase frames based on 4-word lexical bundles, only one 4-p-frame (*the * of the*) out of the 20 most frequent ones overlaps in the CTPs and EPARs. Also, the 20 most frequent 4-p-frames are more productive in the EPARs than in the CTPs. All in all, it was demonstrated that different patterns of language use are linked with different situational and communicative contexts, functions and target users associated with the CTPs and EPARs. Importantly, however, the occurrence of some of the keywords, lexical bundles or phrase frames among the most frequent linguistic items may result from the specific drugs or medicines described in the analyzed texts. Also, the preliminary study showed that a description of the use of phrase frames across different text types may be an effective method of generalization of phraseologies found therein and a promising starting point for further exploration of variability of specific patterns of co-occurring sequences of words.

Due to the limitations concerning the size of this paper, the results of the preliminary analyses are summarized in tables and briefly commented upon only. However, more detailed presentation of linguistic and/or phraseological profile of individual pharmaceutical text varieties, including more comprehensive interpretation of concordances illustrating the actual uses of the most frequent vocabulary and phraseology, shall be developed in the future.

In the future, it is also possible to extend this preliminary study by including other pharmaceutical registers or text types to gain more insight—using similar methodology—into linguistic variation in a particular pharmaceutical text type as compared with other text types, e.g. patient-pharmacist interactions, research articles on pharmacology, academic textbooks targeted at students of pharmacology etc.

(continued)

And last but not least, more research is required in the future to identify the most pedagogically useful vocabulary and phraseology (e.g. Ellis and Simpson-Vlach 2009). Only then is it possible to fully capitalize on descriptions of the most distinctive vocabulary and phraseology by designing effective teaching materials, aimed to increase students' competence in terms of adequate use of lexical and phraseological patterns found across different pharmaceutical text types or registers. This, among other factors, may provide extra pedagogical value for instructors offering or designing specialist language courses on English for Pharmaceutical Purposes—particularly at those institutions specializing in training future pharmacists or pharmacy technicians who are non-native speakers of English (e.g. at medical universities) and/or the ones training specialist translators dealing also with medical or pharmaceutical texts (e.g. at universities offering specialist courses in practical translation).

References

Biber, D. 2006. *University language. A corpus-based study of spoken and written registers.* Amsterdam: John Benjamins.

Biber, D. 2008. Multidimensional approaches. In *Corpus linguistics*, An international handbook, vol. 2, ed. A. Lüdeling and M. Kytö, 803–821. Berlin: Walter de Gruyter.

Biber, D. 2009. A corpus-driven approach to formulaic language in English: Multi-word patterns in speech and writing. *International Journal of Corpus Linguistics* 14: 275–311.

Biber, D., and S. Conrad. 2009. *Register, genre and style.* Cambridge: Cambridge University Press.

Biber, D., and E. Finegan. 1994. Intra-textual variation in medical research articles. In *Corpus-based research into language*, ed. N. Oostdijk and P. de Haan, 202–221. Amsterdam: Rodopi.

Biber, D., S. Johansson, G. Leech, S. Conrad, and E. Finegan. 1999. *The Longman grammar of spoken and written English.* London: Longman.

Biber, D., S. Conrad, and V. Cortes. 2003. Lexical bundles in speech and writing: An initial taxonomy. In *Corpus linguistics by the Lune: A festschrift for Geoffrey Leech*, ed. A. Wilson, P. Rayson, and T. McEnery, 71–92. Frankfurt am Main: Peter Lang.

Biel, Ł. 2011. Integrating professional realism in legal translation classes: translation competence and translator competence. *Meta: Translators' Journal* 56: 162–178.

Biel, Ł. 2013. Phraseological competence in legal translation: How can comparable corpora help train functional translators. Paper presented at methodological challenges for the contemporary translator educators conference, Kraków, Poland, 11 Oct 2013. http://www.kdp.up.krakow.pl/en/mccte2013_conference/mttce2013-abstract-booklet-en/ Accessed 30 Oct 2013.

Bouayad-Agha, N. 2006. The patient information leaflet (PIL) corpus. The Open University. http://mcs.open.ac.uk/nlg/old_projects/pills/corpus/PIL/. Accessed 12 Apr 2012.

Brooks, M. 2001. *Exploring medical language: A student directed approach.* London: Elsevier.

Ciecierska, J., B. Jenike, and K. Tudruj. 1983. *English for Pharmacy (Język angielski: Podręcznik dla studentów farmacji).* Warszawa: Państwowy Zakład Wydawnictw Lekarskich.

Craig, Ch., and R. Stitzel. 2004. *Modern pharmacology with clinical applications*, 6th ed. Philadelphia, PA: Lippincott Williams & Wilkins.

Del Vecchio, F. 2012. What English do you need? Course design for EPP. *Studii si Cercetari Filologice Seria Limbi Straine Aplicate* 11: 109–121.

Donesch-Jeżo, E. 2000. *English for medical students and doctors (part 1)*. Kraków: Wydawnictwo Przegląd Lekarski.

Donesch-Jeżo, E. 2002. *English for medical students and doctors (part 2)*. Kraków: Wydawnictwo Przegląd Lekarski.

Donesch-Jeżo, E. 2007. *English for students of pharmacy and pharmacists*. Kraków: Wydawnictwo Przegląd Lekarski.

Ellis, R. 1997. *Second language acquisition*. Oxford: Oxford University Press.

Ellis, N., and R. Simpson-Vlach. 2009. Formulaic language in native speakers: Triangulating psycholinguistics, corpus linguistics, and education. *Corpus Linguistics and Linguistic Theory* 5: 61–78.

EMA. 2012. European public assessment reports. Online document. http://www.ema.europa.eu/ema/index.jsp?curl=pages/medicines/general/general_content_000433.jsp&mid. Accessed 14 Apr 2012.

Fitzpatrick, S. 2005. *The clinical trial protocol*. Marlow: The Institute of Clinical Research.

Fletcher, W. 2007. KfNgram. Annapolis: USNA. http://www.kwicfinder.com/kfNgram/kfNgram Help.html. Accessed 20 Nov 2011.

Gledhill, C. 1995a. Scientific innovation and the phraseology of rhetoric. Posture, reformulation and collocation in cancer research articles. Ph.D. thesis. The University of Aston, Birmingham. www.isfla.org/Systemics/Print/Theses/Gledhill1995.pdf. Accessed 10 Oct 2012.

Gledhill, C. 1995b. Collocation and genre analysis. The discourse function of collocation in cancer research abstracts and articles. *Zeitschrift für Anglistik und Amerikanistik* 1: 1–26 (cited in Gledhill 1996: 109).

Gledhill, C. 1996. Science as a collocation. Phraseology in cancer research articles. In *Proceedings of teaching and language corpora*, UCREL technical papers, vol. 9, ed. S. Botley, J. Glass, T. McEnery, and A. Wilson, 108–126. Lancaster: UCREL.

Glendinning, E., and B. Holmstroem. 2005. *English in medicine: A course in communication skills*. Cambridge: Cambridge University Press.

Gotti, M., and F. Salager-Meyer (eds.). 2006. *Advances in medical discourse analysis: Oral and written contexts*. Frankfurt: Peter Lang.

Goźdź-Roszkowski, S. 2011. *Patterns of linguistic variation in American legal English: A corpus-based study*. Frankfurt am Main: Peter Lang.

Grabowski, Ł. 2013. Register variation across English pharmaceutical texts: A corpus-driven study of keywords, lexical bundles and phrase frames in patient information leaflets and summaries of product characteristics. *Procedia: Social and Behavioral Sciences* 95: 391–401.

Hoekje, B., and S. Tipton. 2011. *English language and the medical profession: Instructing and assessing the communication skills of international physicians*. Bingley: Emerald.

Hollinger, M. 2003. *Introduction to pharmacology*, 2nd ed. London: Taylor & Francis.

Kierczak, A. 2009. *English for pharmacists*. Warszawa: Wydawnictwo Lekarskie PZWL.

Liu, D. 2012. The most frequently-used multi-word constructions in academic written English: A multi-corpus study. *English for Specific Purposes* 31: 25–35.

Mallick, U., R. Arezina, C. Ritchie, and D. Wang. 2006. Protocol development. In *Clinical trials: A practical guide to design, analysis, and reporting*, ed. D. Wang and A. Bakhai, 23–36. London: Remedica.

Montalt Resurreccio, V., and M. Gonzalez Davies. 2007. *Medical translation step by step. Translation practices explained*. Manchester: St. Jerome.

Paiva, D. 2000. Investigating style in a corpus of pharmaceutical leaflets: Results of a factor analysis. In *Proceeding of annual meeting of the ACL*, 52–59, Hong Kong.

Pickar, G. 2004. *Dosage calculations*, vol. 1, 7th ed. New York: Thomson/Delmar Learning.

Piscitelli, S., and K. Rodvold (eds.). 2005. *Drug interactions in infectious diseases*, 2nd ed. Totowa: Humana Press.

Roemer, U. 2009. English in academia: Does nativeness matter? *Anglistik: International Journal of English Studies* 20: 89–100.

Scott, M. 1997. The right word in the right place: Key word associates in two languages. *AAA: Arbeiten aus Anglistik und Amerikanistik* 22: 239–252.

Scott, M. 2008a. *WordSmith tools 5.0*. Liverpool: Lexical Analysis Software.

Scott, M. 2008b. *WordSmith tools 5.0 help*. Liverpool: Lexical Analysis Software.

Teich, E., and P. Fankhauser. 2010. Exploring a corpus of scientific texts using data mining. In *Corpus-linguistic applications: Current studies, new directions*, ed. S. Gries, M. Davies, and S. Wulff, 233–247. Amsterdam: Rodopi.

Tiedemann, J. 2009. News from OPUS: A collection of multilingual parallel corpora with tools and interfaces. In *Recent advances in natural language processing*, vol. 5, ed. N. Nicolov, K. Bontcheva, G. Angelova, and R. Mitkov, 237–248. Amsterdam: John Benjamins.

Wang, D., and A. Bakhai (eds.). 2006. *Clinical trials: A practical guide to design, analysis, and reporting*. London: Remedica.

WUM. 2014. Medical University of Warsaw. Pharmacy curriculum. Online document. http://wf.wum.edu.pl/sites/wf.wum.edu.pl/files/pharmacy_curriculum.pdf. Accessed 10 Feb 2014.

Lightning Source UK Ltd.
Milton Keynes UK
UKOW06n1338190516

274577UK00001B/53/P